The Culture
of
Education Policy

The Culture

of

Education Policy

Sandra J. Stein

Teachers College
Columbia University
New York and London

Published by Teachers College Press, 1234 Amsterdam Avenue, New York, NY 10027

Library of Congress Cataloging-in-Publication Data

Stein, Sandra J.
    The culture of education policy / Sandra J. Stein.
      p. c.m.
    Includes bibliographical references and index.
    ISBN 0-8077-4480-8 (cloth : alk. paper) — ISBN 0-8077-4479-4 (pbk. : alk. paper)
    1. Poor children—Education—United States. 2. Compensatory education—Government policy—United States. I. Title.

  LC4091.S66 2004
  379.2'6'0973—dc22

                          2004041234

ISBN 0-8077-4479-4 (paper)
ISBN 0-8077-4480-8 (cloth)

Printed on acid-free paper

Manufactured in the United States of America

11 10 09 08 07 06 05 04   8 7 6 5 4 3 2 1

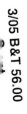

Contents

Acknowledgments

I am deeply indebted to a number of people for their support of my efforts in this book. I was fortunate to have amazing research assistants who worked tirelessly doing both tedious tasks—such as scanning thousands of pages of *Congressional Records*—and more rigorous analysis, such as commenting thoughtfully and critically on my ideas. Jolet Olsen, Stavroula Georgiadou, and Adriano Brata all worked on various aspects of this book, and I thank them for their dedication. The project, however, would have come to a grinding halt a number of times if it were not for the careful, meticulous, and analytically savvy work of Petra Rappoccio. I have been lucky to work with such "gifted and talented" students at Baruch College.

My colleagues at the Baruch College School of Public Affairs provided useful, timely, and challenging feedback on various portions of this book. I thank David Barner, David Birdsell, Marianne Engelman-Lado, Pam Ferner, Diane Gibson, Sarah Sayeed, Robert Kaestner, Sanders Korenman, Doug Muzzio, Jerry Mitchell, Gregg Van Ryzin, Carroll Seron, Neil Sullivan, Lynne Wiekart, and from the greater Baruch College community, David Potash, David Jones, and Shelly Eversley for their thoughtful comments and suggestions. I am particularly grateful for the serious, stimulating, in-my-face, and often hilarious critique provided by Marcellus Andrews, whose comments on the various drafts of my manuscript should be compiled into a book of their own.

Parts of this book are based on research I did for my dissertation project at Stanford University School of Education. I am indebted to Martin Carnoy, Milbrey McLaughlin, Mike Kirst, and David Fetterman for their support and guidance during my dissertation writing.

My colleagues and friends who work in schools and school districts continually remind me why this book matters, and that real people who work in real schools might benefit from reading it. All resisters of policy culture in one way or another, I thank Rhonda Perry, Regina Chiou, Tanya Kaufman, Liz Gewirtzman, and Beth Simmons for providing examples of what is possible in practice, and for being forceful examples of what thoughtful practitioners can do. I also thank all past and current students in the Aspiring Leaders Program at Baruch College; your dedication to equitable public schooling and your willingness to stick with the hard conversations are refreshing and rewarding. I also thank Phoebe Burr, Sara Goldreich, and Claire McIntee for their tireless assistance in proofreading the text; and the NYC Leadership Academy Team for their support and patience during the last stages of this project. At Teachers College Press, I thank Wendy Schwartz for pushing me to craft stronger conclusions, and to Brian Ellerbeck, Aureliano Vázquez Jr., and Siddhartha Deb for their patience and support of this project.

I am deeply grateful for the support of various friends and family members who never made me talk about this project if I didn't want to: Donna Stein, Karen Stein, Jay Stein, Rocío Gonzalez, Rebecca Stein Gonzalez, Sofia Stein Gonzalez, Bob Stein, Stephanie Mendez, Beth Simmons, Shannon Fischer, and Elysa Safran.

Finally, I am in awe of the generous love and support that Matt Lambiase provided me throughout this project, as a brilliant reader, an unwavering fan, a unique revolutionary, and an amazing teammate.

Introduction

Two days before I planned to submit this book to my editor, a colleague of mine promised me a glass of wine and a shoulder to cry on after, inevitably, the newspaper reported something that I would wish I had addressed in this book. I told him that I was so exhausted, I didn't think I'd react to anything related to the topic for a long while. On the day that I planned to submit the book, an article on the front page of the *New York Times* informed me that a lawyer for the White House who advises states on implementing the No Child Left Behind legislation, the latest iteration of the 36-year-old federal education policy at the heart of this book, predicted that "50 to 90 percent of the schools in some states might be found inadequate" (Schemo, 2002, November 27, pp. A1, A18). "Inadequate schools." "Failing schools." I reflected on how earlier versions of this federal education policy framed children in a way that encouraged practitioners to talk about them in terms of their inadequacy, deficiency, and deprivation. Current policy encourages this approach to viewing entire schools. Does my book adequately address this shift? Is my book inadequate? Failing? I thought to call my colleague and ask for that glass of wine and shoulder then.

Then I thought about whether my book, had it been out earlier, might have benefited the current policy construction. The newspaper reports that come out weekly, sometimes daily, about this policy speak to the relevance of the topic, and the lack of consideration of the cultural dimensions of this policy—namely, the language and rituals that it engenders and encourages—continually demonstrate the need for the type of analysis that I provide here. I am writing about a moving target, yet through a lens that challenges the core assumptions of the policy and considers its cultural legacy in both policy documents and practice.

The purpose of this book is to investigate the culture of poverty policy through analysis of the language and behaviors of policymakers and practitioners at various stages of the policy process. Cultural analysis—the explicit attention to the meanings and symbols that guide the construction of categories and shape the use of language—provides a window on the otherwise concealed or unquestioned aspects of policy formation and implementation.

Such analysis considers the systems of meaning revealed through and perpetuated by policies in their initiation and implementation. Here, cultural investigation lays bare implicit standards of normalcy that take shape in the classification schemes used to identify the subjects of policies and shape their lives. The language and rituals of policymaking and implementation define the contours of policy culture. This language is laden with imagery, metaphor, and portraiture. Sentences seemingly culled from a novel such as "by the time he starts to school, he has hardly heard a thing but clanging trash cans, ambulances and monosyllabic vulgarity" (Jacobs, 1965, p. 5742) emerge on the floor of Congress as part of a policy debate on federal education funding. Politicians and practitioners depict the main characters of their policy narratives with purposeful detail, hoping to justify policy prerogatives and performance. The field of cultural and literary policy study (cf. Edelman, 1988; Roe, 1994; Shore & Wright, 1997; Yanow, 1996) provides an analytical option for viewing such policy "texts" as exposing belief systems and organizing thought.

Traditional policy analysis, however, has not focused on such considerations. With investigation of possible relationships between specific policy configurations and discrete outcomes (such as federal compensatory education dollars and student test scores), such analyses tend to reinforce and perpetuate policy categories and classifications (such as "Title I Schools" and "educationally disadvantaged students"). Traditional analytical approaches typically describe the policy "problem" through narrow examination of the subjects of policy: the proposed policy beneficiaries. Policy analysts try to find the proper combination of incentives to motivate certain behaviors in the benefiting population, spurring questions and contextualizing results through rhetorical portraits of policy "targets." In their attempts to describe, propose, justify, and delineate their optimal policy prescriptions, such analysts choose purposeful details to frame their arguments while omitting others, thus effectively coauthoring policy texts with politicians and practitioners.

It is standard for scholarly and legislative debates on poverty-oriented policy to include depictions of individuals living in poverty with accounts of their families, communities, values, and experiences. When cultural considerations arise in policy discussions, they tend to take shape in thin descriptions of the lives and lifestyles of those whom policy aims to address—as opposed to the "thick descriptions" of anthropologists (Geertz, 1973, p. 28)—with a focus on the most provocative characteristics assumed to be policy-relevant. If there is any analysis of culture, it is that of the people living in poverty and, typically, the presumed pathologies that perpetuate their social conditions. The so-called "culture of poverty" is presented as an obstacle to policy success.

In this book, I shift the task of cultural analysis from describing the individuals living in poverty to probing the processes of creating and implementing policies intended to address the conditions of those individuals. Through a case study of Title I of the Elementary and Secondary Education Act (ESEA), the largest U.S. federal education policy intended for children in poverty, I trace the rituals and routines revealed in policy practice from Congress to the classroom. This analysis renders the well-established notion of a culture of poverty as a framework deployed in the culture of policies aimed to address poverty, where characterizations of eligible students and their needs form part of policy practice from political debate to service provision.

FROM THE CULTURE OF POVERTY
TO THE CULTURE OF POLICY

The theory of a culture of poverty is most commonly associated with the work of anthropologist Oscar Lewis (1959, 1961, 1964, 1965). In various books and essays, Lewis provided detailed accounts of families in Latin America and the urban United States with the hope of illuminating the culture—defined as "a design for living which is passed down from generation to generation" (1961, p. xxiv)—of people living in poverty. With a list of nearly seventy interrelated traits that he found among the studied families, Lewis suggested various "universal characteristics" of the culture of poverty, including matriarchal family structures, present-time orientations with limited deferred gratification, frequent spending of small quantities of money with an absence of savings, and a general mistrust of government and politicians (1964, pp. 152–156). Lewis's work, intended as a call for political mobilization on behalf of poor people, was criticized by some for its stigmatization of those living in poverty (see, for example, Foley, 1997; Leacock, 1971; Valentine, 1968; Waxman, 1977), and embraced by others as support for their view of poor people as pathological. Historian Michael Katz (1989) argues that Lewis's framework was "amputat[ed] from its liberal origins" and grew to become a justification for the substandard material conditions of the "undeserving poor" (p. 29). During the mid-1960s, the culture of poverty thesis became a common reference point for politicians and scholars during policy debates, both as a call to action and a way to blame people in poverty for their circumstances. Using Lewis's framework, policymakers defined the problems of poor people and justified proposed policy solutions for their situations. The culture of poverty folded into what I am coining the *culture of policy*.

The concept of the culture of policy is my appropriation and reorientation of the culture of poverty framework summarized above. Conceptualized in somewhat similar fashion as Lewis, this policy culture provides a design for defining and remedying social problems and solutions that is passed between Congress and local governmental entities (such as schools). However, in my adaptation of Lewis's framework, I change the unidirectional nature of a seemingly monolithic cultural transmission model. Rather than seeing this transmission as coming *from* Congress *to* the local entities, I allow for transmission *between and among* the various governmental agencies. This recursive relationship allows for consideration of the influence of local practice on congressional discourse as well as resistance to and adaptation of policy problem and solution definitions at various moments of the policy process.

Akin to Lewis's framework, this policy culture has its own set of interrelated traits and characteristics. These characteristics include a shared conception of policy beneficiaries as deviant from (and usually deficient to) a perceived and often unstated norm; a presumption that government institutions can fulfill a corrective role in the lives of the country's deviant inhabitants; and mechanisms for service provision that provide incentives for identifying, maintaining, and perpetuating a deviant population. Consider these characteristics of the culture of policy one at a time.

Beneficiaries as Deviant from (and Usually Deficient to) the Norm

All social policies provide limited frames for viewing the individuals they are designed to serve. A primary focus on individual attributes and behaviors, rather than on structural or institutional conditions, posits policy beneficiaries as problems that government intervention can solve. As problems, the intended beneficiaries are defined as exceptional, even aberrant to a presumed and often unspoken norm. This presumed deviance can favor or disfavor the policy beneficiaries: policies address both those superior and inferior to the postulated norm (for a complementary argument see Schneider & Ingram, 1993, 1997). Social policies, and particularly those geared toward people in poverty, tend to portray the beneficiaries as lacking or deficient in more than just material resources. The language of education policy debates addressing children in poverty reveals descriptions of the beneficiaries' "culturally deprived circumstances," the presumption of deficiency hinging on the cultures, families, and communities into which the identified populations were born (see Valencia, 1997).

Government as Corrective

As instruments of the state, social policies are predicated on the assumption that the government can remedy the perceived problems of the country's deviant populations. The existence of social policies presupposes that the government can assuage the social problems of policy beneficiaries through funding allocation, bureaucratic design, and/or national focus. Governmental representatives craft policies in keeping with the state's corrective role, refashioning approaches to provide what policymakers consider the most effective and efficient processes toward intended policy goals.

Incentives for Identifying and Perpetuating Deviant Populations

In generating budgetary resources and bureaucratic structures for service provision, policies create incentive structures for the maintenance of deviant populations. Local government agencies and other institutions responsible for service provision receive policy-generated funds with which to develop programs, hire personnel, and purchase materials. These institutions seek to maximize resources, and the identification and maintenance of a deviant population eligible for assistance provides the opportunity to increase resources. The structure encourages those hired to deliver services to the deviant population—the "street-level bureaucrats" (Lipsky, 1976, 1980)—to invest in the maintenance of their clients' deviance. If they are successful at correcting the deviant population, they work themselves out of their jobs.

Characterizations of policy beneficiaries as deviant and government institutions as corrective, articulated at the time of policymaking, are woven into policy mechanisms for funding allocation and service provision. As practitioners in local government agencies implement policy mechanisms, they internalize, interpret, formulate, and reformulate the culture of policy in the language and rituals of practice. Within this framework, a peculiar dilemma emerges. Practitioners aiming to serve the policy beneficiaries in ways that build on their assets, challenge their status as deficient or deviant, and conform to the often lofty goals stated in the policies themselves *must act in resistance to the culture of policy in order to do so.* Without such resistance, those framed as deficient are treated with expectations and assumptions that compromise attempts to serve them effectively.

In the case of compensatory education policies, teachers and administrators who avoid the use of reductive labels to organize service provision and resource allocation, who think holistically about children's educational assets and needs, and who individualize educational programs to build on students' assets often find themselves out of compliance with policy mandates. In such cases, the culture of policy acts as a restrictive force to be resisted through an inattention to policy categories and funding schemes. Thoughtful noncompliance with policy mandates and resistance to the culture of policy emerge as effective practice in the service of the policy beneficiaries. In other words, good teachers know that the most coherent and valuable educational practices for serving the intended policy beneficiaries often require disregard for policy mandates.

WHY COMPENSATORY EDUCATION POLICY?

This framework for the cultural analysis of policy can apply to many government initiatives, particularly those directed at the poor. Compensatory education policies provide a particularly fruitful case for this analysis. Intended to compensate for the perceived deficiencies in the lives and capabilities of children in poverty, compensatory education policies offer supplementary funding to schools serving students growing up poor. Situated at the intersection of childhood, poverty, and government intervention, these initiatives provide a rich and textured example for analysis of the culture of policy. Focusing on children, such policies illuminate the normative expectations of what educational opportunities and resources youth *should* have. Adults involved in various aspects of the policy process convey these expectations through justifications for particular policy proposals and specific configurations for service provision. Policies focused on poverty reveal individual and collective theories of why poverty exists and persists, what might be done to alleviate its consequences (if not eradicate its existence), and what people living in poverty *should* do to improve their lives and those of their children. Finally, all policies communicate values of what the government *should* do for its public, beliefs about what a government *can* do for its public, and theories of which institutional practices lead to the most desirable outcomes, whatever they may be.

Since the mid-1960s, the mainstay of U.S. federal education policy has been Title I of the Elementary and Secondary Education Act. The act, first ratified in 1965, is the largest federal compensatory education policy and provides schools with funds intended for programs to serve the perceived educational needs of eligible students. Initiated as part of President Lyndon B. Johnson's War on Poverty, Title I took shape at a time when national attention focused on the social costs of poverty. Concern for the problems of the poor led scholars and politicians to examine the lives of poor people through observations of cultural traits associated with poverty. "Cultural deprivation" and the culture of poverty became central constructs around which policy discussions were framed. Federal funding would provide a means to address the needs of children who, in Congressional hearings and government reports on Title I, were characterized as "culturally deprived" (W. D. Ford, 1965, p. 5964) and shackled by the "chains of disadvantage which bind them to a life of hopelessness and misery" (National Advisory Council on the Education of Disadvantaged Children, 1966, p. 1; 1969, p. 1).

Within this conceptualization, schools represented a promising site for government intervention. Educational institutions could interrupt the otherwise intractable poverty culture, impart middle-class norms, and break the chains of poverty and disadvantage. Poor students, black students, Latino students, immigrant students, rural students, and urban students, all broadly understood as victims of cultural deprivation, would be beneficiaries of educational policies that could extract them from the poverty cultures into which they were born. Unfortunately, the very characterizations of "disadvantaged youth," most frequently used to justify school funding in their interest, also functioned in ways that stymied the educational processes those funds were supposed to enhance. These characterizations came to provide a filter through which students living in poverty were perceived, as practitioners were required to engage in policy-generated language and rituals. Depictions of students as deficient tied policy-generated money and programs to cultural categories laden with assumptions about students' limited possibilities, potential, and promise.

As with any supplementary government policy or program, service providers were required to identify eligible individuals and demonstrate that they had received specialized services. For Title I, schools were under regulatory obligation to demonstrate attention to the perceived needs of disadvantaged students. In the historical trajectory of Title I, students eligible for funded services through low test scores and/or poverty measures were labeled as "Title I students," "educationally disadvantaged youth" (often referred to as "EDY"), or "at-risk students." Such students were most often provided remedial educational opportunities delivered by practitioners paid exclusively or in part through the school's Title I budget. Services were often delivered in "pullout" programs, in which students were removed from their classrooms to receive instruction.

Reactions to an initial misuse of funds for purposes other than educating eligible students (documented most famously by Martin & McClure, 1969) led to various bureaucratic mechanisms and school-based delivery systems for ensuring compliance (Elmore & McLaughlin, 1988). The result was a complex web of individual programs and accountability measures that spoke more directly to the political obligations of the government to keep track of federal dollars than to the educational needs of the students. On the federal level, the government required evidence that special services reached poor children. Locally, schools and districts vying for any additional revenues were expected to demonstrate regulation compliance to ensure continued funding. To illustrate compliance, programs grew to be quite fragmented in nature and service provision tended to segregate eligible from noneligible students, which often mapped onto race and class (see, for example, Eyler, Cook, & Ward, 1983; Glass & Smith, 1977; Kimbrough & Hill, 1983).

In addition, and perhaps most troubling, policy-driven dollars were commonly used to fund personnel salaries, thus providing funded teachers with an economic incentive to maintain and perpetuate the existence of a deficient student population in order to justify and protect their own employment opportunities. Schools grew to rely on a pool of money generated through student eligibility in order to maintain staff positions. Practitioners, aware that their continued employment relied on student eligibility, were caught in a bind. If they were effective instructors, their students' academic performance might improve, thereby generating less funding toward their own salaries. Depending on the specific configurations of eligibility at various times in the policy's trajectory, schools could maximize revenues through low test scores, high poverty measures, or some combination thereof. Some schools made blatant efforts to expand their budgets through manipulation of such measures. For example, in 1994, the poverty measure used to determine eligibility changed from Aid to Families with Dependent Children (AFDC), a welfare policy involving rigorous qualification processes, to free- and reduced-price lunch eligibility in which parents fill out a form that is rarely validated.

In fact, a Chicago school's magazine reported that while "[p]ublic aid applicants must verify their income; free lunch applicants do not," and then, quoting a representative from the Chicago Lawyers' Committee for Civil Rights, noted, "You can go in and sign up for free lunch and lie" (Anderson, 1997). This approach to Title I eligibility provides a clear disincentive for monitoring free-lunch eligibility practices. An article in a Nebraska news service reported that

> If South Sioux City succeeds in cutting down on abuse in their school lunch program, they'll save the federal government some money, but they'll lose money for their own district, federal dollars that help pay for remedial reading and other programs. (Penner, 1996)

The change in eligibility criteria from AFDC to free lunch produced a predictable rise in reported levels of school poverty. First, eligibility for free lunch pertained to families whose incomes fell within 130% of the federal poverty guideline, whereas AFDC eligibility pertained to those whose incomes were at or below the poverty line. Second, schools had economic incentives to encourage parents to submit free-lunch forms, thus increasing eligibility rates. Some schools even held classroom contests for the most school lunch forms submitted to the school and rewarded returned forms with candy and pizza parties (although I have not seen published documentation of these practices, through personal and professional correspondence with teachers in California and New York, I have learned of their prevalence). With test scores, although blatant attempts to maximize revenues by deliberately miseducating students would be ill-advised to report as such, teachers and administrators were well aware of—and even concerned about—the reliance on student performance measures for revenue generation (chapter 4 will bring these issues to life through the concerns of teachers and paraprofessionals funded through Title I).

Particularly compelling in the case of compensatory education are the central tensions within the culture of policy itself. High expectations for student performance on the part of practitioners are one of the important ingredients in the provision of meaningful educational opportunities. The corrective potential of government is hampered by the mere delineation of an eligible group of substandard and therefore stigmatized students. But without identifying an eligible group, how can all students get services to meet their needs? The conflict is akin to what Martha Minow (1990) describes as the "dilemma of difference." In order to approach legal justice, the law suggests that everybody receive equal treatment. But history teaches that equal treatment affects different people differently. So we create categories of people who we believe should receive some form of special treatment or targeted service. Our constructed categories, although intended to approach a more just arrangement, often become stigmas for the people who occupy them. The categories then reinforce the unjust situation that they were created to remedy.

THAT WHICH FOLLOWS

In the following chapters of this book, I build on the work of policy sociologists and insurgent practitioners who question the language and rituals of policy in their scholarship and daily practice. Through investigation of Title I of the Elementary and Secondary Education Act in both congressional debates and classroom practice, I show how the underlying assumptions and regulatory mechanisms of this policy place constraints on school-based practitioners that actually interfere with both educational processes and the formally stated egalitarian goals of Title I itself.

Using transcripts of congressional floor debates as well as qualitative observations in nine urban elementary schools, this book demonstrates how the culture of policy shapes educational practice. As I explain in the subsequent chapters, the portrayal of policy beneficiaries as weak and deficient can foster educational approaches fundamentally incongruent with the egalitarian goals of well-meaning policymakers, scholars, and practitioners.

The first part of the book examines interpretive approaches to policy analysis, arguing why policies are best understood as organizing principles for everyday life. Building on the work of postmodern theorists and cultural analysts, I put forth my conceptual model for investigating the culture of policy, and then use my cultural analysis approach to frame the evolution of Title I from its inception in 1965 to the present.

In chapter 1, I outline the theoretical premise of this project: the culture of policy influences the routines of practice through both regulatory mechanisms and categorization schemes. I defend the use of cultural analysis to provide rigorous interrogation and interpretation of language and behavior patterns in the policy process.

Chapter 2 provides a historical review of the Title I policy case, using cultural analysis to frame the policy's evolution. Here I describe Title I of the Elementary and Secondary Education Act's origins as part of President Lyndon Johnson's War on Poverty, and how political uses of the culture of poverty theories folded into the original construction of this legislation.

The second part of the book brings the reader into the halls of Congress and of schools. In chapter 3, I analyze the language of Congress during floor debates on Title I of the Elementary and Secondary Education Act from 1965 through 1994. Using qualitative content analysis, I show shifts in how students have been characterized and their needs defined over time. I show changes in the policy language and constructs as the policy evolves through various iterations in the reauthorization process, yet stubbornness in its deficit orientation for students and their potential.

In chapter 4, I move the analysis to the classroom, where I provide intimate, qualitative accounts of nine elementary schools and the adults who work in them, showing the ways in which the culture of policy has taken shape in school practices. I present the language and routines of schooling to demonstrate how practitioners internalize, interpret, formulate, reformulate, and at times resist the culture of education policy in practice.

In chapter 5, I consider the culture of education policy through analysis of two additional equity-oriented policies, desegregation and bilingual education. Through investigation of the simultaneous implementation of these two policies, this chapter provides additional evidence of how the culture of policy creates symbolic systems that can interfere with the policies' educational imperatives.

I conclude the book with consideration of the most recent iteration of Title I as it exists in the No Child Left Behind Act of 2001. This legislation reflects considerable departure from earlier approaches to federal education policy, yet evinces the legacy of past policy constructions. Using this new policy as a springboard, I probe how practitioners might realign policy language and practice at the school level so that policies do not impair our ability to see children in terms of their strengths, assets, and promise. Part of the task, I suggest, is to understand policy as a particular and limited way of seeing that can be questioned, criticized, and challenged.

This book is intended for scholars of education, policy, political science, economics, anthropology, and sociology, as well as for school-based practitioners and policymakers. In my loftiest moments, I see this project as an intervention for both educational scholarship and practice. Through this work, I hope to challenge our assumptions about children in poverty as well as our organizational strategies, both conceptually and practically, for addressing their presumed needs. In my more humble moments, I merely seek to expose some of the inherent tensions in the ways we have conceptualized our policy problems and solutions through reductive assumptions about children, poverty, normalcy, difference, and equity. In my optimistic moments, I believe that if scholars and practitioners could consider policies as pliant and malleable ways of seeing the world, we might evolve our policies and implementation strategies so that they recognize and build on children's intellectual assets rather than rely on and encourage the identification and perpetuation of their deficiencies.

The Culture
of
Education Policy

Policy as Cultural Construct

There are two dimensions to the study of policy culture: first, exploration of the practice of policymaking and analysis; and second, investigation of the language and rituals born of a policy. The first interrogates the systems of meaning reflected in the process of policymaking. How are social problems and solutions defined? Who defines them, and on whose behalf?

The second dimension focuses on the daily language, rituals, and institutional habits shaped by policies. As the symbols, language, and routines of policy in practice take shape as cultural manifestations, questions arise as to how policies promote ways of seeing individuals and provide tools for organizing their lives. How are people eligible for policy-driven services seen by those who provide the services? How do institutions organize to provide services in response to policy regulations? How are those eligible for policy-generated services distinguished from those not eligible? How do policies introduce and build on biases about policy beneficiaries? What is denoted by policy-driven identities such as "welfare mother" or "Title I student"?

This chapter outlines a framework for investigating the culture of policy. First, I present the concept of "the policy dozens," which combines a childhood game of insult-slinging with the policy process. Next, I defend the use of cultural analysis to provide rigorous interpretation of patterns of language and behavior in the policy process. Here I review work in policy studies and interpretive analysis with special consideration of how social problems and solutions are constructed and how those constructions take shape in the language and routines of various levels of governmental agencies and organizations. I then propose a framework for understanding how the interplay between the historical moment of original policy formation and the institutional arrangements for policy delivery shapes the culture of policy at policy initiation. After reviewing the culture of policy framework, I investigate the cultural consequences on policy implementation for the institutions charged with the delivery of equity-oriented, policy-driven programs and services. Through this cultural analysis, I show how the culture of policy plays out in the construction and implementation of equity-oriented education policies.

THE POLICY DOZENS

In his book, *Yo' Mama's Dysfunktional!*, historian Robin Kelley records,

> You would think that as a kid growing up in this world I could handle any insult, or at least be prepared for any slander tossed in the direction of my mom—or, for that matter, my whole family, my friends, or my friends' families. But when I entered college and began reading the newspaper, monographs, and textbooks on a regular basis, I realized that many academics, journalists, policymakers, and politicians had taken the "dozens" to another level . . . I have had kids tell me that my hair was so nappy that it looked like a thousand Africans giving the Black Power salute, but never has anyone said to my face that my whole family—especially my mama—was a "tangle of pathology." (Kelley, 1997, p. 2)

The "dozens," a childhood game of rapid-fire insults, is not a formal feature of the policy process. Policymakers are not schooled in delivering swift, comedic portrayals of policy beneficiaries that last only as long as the conversations themselves. Policy texts do not refer to the dozens in their explanations of how government moves between general "goals and the means for achieving them" (Pressman & Wildavsky, 1984, p. xxi) or the process of turning "policy ideas" into "real-world outcomes" (Kelman, 1987, pp. 6–7). But what Robin Kelley identifies as a new level of the dozens is a cultural convention of the policy process: the portrayal of deficit and deficiency in certain segments of society by scholars, politicians, and policymakers in order to motivate and justify policy proposals.

What distinguishes this new level of the dozens from the dozens of Kelley's childhood is that in the policy process, only those in positions of power get to play, and the insults outlast the conversations in which they are delivered. This new level of the dozens involves the portrayal of individuals and communities as deviant and deficient by people essentially disconnected from those individuals and communities. In the new version of the dozens, the insults are deployed in policy problem definitions, they take root in policy formulations, and they manifest themselves in labels for service delivery. The name-calling practices inherent in the childhood dozens transmute into labeling practices in the policy dozens, the labels becoming stigmatized identity markers in the institutions of policy delivery.

Consider the following example that traces this version of the dozens from the process of policymaking to policy implementation. In the authorizations of Title I of the Elementary and Secondary Education Act (1965)—

the time of problem definition—Senator Walter Mondale (D, MN) (1965) stated, "This bill recognizes that a child from the slums—whether urban or rural—needs supplementary educational opportunities and special programs, to help him overcome his cultural handicaps" (p. 7571). Here, a poor child's culture and community are cast as defective and deficient, indeed a handicap in the way of his or her progress. A subsequent version of the formulated policy born of the bill Mondale was supporting reads:

> ASSESSMENT OF EDUCATIONAL NEED—A local educational agency may receive funds under this title only if it makes an assessment of educational needs each year to (1) identify educationally deprived children in all eligible attendance areas and to select those educationally deprived children who have the greatest need for special assistance. (Education Amendments of 1978, Sec. 124b, p. 2164)

With passage of this bill, schools acquire a monetary incentive to see certain students as "deprived" and to formally identify "deprivation" in the student population. Local institutions attain new motivations to look for, even seek out, deficit and deficiency. And at the time of policy implementation, the labels of deficiency and deprivation become part of the daily vocabulary. Teachers now have language to signify perceived deprivation, as policy-eligible students are marked as "Title I students" or "EDY" (educationally disadvantaged youth) in daily conversation and on classroom rosters. Inside the school, the vocabulary resulting from the policy dozens takes hold in the school culture. When a first-grade teacher comments that "the help at home is so important and our EDY students don't get that,"[1] her colleagues understand the term "EDY" as an identity marker signifying deficiency, lack, and trouble. The policy dozens—in which government representatives cast poor (and in many cases black) children as caught in a "tangle of pathology" or as "culturally handicapped"—form part of the language and rituals of policy, with consequences often at odds with stated egalitarian policy goals. Only through consideration of the symbols, language, and routines of the policy process can we unearth the importance and influence of the culture of policy.

The most instrumental understanding of the policy process goes as follows. A governing body, motivated by interest groups, economic circumstances, and/or international concerns, wants to affect a specific situation, behavior, or condition of its citizenry. In order to do so, it must name a "problem" in need of reform, and put in place rules and regulations to ensure a desired "solution." Through a political process of negotiation among elected officials and interest groups, policies take form, often producing bureaucratic structures, funding streams, and expectations for organizational response. Policymakers aim to construct effective incentives and disincentives to manipulate the behavior of policy subjects and service providers. Policies are judged as "successes" or "failures" based on their measured capacity to produce desired behaviors or outcomes.

To illustrate the above, imagine that a caucus of elected officials decides—after vigorous lobbying efforts on the part of parent and student organizations—that the recent spate of shootings in suburban high schools constitutes a policy problem. They must first name the problem in need of reform and discern the desired solution that a policy could influence. In this case, the desired solution might be as simple as a decrease in school-based shootings. But what is the policy problem? Here, elected officials rely on implicit and explicit theories of cause and effect, influenced by the information that is accessible to them—their lived experiences, anecdotal evidence and testimonials, popular opinion, social science research, and other government reports. So, what are potential policy problems in the case of suburban school shootings? Disenfranchised teenagers who long for attention and belonging, a lack of police presence in suburban schools, and the availability of guns are all potential problem definitions. What are some potential causes of this problem? The values of middle class culture, the parenting styles of suburban adults, the pressures to conform and fit in, the powerful gun lobby? Policymakers might think that the problem is located in individuals, communities, or the structures of society. Each possible problem definition reflects and provides a different lens or way of seeing the policy subjects—children and their parents. Through political negotiations, a sense of the problem coalesces, and proposals for addressing the problem emerge.

Were the government representatives to decide collectively that the policy problem was the disaffected nature of suburban teens caused by bad parenting, they might allocate funds for programs identifying such adolescents and providing interventions for both them and their parents. They might locate programs for the teens and their parents at schools, staff them with trained professionals, and entice participation through incentives they believe attractive to suburban adolescents and adults. They would rely on academic studies of such children and their parents to determine what motivates their behaviors and propose solutions in keeping with the incentives to which this population has been shown to respond. Alternatively, if elected officials were to decide that access to guns was the central policy problem, another program would logically ensue.

Now, imagine that most of the policymakers have never lived in a suburb, know very few people who do, and have either limited or no experiential knowledge of suburban life. Their definitions of the policy problem and potential solutions—no matter how well informed by scholarship or anecdotal testimonial—would emerge from limited, brokered, partial, and distorted perceptions of the daily lives of the folks they aim to serve. Granted, the problem of having limited exposure to middle-class living is not the actual case, as most elected officials are themselves from or now belong to the middle and upper-middle class. The point here is that in every policy case, definitions of the policy problem are influenced by the policymakers' proximity to the issues, their understanding of the local community and economic structures, and their own investment in the matter at hand. What is especially important to remember with poverty-oriented policies is that those defining the contours of the policy problem typically stand far *outside* the communities in which the problem occurs.

Instrumentally, then, policies are systems of thought and action used to regulate and organize behavior. Additionally, when policies define a problem, they construct a way of seeing those affecting or affected by the problem. Policies impart lenses for viewing the people they aim to address. The language of policy reveals who is dominant, who is subordinate, and what controls the dominant should exercise on the subordinate in order to effect desired change. Policy authors condemn certain behaviors and extol others. They intimate claims of normalcy and propose mechanisms for bettering those falling outside the often unspoken and loosely defined norm.

THE RATIONALE FOR CULTURAL ANALYSIS OF POLICY

Within an instrumentalist paradigm, policy analysis typically focuses on the relationships between specific policy configurations and discrete policy outcomes. Grounded in traditional social scientific inquiry, policy analysts of various disciplines devise models—often mathematical—for deciphering the most powerful factors that enhance the behaviors intended or encouraged by a policy. For example, much analysis of education policies has been conducted to determine which policy-generated "inputs" (such as teacher certification, resource allocation, curricular programs, and desegregation arrangements) have some effect on educational "outputs" (most commonly standardized, norm-referenced test scores). Policymakers and politicians rely on the results of such studies to craft arguments for their favored policy proposals.

Recently, however, the field of policy studies introduced an angle of inquiry that challenges the prominent policy paradigm. Interpretive, cultural, or anthropological policy analyses encourage examination of the narrative elements on a policy—what Emery Roe (1994) defines as "the scenarios and argumentation on which policies are based" (p. 2)—through focus on the symbols and language used in the entire policy process, from legislation to local implementation. Cultural approaches to policy analysis promote investigation of policy as a rich and complex system of belief, with all the nuances and subtleties implied therein. It aims to engage and uncover the meanings of policies through analysis of the various modes of communication about them. How do policymakers discuss poverty-oriented policies? How do they represent poor people? What do the written policy documents say? What language is used to characterize those whom the policy aims to serve?

Cultural study of policies directs analytical attention to the multiple meanings that policies engender, through the myriad interpretations of policymakers, policy implementers, policy target populations, and policy analysts. Cultural policy interpretation, then, involves all social actors in the policy process and pays attention to both the historical moment in which a policy develops and the structural realities of institutions responsible for its implementation. Such analysis provides an important dimension for interrogating the assumptions built into policy goals as well as for elucidating certain elements of policy outcomes.

The policy process occupies divergent contexts and spaces. Although all locations of the policy process influence one another in the production of an overarching policy narrative that encourages some shared understanding (Roe, 1994; Yanow, 1996), there is no necessary stability or convergence in the meanings of policy constructed by the individuals engaged in the policy process. Meanings, unlike other elements of policy, cannot be mandated. (This perspective is consistent with the work of communications scholar David Berlo [1960] who argues that meanings are never fixed, as they rely on experiences. Since no two people have identical experiences, no two people have precisely shared meanings.) All contexts, from legislative hearings to service institutions, generate multiple interpretations of the technical/regulatory and cultural/representational dimensions of a policy. Interpretive analysis contributes to the understanding of how policies and the divergent contexts of the policy process interact, shape, and constrain one another.

There are many methodological considerations for this type of policy investigation. Whereas mathematical models aid some scholars in determining the statistical significance of select policy inputs on desired policy outputs, the culture of policy is best examined through systematic attention to the language and behaviors of those individuals performing the policy process. Rather than determine whether test scores went up for students identified as policy beneficiaries at rates significantly higher than like students who were not identified as such, the culture of education policy requires investigation of how policymakers and practitioners communicate about, make sense of, and act on the Title I policy itself. For the study of education policies, two important sites are worthy of consideration: Congress and classrooms.

Congressional floor debates on educational policies, a public aspect of policymaking in which elected officials perform rehearsed speeches or debate core legislative priorities, constitute a definitional moment in the policy process. Federal policies directed at schools carry rules and regulations for the provision of services, as well as funds and mechanisms for targeting funded services to particular populations or subpopulations. Embedded in each policy are assumptions about who the groups or individuals targeted by a policy are and what they need. Naming and defining a policy problem—and those who have the problem, create the problem, or are affected by the problem—are part of the "regularized, repeated actions" (Yanow, 1996, p. 188) that make up policy rituals. Many policies draw boundaries around certain subgroups of the populace, denoting what policymakers and analysts call a "target" population. The representation of target populations and their assumed needs often relies on purposefully crafted characterizations of individuals and groups, what Anne Schneider and Helen Ingram (1993, 1997) call the "social construction of target populations." In equity- and poverty-oriented policies, such characterizations often render policy subjects as deficient or deviant to some unspoken norm. In order to defend the need for certain segments of the population to receive special attention from the government, their social conditions, cultural norms, and presumed values are often depicted as substandard (Foley, 1997). Attention is most often paid to the characteristics of individuals rather than the structures of society that contribute to unequal and inequitable life circumstances. Interrogation of the cultural dimensions of policy unveils the often-obscure assumptions built into policies, and the structural inequalities of power and privilege in which they exist. Cultural analysis reveals how policy provides a limited—indeed distorted—lens for viewing people and their life conditions.

Cultural investigation also allows for interrogation of the ways in which policymakers and practitioners define the needs of policy subjects. Such needs definitions provide insight into the values of a society, as well as the political currency attributed to various causes. Here, the work of political philosopher Nancy Fraser (1989) is useful. Through attention to the "politics of needs interpretation" (p. 292), Fraser encourages analysis of the contested and contextual aspects of needs definitions. Public discourse about needs in various contexts of the policy process (such as Congress or schools) represents a site of societal struggle wherein the "politics of needs" occupy three analytical phases. I will elucidate each phase with concrete examples from the initial 1965 authorization of Title I of ESEA.

The first phase is "the struggle to validate the need as a matter of legitimate political concern or to enclave it as a nonpolitical matter" (Fraser, 1989, p. 294). Considerable debate over the original authorization of ESEA Title I of 1965 focused on whether education was a legitimate federal concern. The conflict between local control and federal control framed the discussion. Those favoring federal involvement in education argued that the central government had not only a legitimate concern but also a moral obligation to the education of students characterized as "poor" or "disadvantaged." For example, Representative Charles Joelson (D, NJ) (1965) urged his fellow representatives to support federal involvement in education with the following remarks on the floor of Congress.

Mr. Chairman, when I was first elected to Congress I was assigned to the House Committee on Education and Labor. Then, as now, I was convinced that the Federal Government has a responsibility to improve the quality of primary and secondary education, and I supported Federal aid to education. It was discouraging and frustrating to me to see the issue bogged down in acrimony and dispute over the years. But today we have taken the ball to the one-yard line, and I urge my colleagues to join together for a touchdown. We owe this obligation to the youth of America. (p. 5987)

Representative Joelson was arguing against his colleagues who opposed federal involvement. Those against federal funding to schools maintained that education was a local matter of rightful interest only to local communities and state governments. For example, Representative Howard Smith (D, VA) (1965) implored:

Mr. Speaker, we apparently have come to the end of the road so far as local control over our education in public facilities is concerned. I abhor that. There is nothing dearer to the American home than the neighborhood school, where you have your PTA and your different organizations, and all take a vital interest in the school and have some control of it. I hate to see that tradition destroyed and that control removed from the little neighborhood in the country and located in the bureaucracy of Washington. (p. 5729)

After extensive debate, attempts to render public education the concern of local communities and not the federal government did not prevail and the central government's role in education took hold. Here, the first phase in Fraser's politics of needs addressed not only whether the educational needs of poor children were a legitimate political concern, but also which level of government should respond to this concern. Folded into the debates about poor children's needs were related considerations of federalism and local control.

Fraser (1989) then suggests that once a "need" is established as a legitimate political concern, the second phase of the politics of need—the "struggle over the interpretation of the need, the struggle for the power to define it and, so, to determine what would satisfy it" (p. 294)—ensues. In the course of interpreting the need, defining it, and proposing solutions to satisfy it, politicians and policymakers interpret and represent those theorized to benefit from government intervention. Portrayals of policy beneficiaries reflect the needs interpretations of elected officials. For example, Representative Sisk (D, CA) (1965) conveys a typical representation of those served by federal involvement in education, noting that under Title I legislation, "[p]ublic schools would be eligible for payments for programs designed to meet the special educational needs of children in school attendance areas having high concentrations of disadvantaged children" (p. 5728).

Here, students characterized as disadvantaged are theorized to have needs that are "special" and that set them apart from other children with implicitly regular or normal needs. The needs themselves remain undefined, but are marked as different from an unidentified norm, and thus reflective of a social problem.

Analysis of the culture of policy inspires investigation of not just how the diagnosis of a social problem emerges from the social fabric of a society, but also the rhetorical portrayal of both social problem and solution. As political scientist Murray Edelman (1988) argues, social problems are constituted by a diversity of meanings associated with an undesirable condition. By constructing a condition as a problem, society names the condition, the government responds to group interests associated with the condition, and these responses (through actions and language) affect the condition, making it either better or worse (pp. 12–16). The naming of a problem occurs within dominant ideological patterns of thought. Some aspects of the social world can be named as problems, while others are left unexamined. For example, if there is ideological support for the unequal distribution of resources through the inheritance of family wealth, then individual life conditions are more likely to be named as a problem than are societal structures of resource distribution. The needs addressed by policy will then likely be named as local—at the community or individual level.

Needs interpretations also expose ideological and political positions on the merits of serving various segments of the citizenry. Representative Smith (D, VA) (1965) provides a cynical interpretation of the needs claims reflected in the Title I policy while portraying the policy beneficiaries and their allies through the lenses of race, class, region, and religion:

> You know, this bill got its steam out of the hysteria that is going on now relative to the minority race. They are the ones they say need education in order to put them on a basis of first class citizenship. They, unfortunately, in great numbers, have been born and raised in poverty, necessary poverty, in the Southern States. Now we see great armies of well-meaning people who want to help those folks. We see them invading the South, marching as Sherman's army marched to the sea 100 years ago. I wonder what their real purposes are? I wonder why ministers of the gospel should desert their flocks and go tramping through the mud on the second Sherman march through the South. (p. 5729)

In referring to the "hysteria . . . relative to the minority race," in questioning the involvement of ministers in the civil rights movement, and in the assertion of poverty as "necessary" in the South, this elected official questions the validity of the federal government's involvement in education for poor and minority youth, with implicit focus on black children in the South. This representative's interpretation of the needs claim suggests that the civil rights movement, which in part legitimated the needs claims for federal involvement in education, mirrors attempts to destroy the South by General Sherman's army during the Civil War. In his challenge to the need for education among "the minority race," he invokes power battles much larger than those reflected in this one particular policy.

As various needs interpretations are communicated, contested, and compromised, the third phase in Fraser's (1989) framework emerges. This phase involves "the struggle over the satisfaction of the need, that is, the struggle to secure or withhold provision" (p. 294). As with many education policies, the struggle over how to address the educational needs of students portrays multiple interpretations of which programs, policies, and approaches might produce the articulated, desired results of increased student learning. For example, Representative Leonard Farbstein (D, NY) (1965) notes quite passionately his desire and commitment to secure provision of federal funding for educational expenditures to resource-poor communities:

> Many States and localities simply cannot meet the enormous tax increases that would be necessary to implement a program of quality education. Therefore, I say there is a need for Federal aid, a burning need, a need we must meet. (p. 5962)

How the provision of such federal funding takes shape is a matter of considerable debate. In every authorization and reauthorization hearing, the funding formula and regulatory guidelines are negotiated, often with impassioned pleas for specific policy proposals. In response to the administration's proposed legislation, congressional representatives put forth amendments that reflect both the overall goals of the legislation and the political incentives to maximize revenues to specific areas, such as states, rural communities, and urban centers. Congressional representatives typically support funding allocation schemes that will favor their constituents (Arnold, 1990; Fiorina, 1974; Mayhew, 1974). Fraser's three phases of the politics of needs hint at the constructed nature of the diagnosis and treatment of social problems.

The acts of naming and defining social problems hold great relevance for how policies shape practitioners' interpretations of their clientele. The very language, terms, phrases, and constructions embedded in policies suggest particular orientations to a given phenomenon. Communications scholar Kenneth Burke (1965) identifies such orientations as "bundle[s] of judgments as to how things were, how they are, and how they may be" (p. 14; see also Kauffman, 1989). Policies reflect and encourage specific orientations on the part of policymakers and service providers. Names for individuals and categories of individuals within a policy text engender multiple meanings reflecting various orientations. They constitute what Pierre Bourdieu (1991) identifies as individual and collective "social judgments" through the attribution of a perceived "social essence" (pp. 121–122).

In the policy process, names are commonly used to identify and characterize populations of people. These names both represent and generate the
social constructions of a policy's intended beneficiaries. Anne Schneider and
Helen Ingram (1993) define the social construction of policy target populations as follows:

> [T]he cultural characterizations or popular images of the persons or groups
> whose behavior and well-being are affected by public policy. These character-
> izations are normative and evaluative, portraying groups in positive or nega-
> tive terms through symbolic language, metaphors, and stories. (p. 334)

Policymakers and policies themselves introduce these cultural characterizations through the names used to identify target populations. In attempts to
direct services to specific groups and frame the nature of the services to be
provided, the policy must first identify (i.e., name) the individuals and groups
to be served. Policymakers suggest various orientations when they develop
policies that serve individuals and groups that they represent rhetorically as
"disadvantaged children," "culturally deprived children," and "educationally disadvantaged youth." Such orientations influence the constructions of
individual practitioners and the meanings that get attributed to eligible students. This phenomenon is not unique to labels that focus on "deprivation"
and "deficiency"; indeed, the language about "gifted and talented" students
communicates rather different orientations from the policymakers' and service providers' perspectives.

Policies directed at schools carry guidelines and regulations for the provision of services as well as funds and mechanisms for targeting funded services to particular students or groups thereof. To ensure that schools deliver
services to a policy's intended beneficiaries, policy-generated dollars are often
accompanied by categorization schemes designed to target services to specific students deemed eligible for or entitled to service provision. These
schemes are also intended to prevent or deter a misuse of funds. The resulting categorization schemes take shape in the language and vocabulary of
schooling. Policies carry both names for groups of eligible students and notions of what those students need. School personnel speak to one another
about students and programs using multiple terms and acronyms, often origi-
nating from a policy measure or specialized funding source. Each term represents a policy or program in the school as well as a shorthand cue for
divergent, and not necessarily shared, worlds of meaning.

Just as the acts of naming and defining give rise to interpretive orientations, categorizations in schools influence how teachers understand and represent their students. Numerous categorization schemes operate in schools
through the lenses of gender, language, race, ethnicity, social class, behavior, age, and achievement. Compensatory and categorical policies add addi-

tional names and labels by introducing program designations, eligibility criteria, and a general sense of policy purpose. Through an act of legislation or the availability of funds, new cultural categories, such as "gifted," "special education," "limited English proficient," and "Title I student" circumscribe the daily sense making in the language and routines of schooling.

As anthropologist Ray McDermott (1996) has argued, the labels acquire students rather than students acquiring the labels. Various scholars and practitioners have raised additional concerns about the use of labels for student designations, arguing that policy-generated labels become a damaging stigma to members of the populations policies aim to serve.[2] Murray Edelman (1988) asserts that "some consequences of the policies pursued are always inversions of the value formally proclaimed as the goal of the activity" (p. 16). Even though educational policies might have clearly articulated egalitarian goals, the stigmatization of those served by the policies quashes the egalitarian objectives by creating teachers' expectations for student failure. These expectations have consequences for the educational opportunities provided to students. Investigation of the cultural dimensions of policy can provide insight into these dynamics.

THE CULTURE OF POLICY FRAMEWORK

In the work of anthropologist Oscar Lewis (1959, 1961, 1964, 1965), poor people and poor communities are depicted as having a slate of interrelated cultural traits, implicitly distinctive from their middle-class counterparts. His work, later picked up rhetorically by Daniel Moynihan and other politicians, became an organizing construct for many of the equity-oriented policies motivated during the War on Poverty and Great Society programs of the mid-1960s. The attention paid to the anthropologically observed or politically presumed cultural traits of those living in poverty surfaced in policymaking discussions, floor debates, and academic arguments.

The culture of policy framework shifts the work of cultural analysis away from observation of the individuals and groups served by a policy to the interrogation of *how the policy process frames the ways we see those individuals and groups*. This shift also exposes how the construction of many equity-oriented policies relies on some of the assumptions built into the culture of poverty framework. The culture of policy, then, examines the procedures and assumptions built into the policy process, while challenging the ways in which policies shape institutional and individual perceptions and treatments of those they aim to serve. Figure 1.1 applies the culture of policy framework to ESEA Title I, detailing how the culture of policy is born out of both historical arrangements and institutional practices, while simultaneously creating recursive consequences that feed into the culture of policy itself.

FIGURE 1.1. The Culture of Policy Conceptual Model

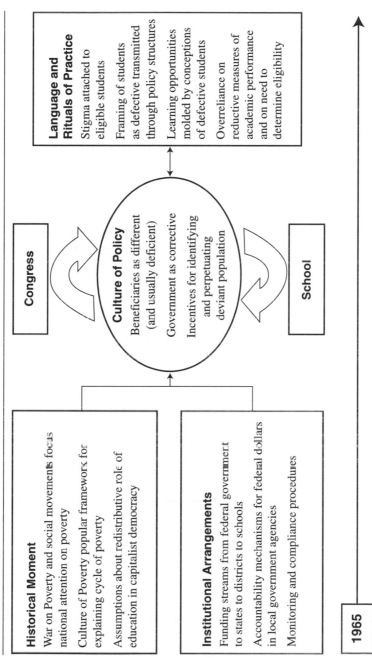

Congress

School

Culture of Policy

Beneficiaries as different (and usually deficient)

Government as corrective

Incentives for identifying and perpetuating deviant population

Language and Rituals of Practice

Stigma attached to eligible students

Framing of students as defective transmitted through policy structures

Learning opportunities molded by conceptions of defective students

Overreliance on reductive measures of academic performance and on need to determine eligibility

Historical Moment

War on Poverty and social movements focus national attention on poverty

Culture of Poverty popular framework for explaining cycle of poverty

Assumptions about redistributive role of education in capitalist democracy

Institutional Arrangements

Funding streams from federal government to states to districts to schools

Accountability mechanisms for federal dollars in local government agencies

Monitoring and compliance procedures

1965

The Historical Moment

Cultural analysis must consider the historical conditions in which a policy emerges. The historical moment of policy formation shapes the framing of policy problems and solutions with contemporaneous notions of policy purposes, government responsibilities, social causality, and national priorities. It also provides context for the ways in which policies are discussed in formal government settings and local implementation efforts.

Consider for a moment the document *A Nation at Risk*, published by the National Commission on Excellence in Education in 1983. The historical context of the Cold War, the Soviet launching of Sputnik in 1957, and international economic competition led politicians and policymakers to put forth impassioned pleas for educational institutions to prepare citizens for international competition. Embedded in these pleas were assumptions about what the government ought to do to ensure the safety, security, and prosperity of the nation. National anxiety about economic growth and competition shaped concerns about educational opportunities. The language of war emerged to justify educational solutions. The second paragraph of *A Nation at Risk* reads as follows:

> If an unfriendly foreign power had attempted to impose on America the mediocre educational performance that exists today, we might well have viewed it as an act of war. As it stands, we have allowed this to happen to ourselves. We have even squandered the gains in student achievement made in the wake of the Sputnik challenge. Moreover, we have dismantled essential support systems which helped make those gains possible. We have, in effect, been committing an act of unthinking, unilateral educational disarmament. (National Commission on Excellence in Education, 1983 [online])

The proposed policy solutions of increased core curricular requirements for high school graduation, heightened performance standards for both high school graduation and college admissions, longer school days and years, and improved teacher preparation all aimed to alleviate the policy problem of a nation made vulnerable by an enemy nation's technological advances. Here, the government's role was to protect its citizens against foreign threat through the preparation of scientists and engineers.

Title I was advanced at an earlier historical moment in which national attention focused on the plight of the poor. In his State of the Union address on January 8, 1964, President Lyndon B. Johnson declared a War on Poverty that aimed the military metaphor inward. President Johnson enlisted volunteers to help fight poverty and its sources through a host of programs aimed at alleviating the perceived causes of poverty. Education was but one of the battlegrounds on which the country would fight the War on Poverty. Employment programs, community action programs, and a plan for continued about farm-animal size further defines the sense of normalcy in knowing certain elements of life outside of the urban environment. Government representatives might not react similarly to the lack of knowledge about the size of subway trains on the part of children growing up in rural or suburban areas.

Similarly, Professor John Silber, then a philosopher at the University of Texas, submitted a letter to Senator Ralph Yarborough (D, TX) about the Head Start and Title I programs that also conjured a middle-class norm. As with various submissions from scholars and practitioners, the letter was read on the floor of Congress and became part of the *Congressional Record*:

> The inability of the desperately poor to profit from these educational and economic opportunities derives in part from the fact that they are partially retarded by the lack of education at a sufficiently early age—by lack of verbal stimulation and experience in symbolic communication *that is a normal part of the childhood experiences of children in middle-class homes* [italics added]. (Silber, as cited in Yarborough, 1965, pp. 7617–7618)

Professor Silber went on to racialize his sense of normalcy by claiming that sufficient verbal stimulation did not take place among black families:

> Children born into Negro families and families whose native language is other than English are not sufficiently stimulated verbally or are insufficiently trained in English to compete successfully in the public schools whose programs are designed for English speaking children. (as cited in Yarborough, 1965, p. 7618)

Public school programs, after all, are designed for the "norm." When children do not benefit from those programs, it is because they fall outside of that constructed norm.

Falling outside the norm is only one element of the casting of policy subjects. The use of language that highlights deprivation, deficiency, deviance, and despair contributes to the framing of policy beneficiaries as inadequate and helpless. The original floor debates about Title I reveal provocative portraits of policy beneficiaries referring to their physical, emotional, even spiritual states. Over and over again, students are described as deprived, their mothers as deficient, and their communities as pathological, with minimal attention to the economic and social structures that create and perpetuate the conditions of poverty. Not only is poverty seen as a disability inherent in the child, but the child's life chances are also presented as curtailed. As noted by Representative Patsy Mink (D, HI) (1965):

> No one doubts the fact that children of the very poor families who live in the slum tenements all across this country suffer mentally as well as physically from this deprivation. Their family life is all but a vacuum of daily subsistence. *There*

economic growth framed the contours of the battle. Educational institutions provided special terrain on which the battle would be fought. Since, as noted by historian Alice O'Connor (2001), poverty was theorized to be caused "not [by] structural barriers but [by] 'certain characteristics'—low education, race, single parenthood" (p. 157) of those living in poverty, educational intervention was deemed necessary. Through public schooling, the state could impart skills, knowledge, and values that would compensate for, if not counter, those taught to poor children at home. As argued by various members of Congress, federal involvement in education—through passage of ESEA Title I—was necessary for victory in the War on Poverty. Hailed as a way to "make the war on poverty effective" (Grabowski, 1965, p. 5994) and as "an integral part, indeed an essential part, of the national war on poverty" (Clark, 1965, p. 7339), supporters of ESEA Title I tied federal involvement in schooling to the ability of the country to address the pressing poverty problem.

At around the same time, academicians of various disciplines turned analytical attention to the lives of the poor. Anthropologists, sociologists, economists, and political scientists all tried to explain the causes and conditions of poverty through scrutiny of the daily interactions and behaviors of people living in poverty. Again, with primary focus on the individual characteristics of the poor, rather than the structural economic and social conditions, scholars such as anthropologist Oscar Lewis (1959, 1961, 1964, 1965) and Michael Harrington (1962) put forth studies of the family structures, spending patterns, and personal relations of the poor. Policymakers embraced the culture of poverty theory as evidence that the poor required government intervention to break free of the individual habits and behaviors understood to perpetuate their conditions. As argued by Alice O'Connor (2001), many liberal scholars and policymakers of the 1960s "had grown more comfortable with the language of psychology, culture, and poverty than with that of political economy and class"(p. 122). The detailed accounts of the daily lives of the poor provided by scholars contributed to the tendency to turn away from considerations of economic structures and divisions along race and class lines. Instead, such accounts encouraged a condemning, paternalistic, albeit rhetorically sympathetic gaze. The popularized scholarship at the time of the War on Poverty provided a lens for viewing policy subjects: children growing up poor were painted as victims of the culture into which they were born.

The historical moment of a policy's inception also reveals concurrent conceptions of the role of government and, in the case of federal education policy, the role of public schools. In a capitalist democracy, public education tends to serve paradoxical roles: the reproduction of a hierarchically differentiated labor force and the democratization of educational opportunities (Carnoy & Levin, 1985; Grubb & Lazerson, 1988). At different historical periods, one role tends to be favored over another. During the mid-1980s, for example, the focus on international competition in the Cold War led to

a concerted effort to raise standards for students in public schools and develop "talent" among those showing "promise" irrespective of the differential access opportunities available to students of different class backgrounds.
During the earlier period of the War on Poverty and Great Society programs,
however, the role of schools as an equalizer or leveler of the metaphorical
playing field gained force. Focus on the state's obligation to serve all students,
to equalize the opportunities available to students, and to "compensate" for
the perceived consequences of poverty rendered educational institutions a
potential site for government intervention.[3] The priorities of a particular
period in time shape the cultural dimensions of policy initiation and adaptation. The historical moment in which any policy is initiated thus plays a
seminal role in the culture of policy framework.

Institutional Arrangements

When a policy is established, it resides within existing institutional and organizational arrangements. These arrangements mold and constrain the ways
in which a policy takes shape both at the level of policymaking and implementation. Government funding is allocated to local educational agencies
through state and district mechanisms. Money moves from the government
through the "multilevel educational bureaucracy" (Comfort, 1982, p. 37)
to the schools. Each level must demonstrate that the allocated funds are being
used as intended: to serve the proposed policy beneficiaries.

Each level of the bureaucracy is held accountable by the one above it. The
Department of Education monitors states. States monitor districts. Districts
monitor schools. Accountability mechanisms include extensive paperwork as
well as on-site visits. Multiple iterations of program budgets, narrative descriptions of program plans, and other documentation of rendered services pass
between levels of government to demonstrate the appropriate use of designated
funds. Additionally, groups of monitors visit educational institutions to observe program implementation, check written documents against practice, and
note whether the use of funds complies with the regulatory guidelines of policy
use. These institutional arrangements aid in the narrow targeting of policy-
generated resources to designated policy beneficiaries. They encourage the
labeling of certain students as eligible, the defense of their eligibility through
conceptions of deficit and deficiency, and the provision of services that are easily
identifiable to outside observers. *Service delivery, then, often conforms to the
need to demonstrate compliance over holistic considerations of what set of
educational opportunities might benefit individual students.* In the case of
Title I, teachers report having to label all curricular materials purchased through
Title I dollars and to ensure that when compliance monitors from the state or
district level visited, only those identified as eligible for services were using those
materials. Some scholars have argued that the fragmented nature of school

programming for Title I service delivery often segregated integrated schools by race, ethnicity, and socioeconomic status through the isolation of students for service delivery (Eyler et al., 1983; Glass & Smith, 1977; Kimbrough & Hill, 1983).

The Culture of Policy in Congress and the Classroom

Both the historical moment of policy initiation and the institutional arrangements for service provision contribute to the culture of policy. My depiction of this policy culture focuses on three interrelated traits: (a) a shared conception of policy beneficiaries as deviant from (and usually deficient to) an often-unstated norm, (b) a presumption that government institutions can fulfill a corrective role in the lives of the country's deviant inhabitants, and (c) mechanisms for service provision that provide incentives for identifying, maintaining, and perpetuating a deviant population.

Beneficiaries as Deviant. At the time of policymaking, policy subjects are commonly portrayed through comparative reference to a perceived or accepted norm. Policymakers most often depict beneficiaries as different from this constructed norm with a substantial tendency toward highlighting their deficiencies, weaknesses, and lacks. Rather than investigate—or even acknowledge—the structural conditions that favor certain members of society over others, elected officials rely on representations of individual and groups of policy beneficiaries. A focus on the structural conditions of a capitalist economy—particularly one in which local community wealth primarily determines school resources—would reframe the policy problem, potentially calling into question the causes rather than the results of an inequitable resource distribution system. Portraits of policy beneficiaries as different, deficient, and needy take center stage as devices to motivate the need for equity-oriented policy.

During the original Title I authorization, congressional representatives defended policy passage by evoking images of both a deviant population and a comparative norm. For example, on the 1965 congressional floor, Representative Quie (R, MN) noted that there are children in the city of Chicago

> who when asked how big a horse or cow was in a picture, answered, "3 to 5 inches." They had not received any experience, no educational experience which they would automatically receive in associating with their parents *if in a middle-class environment* [italics added]. Here is a crying need for Federal assistance. (p. 6019)

Here, the assumption of middle class as the norm is reflected directly. Reference to the "crying need" evidenced in urban children's lack of knowledge

> *is no family effort or ability to supplement the young child's mind with the*
> *wonders of learning and the child is handicapped from this accident of birth*
> *for this socioeconomic disability* [italics added] which in most cases continues
> on as a fetter upon his whole future development. (p. 5765)

In this statement, Congresswoman Mink's representation of the consequences
of childhood poverty focuses not only on the limited material resources available to the child but also on her or his potential for mental and physical
growth. In addition to falling outside the norm, poor children are forever
curtailed by the deprivation into which they were born.

The above quotations reveal both a casting of beneficiaries as deviant and
a larger set of ideological assumptions about race, class, and family on which
such casting is based. In taking for granted certain structural arrangements,
the makers of equity-oriented policy must assume that the poor are deficient.
Otherwise, they are left to address the inherent and necessary inequities in the
structure of capitalist economic and social arrangements. Their representations
of deficiency among the policy subjects form part of the reproduction of social
privilege and domination, even at the time of constructing policies aimed—at
least discursively—at democratizing educational opportunities.

Government as Corrective. Once a pool of defective citizens is identified, the government can position itself as a corrective force. Through
intervention in school funding tied to regulatory mechanisms for service delivery, the government assumes that it can address the perceived problems
of children growing up poor. Passage of Title I conveys an overall sense of
confidence that the government can in essence "treat" poor children through
compensatory funding to their schools. For example, Representative Spark
Matsunaga (D, HI) (1965) supported passage of Title I, asserting that federal intervention could correct the conditions of children growing up poor:

> The proposed legislation dramatizes our national concern over this problem.
> It provides a remedy that is at once immediate, effective, and permanent. . . .
> Let us hope that by correcting educational deficiencies among children born
> to poverty, we will place within their grasp the tools that will enable them to
> live "the American story." (p. 5765)

In the above testimony, federal funding is optimistically portrayed as reflective of the government's corrective potential in the lives of "children
born to poverty." With the romanticized narrative of "the American story"
posited as the norm, federal intervention becomes the corrective device for
those whose life circumstances have led them astray. Through such intervention, perceived deficiencies will be corrected, and policy subjects will
acquire skills and tools, thus enabling them to partake in the promise of
freedom and prosperity.

Incentives for Identification and Perpetuation of Deviant Populations. As long as money to hire personnel for policy implementation exists, so too exist practices of naming and describing policy subjects theorized to need funded services. When the rhetorical portraits of policy subjects promote conceptions of citizen subgroups as different and deficient, and when the government in its corrective role designates funds to fix those citizen subgroups, then incentives for identification and maintenance of such subgroups emerge. In the case of compensatory education, the identification of student subgroups based on achievement test scores or poverty measures encourages a conceptualization of students as lacking in intellect, capabilities, promise, and potential. The policy solution tends to rely on the employment of adults to serve eligible students. Adult employment security then becomes closely linked to student underperformance.[4] Not every practitioner responds in the same way to such incentives, but as long as there are policy dollars coupled with student underperformance, incentives of this nature comprise compensatory policy culture.

These features of the culture of education policy are not stagnant. They are molded and transformed in the interplay between the various levels of government charged with the mandate to "fix" defective students. As schools respond to new government policies and programs, as problems in implementation arise, and as tensions between a policy's stated goal and its actual implementation surface, the school-based experiences feed back into the next iteration of policy. As most policies are revisited every few years, the work and world of the local agencies feed into the work and world of Congress as it reauthorizes policies. The recursive relationship between federal elective representatives and local practitioners suggests an ever-evolving policy culture that emphasizes different dimensions of the culture of education policy during different historical periods.

CULTURAL CONSEQUENCES ON POLICY IMPLEMENTATION

All cultural configurations have consequences for practice. As an organizing principle for daily interaction, policies circumscribe the actions and behaviors of policy implementers as well as policy subjects. The culture of policy can lead to practices that run counter to the intended policy goals. These cultural consequences take form in the language and rituals of practice. In the case of Title I, there are four clear consequences of the culture of education policy on the language and rituals of practice that invert the equity goals of the policy: (a) the overreliance on reductive measures of academic performance and poverty to determine eligibility, (b) the framing of students as defective transmitted to practice, (c) the stigma attached to eligible students, and (d) the molding of learning opportunities based on lowered expectations.

Overreliance on Reductive Measures of Achievement and Poverty

In order to identify members of the defective population needing corrective action and narrowly target resources to address their abnormality, some measure of deviance must be used. Formulas to determine institutional need for policy-generated services rely on the measurement of various characteristics of the policy subjects. In the case of education policies, measures of student performance and family economic circumstances have signaled student eligibility for policy-generated dollars. Earlier iterations of Title I focused on a combination of individual test scores and poverty designations; more recent versions rely solely on school poverty levels. However, all measures are at best imprecise. Educational measurement practices have never effectively captured complex renderings of a child's mind. Even for diagnostic purposes, a composite of various educational performance measures is at best a "union of insufficiencies" (Fullan & Rolheiser, 2001, pp. 31-32)[5] in educators' goals to understand what children know and can do.

Additionally, the advent of using standardized test scores to hold schools accountable for student performance began in large part with Title I legislation. In order to evaluate Title I effectiveness, the bill required "objective measurement of educational achievement" (Elementary and Secondary Education Act of 1965, Sec. 205). The same limited measures, then, were used to determine eligibility and program effectiveness. If the program was effective, the eligibility should decrease and the funds should be cut. Reductive measures of students' capabilities determined both who would generate funds and whether those funds were used well. The incentives for school-based practitioners, of course, were paradoxical. If they could demonstrate program effectiveness, they would lose program revenues. In other words, if teachers could improve student performance, they could lose the resources (or even their jobs) that were central to improving and sustaining that performance.

Similarly, the measurement of poverty is circumscribed by the construction of the concept itself. According to Martin Rein (1970), common definitions of poverty for the purposes of government programs have been based on data concerning the estimated cost of subsistence. Rein argues that such definitions of poverty are "arbitrary, circular, and relative" (p. 458) and laden with ambiguity. The establishment of a "poverty line" based on subsistence definitions of poverty implies that poverty is indeed a measurable condition and that calculations of disposable dollars and dependents can determine whether someone is above or below a poverty threshold. However, that threshold and the methods for measuring whether one is above or below it, let alone where the line should fall, have been hotly contested (Rein, pp. 446–460; see also O'Connor, 2001, p. 324, note 42). Competing responses to the following questions are rarely reflected in the measurement of poverty: What constitutes a comfortable material existence? Does the context in which poverty exists matter? Is poverty most commonly a static or temporary condition? Poverty measures tend to reflect the bureaucratic need to categorize and define groups of people in order to take stock of the citizenry and, at times on the national agenda, provide services. The poverty-line measure cannot capture the complexity of the concept or its meaning for resource-strapped children and families.

Further complicating matters, school poverty measures have at times relied on eligibility for Aid to Families with Dependent Children (AFDC)—which involves a lengthy process of welfare qualification with background investigation—and at other times eligibility for free and reduced-price lunch—which involves the submission of forms reporting income to the school, with no background check. In fact, one school could have considerably different "poverty rates" from using one measure or another.

Transmission of Framing Students as Defective

The language of policy carries with it ways of seeing policy subjects. Policy-generated categorization schemes for dollars, personnel, and eligible students reveal the assumptions and orientations on which a policy is built. Terms such as "at-risk youth" and "disadvantaged children" are written into the policy documents, signaling an association of hazard, danger, and despair with the policy beneficiaries. These terms are carried through written and performed policy interpretations at various levels of implementation. In district offices and schools, for example, students eligible for Title I have been described as "educationally disadvantaged youth," "Title I students," or "Chapter 1 students" throughout the policy's history. More recently, schools have been assigned "Title I" identities as well. These categories of students do not connote natural conditions. One is not born "Title I" or "educationally disadvantaged." Through policy mechanisms, such terms appear in school practice framing the eligible population as defective and in need of corrective treatment.

Stigmatization of Eligible Students

Policy categorization schemes ascribe stigma to eligible students. Through ordinary policy practices, students are marked with labels that carry the associations of defect and deficiency. In Title I's history, teachers have often received lists of policy-eligible students before they even met their classes at the beginning of the school year. Using test scores and poverty measures, district- and/or school-based program coordinators generate lists of eligible students and distribute these lists to classroom teachers. The marks of "Title I" or "educationally disadvantaged youth" and their associated stigma often land on individual students prior to initial face-to-face encounters between students and teachers. And again more recently, such designations are ascribed to entire schools. The origin of the "Title I" or "educationally disadvantaged youth" designations are often forgotten, while the associated meanings of those labels take hold. Practitioners may not remember or be aware of the specific policy requirements that created the Title I designation, but they do associate that designation with some negative condition.[6] Being Title I signals far more than entitlement to policy-generated resources, connecting to notions of ability rather than eligibility.[7]

Compromised Learning Opportunities

Policy-eligibility designations provide information to teachers contributing to their construction of student learning opportunities. When teachers believe that students can perform at high levels, they are more likely to provide rigorous and challenging learning opportunities than when they believe that students cannot perform at such levels. The work of Robert Rosenthal and Lenore Jacobson (1968) in *Pygmalion in the Classroom* demonstrated the connections between teachers' expectations and students' academic performance. In a classic experiment they conducted at an elementary school, teachers were told that some of their students would have an intellectual growth spurt in the upcoming months. The identified students, however, were randomly selected by the researchers and reflected a range of initial academic performance. In what they labeled the "Pygmalion effect," the researchers found that the students identified as expecting a growth spurt did indeed outperform their counterparts with similar initial performance records. According to the authors, negative expectations influence academic opportunities as well. Although Rosenthal and Jacobson's work did not uncover the specific processes that connect teachers' expectations to student performance, subsequent studies have shown how educational opportunities play a key role in linking teacher expectations and student performance (see, for example, Good, 1987; Jussim & Eccles, 1992; Oakes, 1985).

Researchers and politicians have expressed specific concerns about the low expectations that teachers and school personnel might have for students marked as eligible for Title I services (Brophy, 1988; LeTendre, 1991; Slavin, 1991). Although intended to provide services that will bolster their academic performance, casting students as eligible provides information that encourages teachers to compromise learning opportunities, and at worst "dumb down" curricular offerings. These concerns motivated the shifts from individual student eligibility to whole school eligibility in recent reauthorization efforts. Unfortunately, a movement from individual students to whole schools does not guarantee that learning opportunities will not be compromised on a greater scale.

EQUITY POLICIES AND CENTRAL CONFLICTS WITHIN THE CULTURE OF POLICY

The above analysis of the culture of policy exposes central tensions embedded in the ways in which equity-oriented policies influence the language and rituals of schooling. The incentives provided by such policies and their connections to policy-generated material resources place school-based practitioners in a complex bind. As agents of the state, practitioners are expected to assume the corrective paradigm of intervention. Regrettably, however, practitioners who do not subscribe to the language and rituals encouraged by policies find themselves out of compliance with policy mandates and potentially sanctioned for noncompliance.

The culture of policy as described above is a difficult trap for equity-minded policymakers and practitioners. Efforts to overcome this trap have shifted the level or unit of the policy subject—from individual students to entire schools—without addressing the cultural dimensions of the assumptive aspects of defect and deficiency inherent in policy construction. With recent efforts to identify Title I eligibility through consideration of school-level poverty characteristics, the stigma attached to individual students has been relocated to schools and communities. The notion of working in or attending a "Title I school" signals various assumptions about poverty, performance, and school climate. The unit has changed; the stigma has not.

As I will argue in the later chapters of this book, there is a need for critical attention to the policy-influenced language and rituals in schools to avoid the paradoxical and contradictory nature of equity-oriented educational policies. The incentive structures imbedded in policy practice are difficult to break. The negative framing of poor children in policy discourse is hard to avoid. The policy "dozens" may just be an inevitable part of the determination of a legitimate policy need. The schools themselves are the best leverage point for resisting the culture of education policy.

Only through purposeful work on the cultural dimensions of schooling— the language and rituals of practice—can school communities maintain a commitment to an equity imperative. As many policy rituals are at odds with an authentic equity orientation, school-based practitioners need to share strategies for breaking through the traps provided by policies. If the policy dozens remain a part of the policy process, equity-minded practitioners need economic growth framed the contours of the battle. Educational institutions provided special terrain on which the battle would be fought. Since, as noted by historian Alice O'Connor (2001), poverty was theorized to be caused "not [by] structural barriers but [by] 'certain characteristics'—low education, race, single parenthood" (p. 157) of those living in poverty, educational intervention was deemed necessary. Through public schooling, the state could impart skills, knowledge, and values that would compensate for, if not counter, those taught to poor children at home. As argued by various members of Congress, federal involvement in education—through passage of ESEA Title I—was necessary for victory in the War on Poverty. Hailed as a way to "make the war on poverty effective" (Grabowski, 1965, p. 5994) and as "an integral part, indeed an essential part, of the national war on poverty" (Clark, 1965, p. 7339), supporters of ESEA Title I tied federal involvement in schooling to the ability of the country to address the pressing poverty problem.

At around the same time, academicians of various disciplines turned analytical attention to the lives of the poor. Anthropologists, sociologists, economists, and political scientists all tried to explain the causes and conditions of poverty through scrutiny of the daily interactions and behaviors of people living in poverty. Again, with primary focus on the individual characteristics of the poor, rather than the structural economic and social conditions, scholars such as anthropologist Oscar Lewis (1959, 1961, 1964, 1965) and Michael Harrington (1962) put forth studies of the family structures, spending patterns, and personal relations of the poor. Policymakers embraced the culture of poverty theory as evidence that the poor required government intervention to break free of the individual habits and behaviors understood to perpetuate their conditions. As argued by Alice O'Connor (2001), many liberal scholars and policymakers of the 1960s "had grown more comfortable with the language of psychology, culture, and poverty than with that of political economy and class" (p. 122). The detailed accounts of the daily lives of the poor provided by scholars contributed to the tendency to turn away from considerations of economic structures and divisions along race and class lines. Instead, such accounts encouraged a condemning, paternalistic, albeit rhetorically sympathetic gaze. The popularized scholarship at the time of the War on Poverty provided a lens for viewing policy subjects: children growing up poor were painted as victims of the culture into which they were born.

The historical moment of a policy's inception also reveals concurrent conceptions of the role of government and, in the case of federal education policy, the role of public schools. In a capitalist democracy, public education tends to serve paradoxical roles: the reproduction of a hierarchically differentiated labor force and the democratization of educational opportunities (Carnoy & Levin, 1985; Grubb & Lazerson, 1988). At different historical periods, one role tends to be favored over another. During the mid-1980s, for example, the focus on international competition in the Cold War led to a concerted effort to raise standards for students in public schools and develop "talent" among those showing "promise" irrespective of the differential access opportunities available to students of different class backgrounds. During the earlier period of the War on Poverty and Great Society programs, however, the role of schools as an equalizer or leveler of the metaphorical playing field gained force. Focus on the state's obligation to serve all students, to equalize the opportunities available to students, and to "compensate" for the perceived consequences of poverty rendered educational institutions a potential site for government intervention.[3] The priorities of a particular period in time shape the cultural dimensions of policy initiation and adaptation. The historical moment in which any policy is initiated thus plays a seminal role in the culture of policy framework.

Institutional Arrangements

When a policy is established, it resides within existing institutional and organizational arrangements. These arrangements mold and constrain the ways in which a policy takes shape both at the level of policymaking and implementation. Government funding is allocated to local educational agencies through state and district mechanisms. Money moves from the government through the "multilevel educational bureaucracy" (Comfort, 1982, p. 37) to the schools. Each level must demonstrate that the allocated funds are being used as intended: to serve the proposed policy beneficiaries.

Each level of the bureaucracy is held accountable by the one above it. The Department of Education monitors states. States monitor districts. Districts monitor schools. Accountability mechanisms include extensive paperwork as well as on-site visits. Multiple iterations of program budgets, narrative descriptions of program plans, and other documentation of rendered services pass between levels of government to demonstrate the appropriate use of designated funds. Additionally, groups of monitors visit educational institutions to observe program implementation, check written documents against practice, and note whether the use of funds complies with the regulatory guidelines of policy use. These institutional arrangements aid in the narrow targeting of policy-generated resources to designated policy beneficiaries. They encourage the labeling of certain students as eligible, the defense of their eligibility through conceptions of deficit and deficiency, and the provision of services that are easily identifiable to outside observers. *Service delivery, then, often conforms to the need to demonstrate compliance over holistic considerations of what set of educational opportunities might benefit individual students.* In the case of Title I, teachers report having to label all curricular materials purchased through Title I dollars and to ensure that when compliance monitors from the state or district level visited, only those identified as eligible for services were using those materials. Some scholars have argued that the fragmented nature of school programming for Title I service delivery often segregated integrated schools by race, ethnicity, and socioeconomic status through the isolation of students for service delivery (Eyler et al., 1983; Glass & Smith, 1977; Kimbrough & Hill, 1983).

The Culture of Policy in Congress and the Classroom

Both the historical moment of policy initiation and the institutional arrangements for service provision contribute to the culture of policy. My depiction of this policy culture focuses on three interrelated traits: (a) a shared conception of policy beneficiaries as deviant from (and usually deficient to) an often-unstated norm, (b) a presumption that government institutions can fulfill a corrective role in the lives of the country's deviant inhabitants, and (c) mechanisms for service provision that provide incentives for identifying, maintaining, and perpetuating a deviant population.

Beneficiaries as Deviant. At the time of policymaking, policy subjects are commonly portrayed through comparative reference to a perceived or accepted norm. Policymakers most often depict beneficiaries as different from this constructed norm with a substantial tendency toward highlighting their deficiencies, weaknesses, and lacks. Rather than investigate—or even acknowledge—the structural conditions that favor certain members of society over others, elected officials rely on representations of individual and groups of policy beneficiaries. A focus on the structural conditions of a capitalist economy—particularly one in which local community wealth primarily determines school resources—would reframe the policy problem, potentially calling into question the causes rather than the results of an inequitable resource distribution system. Portraits of policy beneficiaries as different, deficient, and needy take center stage as devices to motivate the need for equity-oriented policy.

During the original Title I authorization, congressional representatives defended policy passage by evoking images of both a deviant population and a comparative norm. For example, on the 1965 congressional floor, Representative Quie (R, MN) noted that there are children in the city of Chicago

> who when asked how big a horse or cow was in a picture, answered, "3 to 5 inches." They had not received any experience, no educational experience which they would automatically receive in associating with their parents *if in a middle-class environment* [italics added]. Here is a crying need for Federal assistance. (p. 6019)

Here, the assumption of middle class as the norm is reflected directly. Reference to the "crying need" evidenced in urban children's lack of knowledge about farm-animal size further defines the sense of normalcy in knowing certain elements of life outside of the urban environment. Government representatives might not react similarly to the lack of knowledge about the size of subway trains on the part of children growing up in rural or suburban areas.

Similarly, Professor John Silber, then a philosopher at the University of Texas, submitted a letter to Senator Ralph Yarborough (D, TX) about the Head Start and Title I programs that also conjured a middle-class norm. As with various submissions from scholars and practitioners, the letter was read on the floor of Congress and became part of the *Congressional Record*:

> The inability of the desperately poor to profit from these educational and economic opportunities derives in part from the fact that they are partially retarded by the lack of education at a sufficiently early age—by lack of verbal stimulation and experience in symbolic communication *that is a normal part of the childhood experiences of children in middle-class homes* [italics added]. (Silber, as cited in Yarborough, 1965, pp. 7617–7618)

Professor Silber went on to racialize his sense of normalcy by claiming that sufficient verbal stimulation did not take place among black families:

> Children born into Negro families and families whose native language is other than English are not sufficiently stimulated verbally or are insufficiently trained in English to compete successfully in the public schools whose programs are designed for English speaking children. (as cited in Yarborough, 1965, p. 7618)

Public school programs, after all, are designed for the "norm." When children do not benefit from those programs, it is because they fall outside of that constructed norm.

Falling outside the norm is only one element of the casting of policy subjects. The use of language that highlights deprivation, deficiency, deviance, and despair contributes to the framing of policy beneficiaries as inadequate and helpless. The original floor debates about Title I reveal provocative portraits of policy beneficiaries referring to their physical, emotional, even spiritual states. Over and over again, students are described as deprived, their mothers as deficient, and their communities as pathological, with minimal attention to the economic and social structures that create and perpetuate the conditions of poverty. Not only is poverty seen as a disability inherent in the child, but the child's life chances are also presented as curtailed. As noted by Representative Patsy Mink (D, HI) (1965):

> No one doubts the fact that children of the very poor families who live in the slum tenements all across this country suffer mentally as well as physically from this deprivation. Their family life is all but a vacuum of daily subsistence. *There*

is no family effort or ability to supplement the young child's mind with the
wonders of learning and the child is handicapped from this accident of birth
for this socioeconomic disability [italics added] which in most cases continues
on as a fetter upon his whole future development. (p. 5765)

In this statement, Congresswoman Mink's representation of the consequences
of childhood poverty focuses not only on the limited material resources available to the child but also on her or his potential for mental and physical
growth. In addition to falling outside the norm, poor children are forever
curtailed by the deprivation into which they were born.

The above quotations reveal both a casting of beneficiaries as deviant and
a larger set of ideological assumptions about race, class, and family on which
such casting is based. In taking for granted certain structural arrangements,
the makers of equity-oriented policy must assume that the poor are deficient.
Otherwise, they are left to address the inherent and necessary inequities in the
structure of capitalist economic and social arrangements. Their representations
of deficiency among the policy subjects form part of the reproduction of social
privilege and domination, even at the time of constructing policies aimed—at
least discursively—at democratizing educational opportunities.

Government as Corrective. Once a pool of defective citizens is identified, the government can position itself as a corrective force. Through
intervention in school funding tied to regulatory mechanisms for service delivery, the government assumes that it can address the perceived problems
of children growing up poor. Passage of Title I conveys an overall sense of
confidence that the government can in essence "treat" poor children through
compensatory funding to their schools. For example, Representative Spark
Matsunaga (D, HI) (1965) supported passage of Title I, asserting that federal intervention could correct the conditions of children growing up poor:

The proposed legislation dramatizes our national concern over this problem.
It provides a remedy that is at once immediate, effective, and permanent. . . .
Let us hope that by correcting educational deficiencies among children born
to poverty, we will place within their grasp the tools that will enable them to
live "the American story." (p. 5765)

In the above testimony, federal funding is optimistically portrayed as reflective of the government's corrective potential in the lives of "children
born to poverty." With the romanticized narrative of "the American story"
posited as the norm, federal intervention becomes the corrective device for
those whose life circumstances have led them astray. Through such intervention, perceived deficiencies will be corrected, and policy subjects will
acquire skills and tools, thus enabling them to partake in the promise of
freedom and prosperity.

Incentives for Identification and Perpetuation of Deviant Populations. As long as money to hire personnel for policy implementation exists, so too exist practices of naming and describing policy subjects theorized to need funded services. When the rhetorical portraits of policy subjects promote conceptions of citizen subgroups as different and deficient, and when the government in its corrective role designates funds to fix those citizen subgroups, then incentives for identification and maintenance of such subgroups emerge. In the case of compensatory education, the identification of student subgroups based on achievement test scores or poverty measures encourages a conceptualization of students as lacking in intellect, capabilities, promise, and potential. The policy solution tends to rely on the employment of adults to serve eligible students. Adult employment security then becomes closely linked to student underperformance.[4] Not every practitioner responds in the same way to such incentives, but as long as there are policy dollars coupled with student underperformance, incentives of this nature comprise compensatory policy culture.

These features of the culture of education policy are not stagnant. They are molded and transformed in the interplay between the various levels of government charged with the mandate to "fix" defective students. As schools respond to new government policies and programs, as problems in implementation arise, and as tensions between a policy's stated goal and its actual implementation surface, the school-based experiences feed back into the next iteration of policy. As most policies are revisited every few years, the work and world of the local agencies feed into the work and world of Congress as it reauthorizes policies. The recursive relationship between federal elective representatives and local practitioners suggests an ever-evolving policy culture that emphasizes different dimensions of the culture of education policy during different historical periods.

CULTURAL CONSEQUENCES ON
POLICY IMPLEMENTATION

All cultural configurations have consequences for practice. As an organizing principle for daily interaction, policies circumscribe the actions and behaviors of policy implementers as well as policy subjects. The culture of policy can lead to practices that run counter to the intended policy goals. These cultural consequences take form in the language and rituals of practice. In the case of Title I, there are four clear consequences of the culture of education policy on the language and rituals of practice that invert the equity goals of the policy: (a) the overreliance on reductive measures of academic performance and poverty to determine eligibility, (b) the framing of students as defective transmitted to practice, (c) the stigma attached to eligible students, and (d) the molding of learning opportunities based on lowered expectations.

Overreliance on Reductive Measures of Achievement and Poverty

In order to identify members of the defective population needing corrective action and narrowly target resources to address their abnormality, some measure of deviance must be used. Formulas to determine institutional need for policy-generated services rely on the measurement of various characteristics of the policy subjects. In the case of education policies, measures of student performance and family economic circumstances have signaled student eligibility for policy-generated dollars. Earlier iterations of Title I focused on a combination of individual test scores and poverty designations; more recent versions rely solely on school poverty levels. However, all measures are at best imprecise. Educational measurement practices have never effectively captured complex renderings of a child's mind. Even for diagnostic purposes, a composite of various educational performance measures is at best a "union of insufficiencies" (Fullan & Rolheiser, 2001, pp. 31-32)[5] in educators' goals to understand what children know and can do.

Additionally, the advent of using standardized test scores to hold schools accountable for student performance began in large part with Title I legislation. In order to evaluate Title I effectiveness, the bill required "objective measurement of educational achievement" (Elementary and Secondary Education Act of 1965, Sec. 205). The same limited measures, then, were used to determine eligibility and program effectiveness. If the program was effective, the eligibility should decrease and the funds should be cut. Reductive measures of students' capabilities determined both who would generate funds and whether those funds were used well. The incentives for school-based practitioners, of course, were paradoxical. If they could demonstrate program effectiveness, they would lose program revenues. In other words, if teachers could improve student performance, they could lose the resources (or even their jobs) that were central to improving and sustaining that performance.

Similarly, the measurement of poverty is circumscribed by the construction of the concept itself. According to Martin Rein (1970), common definitions of poverty for the purposes of government programs have been based on data concerning the estimated cost of subsistence. Rein argues that such definitions of poverty are "arbitrary, circular, and relative" (p. 458) and laden with ambiguity. The establishment of a "poverty line" based on subsistence definitions of poverty implies that poverty is indeed a measurable condition and that calculations of disposable dollars and dependents can determine whether someone is above or below a poverty threshold. However, that threshold and the methods for measuring whether one is above or below it, let alone where the line should fall, have been hotly contested (Rein, pp. 446–460; see also O'Connor, 2001, p. 324, note 42). Competing responses to the following questions are rarely reflected in the measurement of poverty: What constitutes a comfortable material existence? Does the context in which poverty exists matter? Is poverty most commonly a static or temporary condition? Poverty measures tend to reflect the bureaucratic need to categorize and define groups of people in order to take stock of the citizenry and, at times on the national agenda, provide services. The poverty-line measure cannot capture the complexity of the concept or its meaning for resource-strapped children and families.

Further complicating matters, school poverty measures have at times relied on eligibility for Aid to Families with Dependent Children (AFDC)—which involves a lengthy process of welfare qualification with background investigation—and at other times eligibility for free and reduced-price lunch—which involves the submission of forms reporting income to the school, with no background check. In fact, one school could have considerably different "poverty rates" from using one measure or another.

Transmission of Framing Students as Defective

The language of policy carries with it ways of seeing policy subjects. Policy-generated categorization schemes for dollars, personnel, and eligible students reveal the assumptions and orientations on which a policy is built. Terms such as "at-risk youth" and "disadvantaged children" are written into the policy documents, signaling an association of hazard, danger, and despair with the policy beneficiaries. These terms are carried through written and performed policy interpretations at various levels of implementation. In district offices and schools, for example, students eligible for Title I have been described as "educationally disadvantaged youth," "Title I students," or "Chapter 1 students" throughout the policy's history. More recently, schools have been assigned "Title I" identities as well. These categories of students do not connote natural conditions. One is not born "Title I" or "educationally disadvantaged." Through policy mechanisms, such terms appear in school practice framing the eligible population as defective and in need of corrective treatment.

Stigmatization of Eligible Students

Policy categorization schemes ascribe stigma to eligible students. Through ordinary policy practices, students are marked with labels that carry the associations of defect and deficiency. In Title I's history, teachers have often received lists of policy-eligible students before they even met their classes at the beginning of the school year. Using test scores and poverty measures, district- and/or school-based program coordinators generate lists of eligible students and distribute these lists to classroom teachers. The marks of "Title I" or "educationally disadvantaged youth" and their associated stigma often land on individual students prior to initial face-to-face encounters between students and teachers. And again more recently, such designations are ascribed to entire schools. The origin of the "Title I" or "educationally disadvantaged youth" designations are often forgotten, while the associated meanings of those labels take hold. Practitioners may not remember or be aware of the specific policy requirements that created the Title I designation, but they do associate that designation with some negative condition.[6] Being Title I signals far more than entitlement to policy-generated resources, connecting to notions of ability rather than eligibility.[7]

Compromised Learning Opportunities

Policy-eligibility designations provide information to teachers contributing to their construction of student learning opportunities. When teachers believe that students can perform at high levels, they are more likely to provide rigorous and challenging learning opportunities than when they believe that students cannot perform at such levels. The work of Robert Rosenthal and Lenore Jacobson (1968) in *Pygmalion in the Classroom* demonstrated the connections between teachers' expectations and students' academic performance. In a classic experiment they conducted at an elementary school, teachers were told that some of their students would have an intellectual growth spurt in the upcoming months. The identified students, however, were randomly selected by the researchers and reflected a range of initial academic performance. In what they labeled the "Pygmalion effect," the researchers found that the students identified as expecting a growth spurt did indeed outperform their counterparts with similar initial performance records. According to the authors, negative expectations influence academic opportunities as well. Although Rosenthal and Jacobson's work did not uncover the specific processes that connect teachers' expectations to student performance, subsequent studies have shown how educational opportunities play a key role in linking teacher expectations and student performance (see, for example, Good, 1987; Jussim & Eccles, 1992; Oakes, 1985).

Researchers and politicians have expressed specific concerns about the low expectations that teachers and school personnel might have for students marked as eligible for Title I services (Brophy, 1988; LeTendre, 1991; Slavin, 1991). Although intended to provide services that will bolster their academic performance, casting students as eligible provides information that encourages teachers to compromise learning opportunities, and at worst "dumb down" curricular offerings. These concerns motivated the shifts from individual student eligibility to whole school eligibility in recent reauthorization efforts. Unfortunately, a movement from individual students to whole schools does not guarantee that learning opportunities will not be compromised on a greater scale.

EQUITY POLICIES AND CENTRAL CONFLICTS WITHIN THE CULTURE OF POLICY

The above analysis of the culture of policy exposes central tensions embedded in the ways in which equity-oriented policies influence the language and rituals of schooling. The incentives provided by such policies and their connections to policy-generated material resources place school-based practitioners in a complex bind. As agents of the state, practitioners are expected to assume the corrective paradigm of intervention. Regrettably, however, practitioners who do not subscribe to the language and rituals encouraged by policies find themselves out of compliance with policy mandates and potentially sanctioned for noncompliance.

The culture of policy as described above is a difficult trap for equity-minded policymakers and practitioners. Efforts to overcome this trap have shifted the level or unit of the policy subject—from individual students to entire schools—without addressing the cultural dimensions of the assumptive aspects of defect and deficiency inherent in policy construction. With recent efforts to identify Title I eligibility through consideration of school-level poverty characteristics, the stigma attached to individual students has been relocated to schools and communities. The notion of working in or attending a "Title I school" signals various assumptions about poverty, performance, and school climate. The unit has changed; the stigma has not.

As I will argue in the later chapters of this book, there is a need for critical attention to the policy-influenced language and rituals in schools to avoid the paradoxical and contradictory nature of equity-oriented educational policies. The incentive structures imbedded in policy practice are difficult to break. The negative framing of poor children in policy discourse is hard to avoid. The policy "dozens" may just be an inevitable part of the determination of a legitimate policy need. The schools themselves are the best leverage point for resisting the culture of education policy.

Only through purposeful work on the cultural dimensions of schooling—the language and rituals of practice—can school communities maintain a commitment to an equity imperative. As many policy rituals are at odds with an authentic equity orientation, school-based practitioners need to share strategies for breaking through the traps provided by policies. If the policy dozens remain a part of the policy process, equity-minded practitioners need to embrace an attitude of resistance to the aspects of policy that limit their effectiveness, and, as I will describe in chapter 6, practice thoughtful noncompliance with inconsistent and contradictory policy mandates. Rather than focusing on the strict mandates provided by policy regulations that counter effective instructional practice, educators need to participate in a radical rethinking of how policy resources might be realigned to address complex considerations of students' strengths and needs. Only through active resistance to the culture of education policy can educators avert the consequences of the policy dozens.

Title I of the Elementary and Secondary Education Act (ESEA) in the War on the Culture of Poverty

> [H]istory (and particularly the history of categories of thought) constitutes one of the conditions under which political thought can become aware of itself. (Bourdieu, 1991, p. 269, note 3)

The specific history of any given policy provides crucial insight into the categories of thought that both reflect and shape policy practice. These categories of thought, or ways of seeing and organizing the social world, form the intellectual strictures that constrain scholars, policymakers, and practitioners as they build and develop their perspectives about those theorized to need government intervention. The names, labels, and descriptive portraits used to identify and characterize policy subjects in political thought and action exist together with the prevalent categories of scholarly and popular thought. This chapter reviews the prevalent categories of thought that shaped the initial conceptualization of Title I policy.

Popular and scholarly conceptions of children, poverty, disadvantage, and government intervention at the historical moment of policymaking are central to understanding the cultural norms and practices engendered by equity-oriented education policies. The historical origins of Title I of the Elementary and Secondary Education Act of 1965 (ESEA) convey the initial foundations of the naming practices inherent in this policy, the categories of thought associated with the policy, and the values woven into those categories of thought through policy formulation.

ESEA Title I was formed in the context of both the War on Poverty and poverty scholarship in the early to mid-1960s. Government reports, congressional debates, and scholarly writings show how political uses of the culture of poverty concept folded into the original construction of Title I legislation. The culture of poverty framework, a popular scholarly perspective at the time, encouraged a vocabulary and orientation that allowed policymakers to address theorized cultural and academic consequences of poverty without confronting the social and economic structures—such as a school finance system based on local property values—that contributed to poverty in the first place. The culture of poverty premise provided a platform on which equity-oriented education policies could be built and justified.

THE HISTORICAL MOMENT

The historical period in which the Elementary and Secondary Education Act was passed has been well documented by scholars of education policy (see, for example, Bailey & Mosher, 1968; Jeffrey, 1978; Meranto, 1967; Timpane, 1978). For purposes of my culture of policy argument, a number of factors are worthy of consideration. For years prior to the passage of the ESEA, numerous congressional representatives had tried unsuccessfully to promote education policy that would allocate federal dollars to local educational institutions and increase the role of the federal government in public schooling. Federal involvement in education, an issue pursued in large part by Democrats, violated the long-standing traditions of local control.[1] A convergence of factors, including a Democratic majority in Congress, growth in the school-age population, rapid urbanization, civil rights activities, and, most important for my analysis, national attention to the plight of the poor, allowed for passage of legislation that brought about unprecedented federal involvement in education. As part of the War on Poverty and Great Society programs, federal intervention in education could be linked to national concern for children in poverty, and local educational institutions could be posited as sites for solving poverty problems by providing services to poor children.

In the context of expanding civil rights activities, including the 1954 *Brown v. Board of Education* decision, the 1963 March on Washington led by Dr. Martin Luther King, and voter registration activities, as well as factors such as black migration to the north and the war in Vietnam, congressional representatives could link support of federal education policy to cultural arguments that reflected collective national concerns. They could vote to generate education funding that would go to their constituencies in the name of the poor, without naming specific racial or ethnic groups as beneficiaries. They could provide funds that would disproportionately serve black children without noting explicitly that their policy would do so. As suggested by Philip Meranto (1967) 2 years after ESEA passage, "[t]he bill provided the Congress with a vehicle for at least partially satisfying the needs of Negroes without appearing to 'knuckle under' to the demands of civil rights groups" (p. 41).

The culture of the poor—and implicitly, or sometimes explicitly, the culture of poor blacks—served as a target for policy intervention. Blacks were organizing around the civil rights issues of equal educational opportunities and voting rights. Many were discouraged by resistance to the *Brown* ruling, and several were failing basic exams for participation in the armed forces. Their "culture," then, served as a powerful diversion away from the damning structures of segregated schooling, the resistance to integration, or the pernicious and lasting effects of school finance practices based on community wealth. Rather than acknowledge the strengths that the organized black community demonstrated in the marches and protests, political organizing, and voter registration activities, Congress instead focused on the cultural deficits and deficiencies identified as part of the poor, and, in the minds of many, poor black culture. Contemporaneous scholarship provided considerable support for this framing.

CATEGORIES OF THOUGHT IN SCHOLARLY DISCOURSE

In the 1940s and 1950s, anthropologist Oscar Lewis (1959, 1961, 1964, 1965) pioneered the study of the family unit as an analytical focal point. Through observations of a select number of families in Latin America and the United States, Lewis (1964) honed and supported his theory that there were various interrelated cultural traits associated with living in poverty. These traits include economic behaviors (such as the frequent spending of small quantities of money), social and psychological characteristics (such as resignation and fatalism), countercultural tendencies (such as a hatred for the police and a distrust of government), and certain feelings (such as helplessness, dependency, and personal unworthiness) (pp. 152–154). One of Lewis's first resulting publications, *Five Families: Mexican Case Studies in the Culture of Poverty* (1959), advanced this framework as an explanatory device to understand how and why poor people are and stay poor. As with most of Lewis's family studies, the author provided an introductory chapter that reviewed his theoretical premises and then many chapters of descriptive biographical narrative about the families or individuals under study. In the introduction to *Five Families*, Lewis presented the notion of "the culture of the poor," noting that this culture "has its own modalities and distinctive social and psychological consequences for its members" (p. 2). Lewis asserted that "the culture of poverty cuts across regional, rural-urban, and even national boundaries," then moved on to note similarities between the poor in various parts of the world—London, Mexico, Puerto Rico—and "among lower class Negroes in the United States" (p. 2).

In Lewis's next publication, *The Children of Sanchez* (1961), he provided a deeper focus on one of the five families of his original book. He also elaborated his theory of a culture of poverty through the definition of culture as "a design for living passed down from generation to generation" (p. xxiv). A later chapter published in a book entitled *Explosive Forces in Latin America* (Lewis, 1964) clarified the theory even further through an extensive list of the economic, social, and psychological traits of the culture of poverty (pp. 152–154). In these works, Lewis proposed that the intergenerational transmission of poverty culture ensures the likelihood that children of poor adults will grow up to be poor themselves. Their cultural proclivities, which he details through the lives of the people he profiles, maintain their poverty status regardless of changes in their material conditions. Lewis again stated that his observations of Mexican families provided "universal characteristics which transcend regional, rural-urban, and even national differences," despite his acknowledgment that his work presented "a provisional conceptual model of this culture based mainly upon . . . Mexican materials" (1964, p. xxv). Although his work thus far had been based on families in Mexico, Lewis argued for the near-universality of the culture of poverty, making explicit comparisons to blacks in the United States, and noting the few exceptions to his theory (namely poor Eastern European Jews).

At around the same time, Michael Harrington wrote *The Other America* (1962), a widely read text that provided a similar cultural argument, but focused on poverty in the United States. Like Lewis, Harrington asserted the existence of a culture of poverty that cut across racial groups (pp. 15–16). However, while Lewis focused on Mexican families and drew parallels to other groups, Harrington focused substantive attention on blacks and Puerto Ricans living in urban centers. In constructing his argument about the "invisible" poor during a time of national prosperity, Harrington noted economic and racist structures as key contributors to the culture of poverty. And although Harrington posited the culture of poverty as a consequence of racism and material deprivation, he presented it as a negative adaptive trait among a mostly black population. For example, after asserting the existence of "an interlocking base of economic and racial injustice" (p. 63), Harrington argued that

> Harlem, as well as every other Negro ghetto, is a center of poverty, of manual work, of sickness, and of every typical disability which America's underdeveloped areas suffer. It is on this very real and material base that the ghetto builds its unique culture. (p. 63)

Although Harrington encouraged readers to see poverty culture as a result of broader racist economic structures, his book popularized the concept of the culture of poverty and ultimately provided an alternative to challenging the economic structures and racist practices that were theorized to cause this culture in the first place. The concept allowed for attention to superficial understandings of culture and theories of how to fix people, namely children, growing up in the culture of poverty.

Like Harrington, Lewis saw the culture of poverty as a response to external economic forces. However, Lewis (1965) also noted differences in his and Harrington's approach (p. xlii). In *La Vida* (1965), Lewis's book on Puerto Rican families living in Puerto Rico and the United States, the author described the culture of poverty as "both an adaptation and reaction of the poor to their marginal position in a class-stratified, highly individuated, capitalistic society" (p. xliv). The remedies he suggested, however, did not address class stratification in the United States. In earlier work, Lewis (1964) encouraged class mobilization against oppressive economic arrangements, but only in "undeveloped countries," advocating instead for "changing the value systems and attitudes" (p. 159) of people in more developed countries. According to the author, a change in the values and attitudes of the poor could interrupt the intergenerational perpetuation of the culture of poverty and eliminate that roadblock to social transformation. Lewis (1965) raised the specific concern that since culture is passed from parents to children, generation after generation, even "the elimination of physical poverty *per se* [italics added] may not be enough to eliminate the culture of poverty which is a whole way of life" (p. lii). By implication, if the government were interested in abolishing poverty, some agency or institution would have to intervene to break the transmission of the culture of poverty to the next generation. Early intervention by agents or institutions outside of the family would be necessary, since according to Lewis (1965),

> [b]y the time slum children are age six or seven they have usually absorbed the basic values of their subculture and are not psychologically geared to take full advantage of changing conditions or increased opportunities which may occur in their lifetime. (p. xlv)

On the heels of these studies came the infamous report entitled *The Negro Family: The Case for National Action* by Daniel Patrick Moynihan. In this widely publicized report distributed by the Department of Labor, and later reprinted in Rainwater & Yancey's edited book titled *The Moynihan Report and The Politics of Controversy* (Moynihan, 1967), Moynihan asserted the Negro family as "the fundamental source of the weakness of the Negro community" (U.S. Department of Labor, 1965, p. 1). Similar to Lewis and Harrington, Moynihan portrayed external factors (in this case white America and the legacy of slavery) as the cause of the structural conditions of black America while paradoxically asserting that the pathologies of the black family were the factors that "perpetuate the cycle of poverty and deprivation" (p. 39). Again, the culture of the poor and, here in particular, the culture of poor black females and their children required government intervention. This document, referred to commonly as "The Moynihan Report," was released to the public while Congress was debating Title I authorization, and according to Christopher Jencks (1965), "[a]fter six months of private circulation among government officials" (p. 39). Jencks's review of Moynihan's work, published in the *New York Review of Books*, noted that the report, "while not an official statement of federal policy, has influenced recent thinking at every level of government" (p. 39).

Indeed, the Great Society and War on Poverty initiatives relied on these scholarly understandings of the poor. Although such understandings were far from common or coherent even to those actively contributing to the scholarship (Moynihan, 1968, p. 19), the notion of a culture of poverty influenced plans and policies for government intervention. "[C]ertain styles of life," namely the cultural patterns of the lower class, were argued to "set limits on what the policymaker can accomplish" (Banfield, 1968, p. 46).[2] Detailing these cultural patterns and implicitly comparing them to a vague notion of the middle or upper class norm provided social scientific rationale for pathologizing poor people and deeming their behavior abnormal.

The notion of the poor as abnormal was not subtle. Scholarly texts described various social, psychological, and cultural attributes of poor people, making explicit comparisons to "the rest of the nation" and the "normal." Michael Harrington (1962) argued that the poor "feel differently than the rest of the nation" and, combining the concepts of culture, feelings, and personality, he described them as "hopeless and passive, yet prone to bursts of violence . . . lonely and isolated, often rigid and hostile" (p. 122). Daniel Moynihan in the report for the U.S. Department of Labor (1965) described the Negro family as a "tangle of pathology"[3] (p. 39), and Edward Banfield's book *The Unheavenly City* (1968) defended this view, stating that "[t]he implication that lower-class culture is pathological seems fully warranted" (p. 54). In fact, Banfield noted that throughout his book he would use the term "*normal* . . . to refer to class culture that is not lower class" (p. 54). The scholarly concept of an abnormal culture of poverty—although contested by a number of intellectuals at the time who instead focused on the critical analysis of economic structures, racism, and stigma (see, for example, Leacock, 1971; Valentine, 1968; Waxman, 1977)—gained considerable popularity and experienced "rapid diffusion into the rhetoric of the War on Poverty" (Rossi & Blum, 1968, p. 41).

The culture of poverty theory proved provocative and compelling to many elected officials and policymakers of the time. It both reflected and encouraged political attention to the individuals living in poverty rather than the socioeconomic structures that contribute to its existence (for a similar argument, see O'Connor, 2001, pp. 121–123). Those concerned with the plight of the poor could fight the War on Poverty in part through fixing the cultural tendencies of poor people and without needing to address or alter the economic or social structures that even some proponents of the culture of poverty framework (such as Harrington, 1962) identified as determinative. The government could instead direct its resources toward policy that would address some notion of poverty culture as lived by individuals and interrupt the transmission of this culture to future generations.

If poverty culture was indeed transmitted from generation to generation, perhaps government institutions could intervene to interrupt that transmission and prevent the passage of poverty from parents to children. One of the central features of the War on Poverty could be a war on the culture of poverty. But where could that war be fought? Educational institutions provided an obvious opportunity for corrective intervention. If poor parents were inevitably going to teach their children the culture of poverty, which according to Lewis's theory could make or keep people poor despite the elimination of the material poverty, then the schools could impart a cultural alternative. Local educational agencies throughout the country could change the dynamics of persistent intergenerational poverty by compensating for the cultural deficiencies of the poor through supplementary educational services. Educators could pass on middle-class culture, thus replacing the ghetto culture that doomed a child to a life of poverty with an alternative design for living.

Education was only one battleground on which the War on Poverty was fought. However, this national policy domain received considerable emphasis, as it was understood as a key to social mobility (Miller & Roby, 1968, p. 72). Educational scholarship in the early 1960s highlighted the plight of poor children in schools (see, for example, Passow, 1963; Riessman, 1962). These studies influenced both the passage and conceptualization of the Elementary and Secondary Education Act and particularly Title I of that act (Meranto, 1967). After decades of political resistance to substantial federal involvement in education, one of the key factors that encouraged passage of such an unprecedented and substantial federal education bill was the "rediscovery of poverty" among scholars and elected officials (Meranto, 1967, pp. 16–20; see also Thomas, 1975, pp. 27–28).

Scholars posited educational institutions paradoxically as part of both the poverty problem and solution. While education represented a means for escaping poverty, some scholars noted that poor children by and large attended substandard schools (see, for example, Conant, 1961). Additional government support, then, was theorized to aid substandard schools through funding that could be targeted to poor, disadvantaged, culturally deprived students. There was considerable confidence in both educational scholarship and among congressional representatives that educational institutions could correct the poverty problem. In comments that typify the sentiments of the time, Representative Madden (D, IN) (1965) espoused:

> If similar legislation was enacted 15 or 20 years ago, millions of American youth who are now unemployed, living in poverty or following a life of idleness or crime would now be on their way to financial independence and enjoy American abundance and prosperity. (p. 5732)

However, most scholarly approaches to compensatory education did not focus on the problems of schools as institutions, but rather the deficiencies of the students attending them (Jeffrey, 1978, pp. 12–13). This scholarly focus on the individuals living in poverty was echoed in the categories of thought used to understand, organize, and serve children in policymaking and implementation. The language of policymaking legitimized and institutionalized these categories of thought through legislation that eventually required their use in the identification and service of students.

LEGISLATING WAYS OF SEEING

The categories of thought reflected in the culture of poverty theory were echoed on the floors of Congress during initial policy debates to authorize the Elementary and Secondary Education Act (1965), and particularly Title I. Talk of cultural deprivation, the vicious cycle (or circle) of poverty, and the role of culture as a *cause* of poverty framed the arguments used to advocate passage of the bill. Ratification of Title I represented the government's ability to correct the deviant poor by interrupting the transmission of cultural norms from one generation to another, although in the congressional debates, the notion of culture was vague and ill-defined. Members of Congress focused on "cultural experiences" (e.g., visits to libraries and museums) and "cultural skills" (e.g., language and social grace). Neither conform to the anthropological sense of culture as, according to Clifford Geertz (1973), "an historically transmitted pattern of meanings embodied in symbols, a system of inherited conceptions expressed in symbolic forms by means of which [humans] communicate, perpetuate, and develop their knowledge about and attitudes toward life" (p. 89). Nonetheless, passage of Title I was posited as a way to "help break the vicious chain of hereditary poverty—the poverty that stems from cultural deprivation" (Gilbert, 1965, p. 5970).

In the controversial expansion of what had been almost nonexistent federal involvement in education, members of Congress portrayed passage of ESEA as a way to address or correct the culture that poor children (often described as those living in slums) received at home. This culture was not only conceived as a detriment to children born into poverty, it was also a threat to individual and national security. Draft rejection rates and criminal activity due to "educational deficiencies" provided additional rationales for an increased federal role in education. According to members of Congress, if students in poverty did not overcome their deficiencies, there would be fewer soldiers to defend the nation and crime would be on the rise (see, for example, Fong, 1965, p. 7568; Madden, 1965, pp. 5332–5733; Reid, 1965, p. 6135; Sisk, 1965, p. 5727; White, 1965, pp. 6148–6149). Educational intervention could protect the country's citizens both internally and externally.

In portraying the theorized needs of the policy beneficiaries, the primary focus of the debates was on the cultural rather than academic skills of poor children. Although members of Congress did not entirely ignore the role of educational institutions in developing students' basic academic skills, they more commonly posited the presumed cultural handicaps of children growing up in poverty. In the cumulative debate text with substantive focus on Title I (which reflects over 350,000 words), members of Congress mentioned *skills* only 41 times. And, of those 41 mentions of skills, only 18 referred to the skills that students could or should develop through provision of Title I–funded instructional services (the remainder of the references to skills referred to those of general citizens, as in vocational skill; teachers, as in the skills needed to work with various groups of students; and mothers, as in cultural skills). In fact, two of these mentions named "cultural skill" explicitly. In contrast, members of Congress mentioned *culture* or cultural factors 86 times, 61 of which referred to a child's cultural disadvantage, deprivation, or need for cultural training (the remainder of the references to "culture" refer to cultural pride, cultural resources, cultural leadership, cultural interests, and cultural disadvantage in more generalized terms). In the debates, then, the need to address the *culture* of the children was three times as prevalent as the need to address their academic *skills*.

As conjectured by various members of Congress, federal education policy could make up for the disadvantages of children who did not learn middle-class culture at home. Echoing concern over the intergenerational transmission of poverty found in the scholarship of the time, poor parents, and in particular mothers, were portrayed as ill-equipped to prepare their children for productive and poverty-free lives. Motherhood received particular attention, as the transmission of culture was assumed to be from mother to child, and fathers were assumed to be gone. Government intervention in general and Title I more specifically was thought capable of compensating for bad mothering, "in a cultural sense," by providing poor children with what Congressman Jacobs (D, IN) referred to as "remedial cultural training." But training the children of poverty would not be enough. Jacobs (1965) further theorized that remedial cultural training tends to be literally lost on deaf ears if the twiglike child cannot discriminate among the subtle sounds of his language, indeed his mother tongue. . . . And if neither he nor his early adult associates can well comprehend the language, how shall he learn of the beauty of gentleness he will never have touched in the first 6 years of his life? (p. 5742)

Poor mothers, too, would have to be trained. Describing a government intervention program that provided cultural corrections, Jacobs assured that "[e]ven the culturally deprived mother, lacking in cultural skills, in most cases, proves to be an angel mother once she is motivated to participate in breaking the chain of poverty and ignorance, between her generation and the next" (p. 5742). Jacobs continued to hold forth on how the government had provided mothering skills to women of preschool-age children:

First, officials interview the culturally deprived parents, or rather "parent," since in most cases the father has deserted. And they remind the parent that she is unable to give her children the lessons in grammar and social grace which they need, but that, nevertheless, she can help by encouraging her little children to go a few hours a day to the nursery school. And by asking the children questions about the school when they come home, and even if the mother might not understand her children's answers, at least she would show an interest, and thereby encourage them to achieve. (p. 5742)

Here Jacobs posited educational institutions as better prepared to mother than poor women. Similar to the Moynihan Report, the Jacob's testimony portrayed "culturally deprived" (read black) mothers as ill-equipped, alone, and, after government intervention in the education of her children, less knowledgeable than her preschool child. Although preschool itself may benefit most children, regardless of class background, here it provides another opportunity to disparage poor mothers.

Senator Ralph Yarborough (D, TX) (1965) raised a similar sentiment through his inclusion of a paper entitled "Proposal for a measure attacking poverty at its source," written by John Silber, then chairman of the department of philosophy at The University of Texas, in the *Congressional Record*. According to this paper, "the stultifying atmosphere in which slum children live must be transformed. . . . [T]heir family lives must be improved through the education of slum mothers and the development of male counselors for these children" (Silber, as cited in Yarborough, p. 7618). Silber then proposed various steps toward the transformation of the lives of slum children, depicting male tutors as another potential intervention strategy: "The tutor, a 'preventive parole officer' and academic counselor, should, if possible, be a male schoolteacher. . . . This male figure will, in part, be a father surrogate, since a large percentage of slum children live in fatherless families" (p. 7618). In this senator's inclusion of a philosopher's comments as part of his testimony toward passing a bill on the floor of Congress, the pathologies of the matriarchal black family presented in the Moynihan Report and the culture of poverty theories of Lewis and Harrington were woven together in a seamless whole. Scholars and politicians colluded in seeing culture as the foundation of poverty, with government intervention—through transformation of the mother or provision of a government-sponsored male figure—as a viable way out.

The notion of culture as the foundation of poverty received considerable support throughout the Title I debates. Politicians repeatedly characterized the policy beneficiaries in terms of deficit and disadvantage, referring to them as "paralyzed by poverty" (Byrd, 1965, p. 7708) and "handicapped by cultural experiences" (Yarborough, 1965, p. 7616). Communities with concentrations of poverty were described as "poverty-impacted and backward areas" (Anderson, 1965, p. 5732). Speeches clarifying, supporting, or denouncing the federal role in education, the separation of church and state, and the various funding formulas presented during the debates again revealed conceptions of poverty rooted in individuals and communities, rather than political and economic structures. Not only were the structural features that create the conditions of poverty often overlooked when characterizing the poor, at a number of points throughout the debates, the policy beneficiaries and their families were described as a "burden" on the country. Schools with high concentrations of "educationally deprived" students faced an inordinate burden that the government could address. As relayed by Representative Perkins (1965), a group of educators who had met with President Johnson about the role of the federal government "decided that the Nation's first job was to help the schools serving the children from the very lowest income groups. These families constitute the No. 1 burden in this Nation on our public school system" (p. 5736). The rationale behind casting the poor as a burden, rather than a client, consumer, or simply participant in compulsory public education, was borne out of the reliance on local property taxes to fund schools. Representative Perkins (1965) noted the following:

> These families, we know, cannot bear their share of the taxes to help pay for their education, and unless their children get a good education we know that they become, as President Johnson has said, "tax eaters instead of taxpayers." That is why this administration has placed top priority on breaking the vicious cycle that today threatens the future of about 5 million children in this, the richest Nation on earth. (p. 5736)

The above logic reveals the sense of promise that schools could take the children of resource-poor communities and, through some type of educational intervention, produce future taxpayers who could adequately finance public schooling. In fact, education was theorized to be a solution to poverty. As stated by Congressman Alphonzo Bell (R, CA) (1965) in support of this bill, "[e]ducation is an area in which we strike poverty right on the head. Education is really the answer to the problem, with respect to the state of our poverty today" (p. 5961).

But such students and families were not only cast as burdens for tax purposes. They also, according to Representative Patsy Mink (D, HI) (1965), created "special burdens upon the school system and upon the teachers who are called upon to devote extra effort for these children, sometimes at a sacrifice of others in the classroom" (p. 5765). Indeed, poverty, as a category unto itself, was thought to be a burden to the educational system. As noted by Representative Albert (D, OK) (1965), the Elementary and Secondary Education Act itself "recognizes that wherever poverty is found, in whatever degree, it places a burden on the educational institutions of the country" (p. 6130). Poverty, families living in poverty, and the children born into poverty were characterized through the metaphor of burden: at best a load to be carried and at worst a drain on the resources of middle-class society.

The specific burden that Title I policy was to alleviate had to be defined clearly so that resources could be distributed appropriately. The technical and conceptual definition of the policy beneficiaries was a topic of considerable debate. Members of Congress attempted to clarify the construct of "educational deprivation" through discussions of its relationship to "economic deprivation" and various conditions related to learning. A great deal of this debate hinged on the determination of a funding formula for allocating money to districts and schools. The Johnson administration had proposed a funding formula that defined policy-generated program eligibility in terms of family income, with less than $2,000 ($11,683 in 2003 based on the Consumer Price Index) annual family income signaling an eligible student. This formula was challenged during the hearings leading up to the floor debates and disputed on the congressional floor.

Some congressional representatives argued for consideration of factors beyond the sole criteria of family income. Perhaps school location, concentrations of eligible students, and educational abilities should be taken into consideration. For example, early in the floor debates, Senator Peter Dominick (R, CO) (1965) expressed concern over the convention of defining educational deprivation in terms of family income:

> It is only fair to ask, What is an educationally deprived child? How do we define him or her? What should he or she be? How are they to be classified? There is only one classification set forth in the bill. An educationally deprived child is deemed to be such because his family has an income of $2,000 or less. (p. 7331)

Senator Dominick (1965) noted that during hearings prior to the floor debates he challenged the then U.S. Commissioner of Education, Francis Keppel, and other witnesses on this definition, asking whether a child "whose family had the misfortune of having an income of $2,000 or less" but who attended "a highly qualified and very able school district" (p. 7331) should be considered educationally deprived. The answer the congressman received from the witness was that "there is a correlation between poor educational ability and low income" (p. 7331). Senator Dominick accepted this reasoning, stating, "I do not know about that type of analysis, but it seems to me to be a reasonable approach to the problem" (p. 7331). By extension, individual poor students, rather than the schools that they attended, harbored the problem of educational performance. The problem was located in the poor students themselves and not the institutions that served them.

An earlier exchange between representatives Robert Griffin (R, MI) and Carl Perkins (D, KY) suggests the tensions in where to locate the problem that Title I aimed to solve. Congressman Griffin (1965) asked directly, "Are educationally deprived children the same as economically deprived children?" (p. 6004), to which Congressman Perkins (1965) replied, "There is certainly a high correlation between low income and educational deprivation if they meet those standards" (p. 6004). When asked what standards he was referring to, Congressman Perkins explained:

> If large numbers of children from low income families attend a school, all evidence points to the fact that you will find large numbers of educationally disadvantaged children in that school. The funds under this bill will be concentrated in those schools, as the distinguished gentleman knows. (p. 6004)

Here the concept of educational disadvantage is identified with the concentration of poor children in a school.

Throughout the debates the tension between defining Title I beneficiaries through the lens of poverty and through the lens of academic performance grew. For example, Senator Winston Prouty (R, VT) (1965) contributed to this definitional quandary by asking, "[W]hat is the object of Title I of this bill? Is it to remedy poverty, or is it to remedy educational deprivation?" (p. 7625). He then read a section from a staff memorandum that stated, "In this legislation, we are not concerned with poverty per se. We are primarily concerned with low educational attainment" (p. 7625). Prouty went on to assert that

> the target of title I of this bill is not the poor child, as such, but the educationally deprived child. . . . The special kind of aid it contemplates is designed for and aimed at a special kind of child—one who is educationally deprived or, to use an equivalent term, culturally disadvantaged. (p. 7625)

In this testimony, Prouty distinguishes between poverty and academic performance, but returns to the equation of educational deprivation (i.e., performance) and cultural disadvantage (i.e., poverty). The prevailing

understanding throughout the debates was that poverty predicted poor performance and that poor children should be seen as the beneficiaries of
Title I irrespective of the schools that they attend or the educational opportunities they receive.

This problem definition reflects various biases at the heart of Title I's
development: Poor children are assumed to have poor performance, to have
less relevant skills and knowledge, and to need remedial education. The
schools that poor children attend, the expectations that educators have of
them, and the instruction that they receive all garnered less attention than
the individual attributes and assumed deficiencies poor children theoretically
exhibit. The students themselves harbored the problems that policies aimed
to solve. Poor children were assumed less capable at the time of policymaking.

Although not stated explicitly, the racial implications of these assumptions are no less present. The intersection of race and class made easy the
association of poverty culture with black culture, and the then-popular work
of Harrington and Moynihan strengthened the conceptual and practical
convergence of these race- and class-based categories. This race–class intersection was openly acknowledged by Senator Robert Kennedy (D, NY) (1965)
in his assertion that "[w]e all know that Negroes are twice as likely to be
poor as whites" (p. 7330) and by Representative Howard Smith (D, VA)
(1965) in his statement that members of "the minority race, unfortunately,
in great numbers, have been born and raised in poverty, necessary poverty,
in the Southern States" (p. 5729).[4] Overall, however, the widely accepted
culture of poverty premise provided a vocabulary for the racial logic of differentiated capabilities without the need to single out any particular racial
or ethnic groups. "Cultural disadvantage"—a term that was used frequently
but only implicitly and vaguely defined—was framed as a policy problem,
and policy-afforded "cultural training" as part of the solution.

For the most part, however, claims of cultural disadvantage or deprivation were not overtly linked to a specific racial or ethnic group. Direct mentions of the "Negro" population on the congressional floor tended to be part
of some comparison with whites (such as for draft rejection rates) or as part
of a litany of policy beneficiaries, as in Representative Adam Clayton Powell
Jr.'s (D, NY) (1965) following statement:

> Let us teach every white boy walking down every dusty road in Georgia that
> America belongs to him. Let us teach every black boy out of the slums of Harlem
> that America is his. Let us teach every poor white in the mountains in Ken-
> tucky that the joys of America belong to him. (p. 5735)

Similarly, Senator Walter Mondale (D, MN) (1965) proclaimed:

> I support this proposed legislation . . . because of what it will do for the share-
> cropper's child in South Carolina, the Negro child in Harlem, or the child of

Mexican descent in Phoenix—as much as for what it will contribute to the future of the child of a widow in Minneapolis. (p. 7571)

In the debates overall, however, the conceptual connection to the "black boy out of the slums of Harlem" was far more prevalent than to any of the other groups mentioned in Mondale's comments above. Indeed, "poor whites" were mentioned only one time in the entire Title I debate, whereas "slums" were mentioned 58 times.

Some members of Congress even made explicit claims that poverty was not associated with any one particular racial group. For example, Senator Edward (Bob) Bartlett (D, AK) (1965) spoke directly to the contrary:

Poverty, whether it be financial or social, is not selective. It is a disease which afflicts people of all races, colors, and creeds. . . . If we are ever to succeed in eradicating it, we must attempt to work with all the children affected. (p. 7326)

Senator Fulbright (D, AR) (1965) later noted that "race is not a factor in the consideration of this bill" and moved on to the connection between this bill and desegregation implementation, claiming that "[i]n fact, many school systems will be helped immeasurably in meeting the problems of desegregation with the programs which can be financed by title I grants" (p. 7625).

The relationship between Title I and desegregation policies raised important and complicated issues for Congress. In thinking through the implementation issues that local practitioners might face, some representatives addressed directly the potential for segregating eligible students. For example, Representative Frank Bow (R, OH) (1965) posited how a district serving "educationally deprived children" could serve these students through special programs, stating, "[I]t is possible to segregate in some manner the children from low income families who could be classified as 'educationally deprived' and spend this amount of money in their behalf next year" (p. 5993). Here the representative portrays segregation of poor children as a viable delivery strategy for Title I. Concern over this very approach was addressed in a letter included in the debates by Congresswoman Edith Green (D, OR) (1965) from Albert Shanker, the then-president of the United Federation of Teachers in New York City. Shanker urged the congresswoman to vote against passage of ESEA precisely because he thought this policy would, among other things, "increase segregation of public schools" (p. 5989).

At issue here were two potential types of segregation: one by class, and the other by race. Although the segregation of poor students was not technically unconstitutional, the overrepresentation of black students among the poor would potentially lead to within-school racial segregation in desegregated schools. Since, based on the logic of Brown v. Board of Education of

Topeka (1954), a policy of segregating by race "is usually interpreted as denoting the inferiority of the Negro group," segregating students by race or class could denote the inferiority of the stigmatized group. In fact, the *Brown* ruling asserts that this sense of inferiority

> affects the motivation of a child to learn. Segregation with the sanction of law, therefore, has a tendency to [retard] the educational and mental development of Negro children and to deprive them of some of the benefits they would receive in a racial[ly] integrated school system.

By extension, the segregation of poor students could lead to a similar effect. The above excerpts of the *Brown* ruling precede the famous footnote 11 in which the social scientific contributions of Kenneth Clark and others on the psychological effects of segregation were used to defend the claim that segregation itself caused decreased motivation to learn and stunted intellectual development on the part of Negro students. Concern over class-based segregation, however, was not treated on the floors of Congress with similar levels of concern. In fact, the framing of poor children as culturally inferior was not deemed problematic.

Instead, this framing of children in terms of their perceived cultural disadvantage was, in part, a rhetorical device used to persuade members of Congress to pass the ESEA legislation. Members of Congress leveraged popular and scholarly conceptualizations of children to convince each other and the public of the value of this bill. Once the voting did take place, ESEA passed easily in both the House and Senate.[5] After passage, information about the bill was disseminated to educators. Along with this information came the ways of seeing children in poverty advocated on the congressional floor.

DISSEMINATING WAYS OF SEEING

As evidenced in the words of both scholars and politicians, the culture of poverty thesis drew considerable concern over the intergenerational transmission of poverty culture. My culture of policy thesis draws a parallel concern over the interagency transmission of *policy culture*. Through documents produced by the government, local educational institutions inherit the categories of thought solidified in Congress. In practice, these policy-driven categories of thought introduce, build on, or reinforce ways of seeing and organizing children in schools. Indeed, they provide the vocabulary for discussing and serving students, and reward its use with federal dollars.

Government documents that were distributed to educators reflected portrayals of the policy beneficiaries similar to those put forward in Congress, tying the belief in the nobility of government intervention to the plight of the poor. For example, the title of an early government publication about Title I funding, *Education: An Answer to Poverty* (U.S. Office of Education & Office of Economic Opportunity, n.d.), typifies the belief that schools could somehow undo poverty and that poor children could be fixed by proper educational intervention. A photograph on the front page of the booklet shows a young girl with dark eyes, skin, and hair, perhaps of Latin American, South Asian, or Middle Eastern descent, smiling broadly. She represents the adorable yet defective policy subject.

The inside cover of the booklet is written in memo form, addressed to "School Administrators, School Board Members and Others Concerned with Good Educational Programs." The memo is from Sargent Shriver, the director of the Office of Economic Opportunity and Francis Keppel, the commissioner of education. The memo's title reads "Good Ways to Improve Teaching of Poor Children." The publication date is not listed, although the text of the memo announces a deadline for the usage of ESEA funds as August 30, 1966. The table of contents reveals that the booklet profiles programs at various stages of the educational process in different educational contexts. Before these profiles and after a brief foreword, the booklet begins with a chapter entitled "Can We Understand Them?" (U.S. Office of Education & Office of Economic Opportunity, n.d., p. 4). Here, "we" refers to a generic "American," a middle-class norm, a group of educators charged with the delivery of services to a monolithic "them." "Them" refers to the children of poverty, a vague class of children characterized by extreme physical hunger, but no intellectual curiosity. Their experiences are described as devoid of knowledge, their worlds depicted as lacking in learning. Early in the document, it reads:

> It is a standard American complaint that four-year-olds are forever asking, "Why this? Why that? Daddy, Mummy, tell me why." Not these children. They do not wonder why. Curiosity, the marvel of observing cause and effect, the joy of finding out—which power the development of knowledge—have laid no deep mark on their lives. (p. 7)

Although the brochure is directed at improving *programs* serving students, the first few pages tell educators what is wrong with the *students* themselves, rather than how educational programs have not been able to recognize their strengths, build on these capacities, and teach the students well. In these documents, the students harbor the problem. They have no curiosity. They have no joy of finding out. They are less able to learn. The document goes on to contrast the culture of the poor recipients of federal funding with "standard American values" (p. 9) and the "middle-class American notion of the value of time" (p. 8). The notion of a middle-class norm was not subtle here;

children "from poor families" were contrasted directly with "normal" (p. 24) children in the program descriptions.

In keeping with its title, the entire document envisions schools as the saviors of poor children. However, the brochure also asserts that schools cannot save the children of poverty on their own. Federal funds could support the schools in their efforts to "undo the overwhelmingly negative, mind-closing oppressiveness of the out-of-school world of the impoverished child" (U.S. Office of Education & Office of Economic Opportunity, n.d., p. 10). Although these funds could support programs such as those featured in the booklet, they could not overcome the terrible "mind-closing" effects of poor families. The use of the word "mind-closing," as representative of the entire document, is particularly poignant here. How can an educator provide instruction for a student who has been identified in a government document as living in a world that is closing her or his mind? This brochure, along with many other well-meaning publications of the time, provides the educator with ideas for programs for disadvantaged students but also with limited expectations and excuses for student underperformance caused by ineffective instructional practice. By introducing or nurturing preexisting biases among educators in receipt of this booklet, the government transmits its own categories of thought to local agencies. And in so doing, it eviscerates its stated democratic, egalitarian, and antipoverty purposes by casting the children it proclaims to serve as defective, deficient, and abnormal.

A number of similar documents were produced and circulated during the early years of Title I. The covers of such documents often carry photographs of children, a visual representation of the policy beneficiaries. One document entitled *Improving Education Through ESEA: 12 Stories* (U.S. Department of Health, Education, and Welfare, 1970) shows a black boy in the arms of a young white woman. The boy, looking forlorn, rests his head on the woman's shoulder. The woman holds the boy, her straight blonde hair held back by a wide headband. Both gaze off into the distance. The image is familiar; the Madonna comforts the suffering child. More specific to this document, the white Madonna comforts the suffering black child. Through the dissemination of government publications about Title I, the depictions of children living in poverty reflected in congressional debates spread to the practitioners responsible for their education, reinforcing or introducing biases about poor children, particularly poor black children, and what they were capable of doing.

These conceptions, presented in the form of government publications that were circulated to local schools, influenced the language and rituals of schooling. As early as 1966, one year after initial authorization of ESEA, Congress reconvened to modify and reauthorize Title I. During this reauthorization, Representative Bert Bandstra (D, IA) (1966) presented a letter from a principal of an Iowa high school as part of his remarks. This letter highlights how the creation of this policy led to the categorizing of students based on policy regulations. The principal's letter, in support of ESEA reauthorization and expansion, reads, "Under the formula set up by the Office of Education, we were to identify 81 culturally and educationally deprived students from our High School and to set up a program to best reach these 'deprived' students" (Clark, as cited in Bandstra, 1966, p. 12984). The principal moves on to note that "there were really more [deprived students], but under the O.E. Formula and money available, we chopped it off at 81" (p. 12984). The principal further explained that in order to implement the Title I program, the identified students were segregated from their nondeprived peers in "special sections of the same courses they had been in all years . . . [making] sure that they were with students of like ability" (p. 12984).

What is particularly fascinating about this letter and its inclusion in the 1966 floor debates is that it demonstrates how Title I provided an opportunity to blame poor students for their low academic performance. Although the principal asserts that traditional instruction—which he described as "stick[ing] the kids between four walls, giv[ing] them a textbook to read, and let[ting] the teacher recite to them what they have already learned by reading the text"—caused "[t]he good students [to be] bored to death and completely unchallenged, and the poor students [to be] lost after the first week," he also manages to disparage the skills of the poor, deprived students, noting that "we were not reaching them with the conventional textbook-teacher lecture method, mainly because most of them were poor readers, poor listeners, and had short attention spans" (Clark, as cited in Bandstra, 1966, pp. 12984–12985). Although Clark acknowledges that the instructional methods were "outdated, inadequate, and very dull," he still focuses on the poor skills of the 81 newly categorized "culturally and educationally deprived students" (pp. 12984–12985).

This form of implementation was not unique to one Iowa principal's school. According to Carl Kaestle and Marshall Smith (1982) in an article published nearly 20 years later,

> [i]mplementing Title I . . . required an organizational structure for the delivery of services that was independent of the regular school program. Separate administrative structures were developed in school systems and in schools. Title I personnel were hired and paid for only with Title I funds and were required by law to work only with Title I students even in the halls and in the schoolyard. In classrooms the segregation of Title I from the regular school was almost as complete. (p. 400)

The transmission of the culture of education policy from Congress to the classroom encouraged the language and rituals of naming and segregating eligible students.

However, as with all cultural transmission, there is resistance to the language and rituals of policy culture. Within scholarly publications, the popular press, and even on the floor of Congress, there is evidence of resistance to the dominant categories of thought deployed in policy practice. Critics at the time made arguments against the culture of poverty thesis and compensatory education programs. One scathing critique of the dominant ways of seeing came from William Ryan, a Boston psychologist, in a 1965 article published in *The Nation* and later reprinted in an edited volume by Lee Rainwater and William Yancey (Ryan, 1967). Ryan wrote, "For the fact is that the Negro child learns less not because his mother doesn't subscribe to *The Reader's Digest* and doesn't give him colored crayons for his third birthday, but because he is miseducated in segregated slum schools" (p. 464). Moving on to criticize popular conceptions of compensatory education, Ryan continued:

> [W]e must be clear what we mean by "compensatory programs" and we must face directly what we are compensating for. . . . For the millions of grown and half-grown Negro Americans who have already been damaged, we must make up for the injury that we did to them. This is what we must compensate for; not for some supposed inherent or acquired inferiority or weakness or instability of the victim whom we injured. (p. 466)

Despite this public protest in an alternative journal, the dominant portrayal of the policy subjects reflected assumptions about the inferiority, weakness, and instability of the poor. These assumptions laid the groundwork on which all future reauthorizations of ESEA Title I were built. The next chapter follows these assumptions and their conceptual consequences through the next 3 decades of Title I congressional floor debates.

Congressional Framing of Children in ESEA Title I Debates, 1965–1994

This chapter explores how the problem definition of poor, culturally deprived students persisted, underwent revisions, and was in part transformed by congressional decisionmakers as they reauthorized Title I for the first 30 years after its initial passage. The ensuing analysis illustrates how Title I beneficiaries were constructed and characterized through the first 3 decades of the policy's history. The initial conceptualizations of the policy beneficiaries and the ways in which federal policy might correct their deficiencies were anchored in the culture of poverty framework. Careful investigation of the language of Congress as the policy was reauthorized reveals that while still embedded in the initial cultural constructions of the poor, the terms and concepts employed in policy debates evolved over time. The language of policymaking is not taken lightly.

The following passage, taken from a newspaper report and presented in the floor debates by a member of Congress, captures a moment in which the then–minority staff director, Charles Radcliffe, made last-minute modifications to the proposed text of the Elementary and Secondary Education Act (ESEA) for its 1981 reauthorization:

> Radcliffe sank into the couch, penciling changes in the bill. To meet complaints from Rep. Shirley Chisholm (D-NY), he changed the words "educationally deprived" on page 69 to "children from low-income families"—to make sure the extra bucks don't head toward rich kids who happen to be doing poorly in school. (Peterson, as cited in LaFalce, 1981, p. 15272)

The reauthorization process had been daunting. The Reagan administration proposed to consolidate various compensatory programs into block grants, a plan resisted by the Democrats. Harried congressional aides and staffers worked to produce legislation upon which a majority could agree.

Characterizing the students appropriately was a source of battle. The problems that this policy aimed to address were not simply about "educational deprivation," whatever that was intended to mean; they were also about poverty status.

Specific change, the replacement of "educationally deprived" with "children from low-income families," reflects the deliberate nature of the terms used to characterize a policy problem. Members of Congress frame these problems with carefully chosen sets of terms that reflect their lenses for viewing the social world. Their language reveals the systems of meaning that are deployed and strengthened through the policy process. The above excerpt reveals conflicting conceptualizations of the policy problem addressed by the act. Poverty, Representative Chisholm seems to maintain, should be the focus of ESEA Title I policy. Others, however, suggest that low academic performance regardless of family wealth should be the primary eligibility criterion. The excerpt above also reflects some of the core assumptions built into Title I policy. Whereas rich kids might just "happen to be doing poorly in school," poor kids, through this policy lens, should receive "the bucks" regardless of their performance. Perhaps they are assumed to have low performance. Perhaps, given the inequitable funding mechanism for education, they are deemed worthy of additional resources regardless of their performance.

As argued in the last chapter, the original framing of Title I policy casts poor children as academically deficient by virtue of their family's socioeconomic status. Poor kids and the cultural deficiencies of their homes—rather than the economic or instructional resources of their schools or communities—were the focus of the policy discourse and ultimately the implementation of educational interventions. Poverty status in and of itself came to signify poor academic performance. Expectations for the potential of the policy beneficiaries were set reproachfully low as the contours of the culture of poverty theory took root in the culture of policy. The categories of thought launched in the culture of policy, and most poignantly the categories of children constructed for policy purposes, were debated over the next several decades of Title I's existence.

My treatment of the historical trajectory of the categories of thought launched in policy debates relies on the discursive arena of the congressional floor. Floor debates, which usually take place after considerable testimony and negotiation in committee and subcommittee hearings and conferences, typically consist of prepared statements by elected officials in the House and Senate. These statements, often written by congressional aides, reveal the political perspectives and priorities of elected representatives and, presumably, their constituents. The legislative arena is one of any number of available sites that provide insight into the culture of policy. However, considerations of data availability limit where one can look for such discursive practices. While the halls, back rooms, and even bathrooms of Congress might be the places where the most revealing representations are communicated, such conversations are not recorded, documented, or made publicly accessible. This analysis, therefore, focuses on the official records of congressional floor debates, which, at the very least, are informed by the backroom conversations, local hearings, and behind-the-scenes bargaining.

This arena provides insight into the ways in which politicians construct the policy beneficiaries and define their needs not only at the time of initial policymaking, but throughout a policy's tenure. There are a number of observations that we might make about how members of Congress represent poor children and define their needs. For example, given the time-honored American script of individual potential, possibility, and achievement, elected officials might be more likely to focus on the private weaknesses wrought by disadvantage and poverty instead of the public economic arrangements that ensure at least some measure of these conditions. Faith in the individual leads to remedies of identified children through services in their schools, rather than the structural features of school finance or broader issues of the distribution of educational opportunities. However, members of Congress are rarely of one mind. As this chapter demonstrates, the rhetorical portraits launched in Congress bare concerns about how children are cast in the policy process, and how the various categories of thought deployed in policymaking represent them. Both the range of rhetorical portraits and those portraits rendered dominant provide important information for the construction of the categories of thought used in the policy process. They also influence the consequences of these conceptual categories for the individuals placed in them.

THE 1960S: SAVING THE POOR THROUGH EDUCATION

Within the second half of the 1960s decade, Congress reauthorized the ESEA twice, first in 1966 and again in 1967. During these debates, various politicians argued for expanding eligibility criteria so that federal funds would reach more children. They also debated the virtues of general versus categorical aid. With the Vietnam War as a backdrop and the War on Poverty in the foreground, the debates over this federal education policy were heated. Members of Congress spoke passionately about the importance of education as a means to save poor children and develop their communities.

1966: Defining Deprivation and Disadvantage

In 1966, members of Congress reconvened to amend the Elementary and Secondary Education Act of 1965. Less than a year after the policy's inception, Congress was to evaluate the program's quality and determine whether to develop, maintain, or discontinue this federal education intervention. An excerpt from the administration's proposed 1966 legislation reads, "Educational deprivation cannot be overcome in a year. And quality cannot be achieved overnight" (Perkins, 1966a, p. 4426). With so little time to evaluate the program's effectiveness in terms of student performance and with a Democratic majority in favor of the act, Congress was likely to reauthorize ESEA with amendments that reflected the desire to expand the policy's reach. One of the key amendments to the act was a change in the funding formula. Whereas the 1965 legislation defined students at the poverty level as those whose household income was less than $2,000 ($11,683 in 2003 using the Consumer Price Index) and those receiving Aid to Families with Dependent Children (AFDC), members of Congress proposed in 1966 to amend the legislation so that children in households with less than $3,000 ($17,037 in 2003 based on the Consumer Price Index) annual income, as well as children receiving AFDC, would be eligible for services. Proposed amendments also included provisions for children on Indian reservations, children of migratory agricultural workers, and foster children. Each group was theorized to need Title I–funded services due to home or family environments.

The change in funding formula demonstrates how constructed categories of thought become policy markings with seemingly objective, quantifiable measures, yet porous definitional boundaries. After all, the location of the "poverty line" at $2,000 or $3,000 was arrived at through discussion, persuasion, and precedent. The actual figures are arbitrary markers, disconnected from the number of people in a household or the financial needs of those individuals (for a similar argument, see O'Connor, 2001, pp. 182–185). In discussing the reauthorization of ESEA, Senator Jacob Javits (R, NY) (1966) illustrates how these constructed categories can be defined inconsistently from person to person and policy to policy:

> Maintaining the income level at $2,000 [as was the case for Title I] presents us with the anomaly of a youngster being at the poverty level under present Federal programs during his preschool and college years if he comes from a $3,000 annual income family [as was the case for other federal poverty policies]; but being considered at the poverty level during his elementary and secondary school years only where his family earned $2,000 or less. (p. 7956)

Even between policies, the seemingly objective measure of poverty was not consistent. Additionally, changes in the measurement of "poverty" or "low income" show the imprecise and arbitrary nature of labeling the policy beneficiaries themselves. Whereas during the first year of the policy's existence, students whose families in 1965 earned between $2,000 and $3,000 ($11,683 and $17,523 in 2003, respectively, based on the Consumer Price Index) were not considered "educationally deprived," irrespective of the number of children in the families, the following year those same students were considered to be victims of educational deprivation. In the original 1965 authorization debates, the difference between $2,000 and $3,000 was questioned for its relevance. Senator Prouty (R, VT) (1965) noted that "[t]he selection of a low income factor in the distribution formula is based on the need for an objective and administratively workable definition of 'educationally deprived child'" (p. 7321). Although he went on to explain that "[n]o one suggests that the $2,000 line or the $3,000 line or any other line divides the educationally deprived child from his more fortunate colleagues" (p. 7321), the use of the low-income factor as an "objective" definition of educational deprivation transfers the arbitrariness of the poverty line measure to the educational domain. Certainly, family income is a useless measure of academic performance, educational capability, or instructional need. However, since initial construction of ESEA policy was framed as a remedy to poverty, children in poverty—rather than those struggling in school—were framed as the "educationally disadvantaged" and "deprived."

The constructs of "deprivation" and "disadvantage" remained central in defining the policy problem in the 1966 debates. Similar to the original authorization, elected officials referred to the concept of "educational deprivation" without ever defining it beyond reference to the poverty line. Nor did the members of Congress delineate the meaning of the vague and ubiquitous phrase "special educational needs." Compared to the extensive efforts on the floor of Congress to amend or propose definitions of other key constructs, such as "current expenditures," "educational agencies," "handicapped children,"[1] and "poverty," the lack of a clear, cogent definition of the policy beneficiaries on the floor of Congress provided little guidance for coherent policy construction. The meaning of the term "educational deprivation" continued to be interchangeably academic, economic, and cultural. Representative Quie (R, MN) (1966) highlighted the ambiguity of the concept of educational deprivation:

> The reason for this legislation is to help educationally deprived children and not just poor children. Poor children are counted in order to get the money into the school districts. The whole thing is mixed up, especially since there is no definition of "educationally deprived" in the act. (p. 25337)

Although not in the act itself, there was a definition of the term "educationally deprived children" in the federal regulations that governed the ESEA of 1965. That definition read:

> "Educationally deprived children" means those children who have need for special educational assistance in order that their level of educational attainment may be raised to that appropriate for children of their age. The term

includes children who are handicapped or whose needs for such special educational assistance result from poverty, neglect, delinquency, or cultural or linguistic isolation from the community at large. (45 C.F.R. [Code of Federal Regulations], as cited in Martin & McClure, 1969, p. 66)

This definition, focusing on low academic performance, but then including children with conditions theorized to result in low academic performance, leaves interpretation of the concept of educational deprivation wide open. Representative Quie intimates that educational deprivation is different from economic deprivation, but notes that the policy requires school districts to discern students' Title I eligibility through poverty measures primarily. By implication, then, educational deprivation was assumed to exist within poor children.

The use of low income and educational deprivation synonymously reflects the overall acceptance of what Congressman Fogarty called "the interrelated problems of poverty and educational deprivation" (p. 2091). Absent common acceptance of what the term "educational deprivation" signified, Congress passed new amendments that changed the technical definition of poverty and used that definition to signal educational deprivation.

This change in the technical definition of poverty, coupled with the interchangeable use of "low-income" and "educationally deprived (or disadvantaged)" to describe policy beneficiaries, demonstrates how categories of thought evolve and converge. While the concept of *educational deprivation* had no clear substantive content or connection to any generally accepted indicators of student academic performance, the technical measurement of *poverty* could be understood, measured, and expressed in concrete dollar amounts. The use of a simple measure of family income and the assumption of its connection to poor academic performance brought together the categories of low-income families and educational deprivation in ways supported by the culture of poverty thesis. In this policy script, poor students were continually expected to do poorly in school, and ESEA Title I was to somehow remedy poverty.

As a remedy to poverty, the Elementary and Secondary Education Act funded programs that provided additional educational services and "cultural opportunity programs" (Conte, 1966, p. 25344; for similar references to cultural enrichments see Fogarty, 1966, p. 2092; Morse, 1966a, p. 5092). In the 1966 debates, children were still cast as the victims of poverty, but, unlike in the prior year's debates, the family was not posited as the primary locus of responsibility. In similar language used in the original authorization, Representative Carl Perkins (D, KY) (1966b) cast Title I beneficiaries as "the children of urban ghettos and rural outposts, the children from backgrounds of poverty and cultural deprivation which all too often precludes [sic] them from receiving the full benefits of standard educational programs" (p. 25328). However, Representative Perkins also looked to the schools as a source of the problem: "The lack of an educationally favorable home environment has not been the only impediment standing in the way of educational achievement for these children; inadequate educational programs must share part of the blame for their failure" (pp. 25328–25329). Here concern for the "culturally deprived" and the "cultural deprivation" of the poor still received attention, as did the institutions—cast similarly as "educationally deprived school districts" (Yarborough, 1966a, p. 12716)—that were supposed to serve them. The 1966 reauthorization debates contain descriptions of the presumed culture in which poor children were immersed, similar to those introduced in the initial authorization, but with more focus on the programs available to such students. Now the challenge for policy supporters was to justify program expansion rhetorically.

Program expansion, of course, would require more federal dollars. In order to argue for additional funding, some members of Congress used the war in Vietnam as an emotive rhetorical device. The war provided a poignant comparison that some congressional representatives employed to challenge the nation's priorities. By juxtaposing funds for the education of American children with the "blood money" (Morse, 1966b, p. 25261) used in the "killing program in Asia" (Morse, 1966b, p. 25262), elected officials created stirring accounts of the policy choices available to them. For example, Senator Wayne Morse (D, OR) (1966b), the Chairman of the Subcommittee on Education, argued the following:

> [T]he President of the United States has not faced up to his responsibilities in bringing to Congress a tax bill that would have this war paid for by those who are making the money out of the blood that is being spilled. But it is much easier, apparently, for President Johnson, to have the schoolchildren and the poverty-stricken people of America pay for this war. (p. 25471)

Senator Ralph Yarborough (D, TX) (1966b) went further to compare the costs and benefits of the war with those of the schools when he questioned whether "the education of the youth of America, . . . which is approximately one-twelfth the cost of the war in Vietnam, . . . is at least one-twelfth as valuable as the cost of the war in Vietnam" (p. 25479). The diminishing popularity of the war became a prevalent tool for supporting education policy expansion.

The shift between the 1965 and 1966 debates is subtle. Within one year, the policy justifications evolved away from a focus on the culture of the policy beneficiaries as the primary justification for the policy to reports of the promise and value of the established policy in addressing the culture of poverty. Despite this observed shift, ESEA Title I was still considered to be an answer to poverty through educational and "cultural" opportunities for poor children, and the culture of poverty thesis was woven into the fabric of each policy amendment. Not even one full year after the original passage of ESEA, the discourse reflected a generally accepted definition of the policy beneficiary grounded in assumptions about deficit and deficiency, poverty, and performance.

1967: Detailing Desperation and Despair

In the 1967 reauthorization debates of ESEA (the actual bill passed in December 1967 and was approved in January 1968), poignant images of cultural deprivation, similar to those launched in the 1965 debates, resurfaced as the Democrats attempted to retain the focus and federal oversight of Title I policy.[2] These portraits formed part of the defense against an amendment supported by Representative Albert Quie (R, MN). The Quie Amendment proposed to consolidate the categorical grants in ESEA that made specific provisions for distinct groups of students (the educationally deprived, the handicapped, the Indian children, the migratory children) and replace them with a block grant intended to serve all students based on local discretion. Representative Quie also sought to change the funding formula so that the states, rather than the federal government, would determine the number of eligible students and distribute the funds accordingly.

Democrats and various education interest groups opposed the Quie Amendment on the grounds that the shift in control from the federal to the state government would not guarantee the appropriate use of policy dollars for the "disadvantaged." Metaphors of the "handicapping" and "crippling" effects of the "vicious cycle of poverty" on the "culturally deprived children" living in the "ghetto slum," the "poverty-stricken rural" areas, or "the invisible prison of poverty" proliferated in the debates as Democrats argued against Representative Quie's proposal. Defending the categories of thought embedded in the original policy, members of the Democratic majority insisted that a general aid bill that "eliminates the concept of poverty" (Calkins as cited in Feighan, 1967, p. 12659) would not serve the "educationally and culturally deprived" students as intended in the original legislation.

Not only were the "educationally and culturally deprived" at risk of losing important resources and learning opportunities under the proposed amendments, according to one representative, "the advantaged" stood to suffer as well. Congressman Andrew Jacobs Jr. (D, IN) (1967) pushed the rhetorical justifications for federal money to poor children in his assertion that the policy "problem" that ESEA addressed was not simply the "poor children," but it also addressed "what those culturally disadvantaged children could grow up to be and to do to the advantaged children" (p. 13844) later in life. Representative Jacobs implored:

They all start as twigs. But by 6 years of age if the twig has not had the advantage of adequate standards of culture and education in his home, in more cases than not he is already headed toward being the kind of adult most likely not to have sufficient self-control to live peacefully and productively in our communities. (pp. 13844–13845)

Through maintenance of this policy in its categorical form, Jacobs insisted that "[t]he disadvantaged would be saved from ignorance and empty lives," and that "[t]he advantaged would be saved from being surrounded 10 years hence by an ocean of ignorance in which it might truly be folly to be wise" (p. 13845).

Throughout the debates, textured descriptions of the policy beneficiaries and their lives defined the contours of the concept of "educational deprivation" more than the formal, technical definition provided by the federal regulations. Similar to original debates of 1965, the portrayals of policy beneficiaries relied on the material conditions of poverty more forcefully than concrete aspects of academic performance or school-based learning opportunities. For example, Senator Ted Kennedy (D, MA) (1967) put forth a casual, folksy definition of the policy beneficiaries that portrayed their daily nonschool lives:

> [P]oor children do not have books read to them. They do not go away in the summer. They do not eat three good meals a day. They do not wear shoes that fit. They are not visited by a doctor when they are sick. They do not have their own bedrooms—or their own beds. These are the educationally disadvantaged children. These are the children compensatory education programs are designed for. (p. 35715)

According to Kennedy, compensatory education, in the form of narrowly targeted categorical aid, should compensate for the "heritage of cultural depravity" (p. 35715) shared by poor children. As in the original authorization, the children were portrayed as "deprived of any cultural stimulation or any incentive to learn" ("Teaching Teachers," as cited in Holland, 1967, p. 10534) in attempts to secure demarcated funds that could compensate for the misfortune of their lives. By original design, ESEA policy "focused on the disadvantaged child rather than on the institution the child was attending" (Moorhead, 1967, p. 13822). The rhetorical justifications put forth by members of Congress, then, logically focused on the deprivation of the poor child rather than the capacity of the school or the other public institutions that shaped the child's life.

Additionally, specific subgroups within the category of "disadvantaged" and "deprived" received special attention during the debates. Since the Quie amendment did not name individual groups of students, concern for the future of monies designated for "Indian children" and "migratory children" led to pointed appeals for consideration of their plights. For example, Representative James Haley (D, FL) (1967) read a statement written by Stewart L. Udall, the then–secretary of the Interior, that cast Indian children as "handicapped educationally, economically and geographically through physical and social isolation from the mainstreams of American life" (p. 13817). Similarly, Representative Burt Talcott (R, CA) (1967) cast migrant students as "culturally deprived, asocial, or semiliterate" (p. 13853). Facing proposals for the combination of earmarked funds into a general fund package, some members of Congress were impelled to revive portraits of despair and deprivation and locate them in terms of the deficiencies perceived to exist in specific ethnic groups as well as in the labor conditions of students' parents. Again, to defend the need for marked federal money for certain children, the perceived weaknesses of those children were depicted with only vague and superficial references to their academic performance or the conditions of their schools.

That is not to say that members of Congress did not discuss children in terms of their academic performance or the conditions of schooling conducive to effective teaching and learning practices. Various legislators did highlight school-based features such as class size, facilities, instructional materials, and teacher quality that could lead to observable outcome improvements for students. However, the widely accepted connections between poverty and academic performance provided the context for these conversations. Senator Morse (D, OR) (1967a) typified the general theoretical premises that framed such considerations in stating, "It has long been recognized that children from impoverished homes commonly suffer physical, intellectual, and cultural handicaps which impede their academic achievement and help perpetuate a cycle of poverty" (p. 13799). The 1967 reauthorization debates led to the ultimate defeat of the Quie amendment and the maintenance of the category of "educational disadvantage" that framed the ways of seeing children in poverty.

Besides the Quie amendment, another important focus of the 1967 debates that launched various characterizations of the policy beneficiaries was the National Teacher Corps program. Contained originally in the Higher Education Act of 1965, the Teacher Corps program was established to address the national shortage of teachers through university training. The 1967 legislation proposed by the administration transferred part of the authorization of the Teacher Corps to the Elementary and Secondary Education Act. Some Republicans resisted this transfer and opposed the program altogether on the grounds that it was ineffective at addressing the labor shortage of teachers and should remain in the domain of higher education. The Teacher Corps program recruited participants—portrayed on the floor of Congress as "young," "dedicated," "committed," and "idealistic"—specifically to teach "disadvantaged children." One of the purposes of the program was to "channel the idealism and energy of young men and women into the teaching profession in order to reach children who had never been motivated" (Ryan, 1967, p. 13874) and to "go into the most difficult educational circumstances and try to help and bring these youngsters up to better cultural and educational levels and to make them meaningful citizens" (Pucinski, 1967, p. 13870). Here the young teachers, portrayed as dedicated and idealistic, were to teach the young children, represented as unmotivated and culturally substandard. In order to justify the inclusion of the program in ESEA policy, various members of Congress launched imagery of the children rooted in deprivation and deficiency. The language of the policy debate focused the lens for seeing poor children as deviant, peculiar, uneager to learn, and difficult to teach. For example, Representative Dante Fascell (D, FL) (1967) defended the Teacher Corps program, stating:

> [T]he American educational system is based on the premise that all students want to learn. Very little is known about the lethargic child, the child who lacks the psychological ingredients that make him an eager student. Very little is known about how to reach the poor child in our Nation's ghettos.
>
> Only recently has Florida and the rest of the Nation begun to develop methods specifically designed to instruct teachers in how to meet the special problems of the disadvantaged child. In the forefront of this important new area of teacher education is the Teachers Corps. (p. 13597)

With the aim of supporting the Teacher Corps program, Representative Fascell and others described the children served by the program as lethargic and lacking. Fascell, although claiming that little is known about children growing up poor, asserts that poor children do not *want* to learn. In extolling the Teacher Corps program, he denigrates the children that it serves, and calls into question their interest in gaining knowledge and skill.

In rare contrast to the derogatory casting of the Title I policy beneficiaries, Senator Wayne Morse (D, OR) (1967b, 1967c, 1967d) discussed federal education as an investment in the "brainpower" of future generations. Rather than describing deficits, Senator Morse highlighted the potential of young children and the government's obligation to develop that potential (p. 34910, 35074, 37034, respectively). Overall, however, the 1967 reauthorization debates evince considerable reliance on portraits of desperation and despair akin to the original authorization. In support of continued resources to specific programs and groups, members of Congress diminish the theoretical potential of children growing up poor through claims of their weaknesses and limitations. Vague claims of disadvantage and deprivation infuse the entire debate while the academic performance of the policy beneficiary in terms of eligibility remains unspecified. The reauthorization hearings of the 1970s build on these ways of seeing.

THE 1970S: REFINING POLICIES AND PROGRAMS

The Title I reauthorization debates of the 1970s demonstrate a movement toward evaluation and programmatic oversight. After a number of years of federal education funding, members of Congress and the taxpaying public wanted to see measurable results in government spending. And with actual Title I programs to evaluate, congressional debates turned to the measurement of policy effectiveness. Throughout this decade, the debate over the conceptualization of the policy beneficiary continued and included new considerations of eligibility through the adoption of poverty measures that accounted for additional facets of the lives of poor people. Although still focused on the policy beneficiaries and their need for compensatory educational services, the debates moved away from predominantly cultural renditions of the children to descriptions grounded in academic performance. This conceptual repositioning of Title I raised questions about the policy's aim: should it address poverty or target education?

1970: Diffusing Poverty's Ills Through Evaluation and Oversight

In the year prior to the 1970 reauthorization, the Washington Research Project and the Legal Defense and Education Fund of the National Association for the Advancement of Colored People released a report entitled *Title I of ESEA: Is It Helping Poor Children?* (Martin & McClure, 1969). This study, based on interviews with and observations of Title I officials, coordinators, principals, teachers, and parents in nine states, found that "[t]he intended beneficiaries of Title I—poor children—are being denied the benefits of the Act because of improper and illegal use of Title I funds" (p. ii). Citing "gross" misuses of Title I money for general school purposes—including the renovation of "superintendents' offices with paneling, wall-to-wall carpeting and color televisions" (p. 57)—the document called for stronger administration and oversight of the program so that the general education community and the country at large could fulfill "a long-needed promise to our Nation's poor children" (p. 58).

Although the authors asserted their strong support for Title I policy and its commitment to students whom they described as "educationally deprived children—black, brown, white, and Indian children" (p. ii), the study highlighted how the monies were not reaching the intended beneficiaries or serving their "special educational needs" (p. 29). Interestingly, the authors of this report refer to these educational needs as varying between communities and assert that "special educational problems might be low reading levels, inability to speak English, need for greater individual attention, or need for instruction *more relevant to a child's cultural background* [italics added]"

(p. 29). This approach to the child's culture in terms of its educational relevance stands in stark contrast with the overall focus of congressional discourse, in which instruction was to *overcome* the child's cultural background.

Around the same time, various evaluations of Title I began to appear in education journals and the mainstream media. The results were mixed. Although Title I had indeed provided additional funding to resource-strapped school systems and had purchased some educational services, few programs could demonstrate measurable improvements in educational performance (McLaughlin, 1975). The studies, typically of a select number of Title I–funded programs, schools, or districts, celebrated the new resources and funded services in schools (see, for example, Connecticut State Department of Education, 1967; Indianapolis Public Schools, 1970; Joiner, 1970; Ohio State Department of Education, 1970; Spraggins, 1968) and/or noted a lack of improvement in performance measures, typically reading achievement test scores (see, for example, Dentler, as cited in Jeffrey, 1978; Glass, 1970; Gordon & Jablonsky, 1968; Hawkridge, 1968; Mosbaek et al., 1968).[3]

Program evaluation and oversight, then, were deemed necessary to determine whether the dollars were reaching the right children and were being used effectively toward their education, and to ensure that Title I was being used to "supplement, not supplant" local educational programs.[4] Members of Congress crafted their notion of appropriate beneficiaries in the vague and similar terms of "educational deprivation" and "disadvantage." The low-income factor, which still served as the technical definition of "educational deprivation" for policy purposes, was increased in the 1970 reauthorization to $4,000 ($20,055 in 2003 based on the Consumer Price Index) without much discussion. After the reauthorizations of the late 1960s, adjustment to this measure of poverty and Title I eligibility was presented as necessary simply due to inflation and cost-of-living increases. The change passed without debate.

In addition to the typical constructions of the policy beneficiaries as disadvantaged and deprived, the 1970 reauthorization debates contained various metaphors of civil unrest, destruction, and violence. The most powerful uses of these metaphors were launched in efforts to demonstrate the "desperate need" for the Title I program. In excerpts from hearing testimonies of superintendents and school board representatives nationwide that were presented on the congressional floor, Title I was posited as "the difference . . . between riot and disruption" in one community (Kottmeyer, as cited in Perkins, 1969a, pp. 4179–4180) and a way to keep the "social dynamite" of poorly educated inner-city children from exploding (Mitau, as cited in Perkins, 1969a, p. 4182).[5] This "social dynamite" was composed of potential future criminals or, as some representatives described them, "predelinquents" (Goodell, 1970, p. 2580).

"Predelinquency," a new category added to the legislative landscape in the 1970 reauthorization, referred to children with the potential for causing trouble or breaking the law. When the category of "predelinquent" was first introduced on the floor of Congress, Senator Peter Dominick (R, CO) (1970) inquired about its meaning, stating that he did not "mean to be facetious, but . . . was intrigued with the wording . . . 'predelinquent juvenile'" (p. 2581), and proceeded to ask about the origin of the term. Senator Charles Goodell (R, NY) (1970) replied that the term was "fairly well accepted . . . among people who work in this field" (p. 2581). Senator Goodell continued honing a definition of predelinquency as children who "have not been adjudicated delinquents nor have they been before a court, and yet they are what might be termed disruptive troublemakers or potential delinquents" (p. 2581). Although they have not yet had problems with the law, he asserted, "[t]hey are very close to the category of having committed offenses or charged with criminal offenses" (p. 2581). Responding to this definition, Senator Dominick expressed apprehension and criticized the implications of recent research that tied criminal behaviors to the genetic makeup of incarcerated individuals.[6] He explained that "recently a number of people have maintained that children with, for instance, a triple Y chromosome are more likely to be criminals when they grow up than children with a double Y chromosome" (p. 2581). Claiming to be a "defense lawyer by nature" (p. 2581), Dominick wondered whether teachers might inappropriately prejudge their students as being "guilty before an event happens":

> I wonder if we might be getting into a similar problem where someone in an educational system might say, "I do not like young Johnny, down there. He is raising Cain. I think he is a predelinquent and needs special instruction."
> (p. 2582)

Senator Goodell replied that he did not "intend to get into the question of chromosomes" and that there were "ample overt signs of predelinquency that can be used and have been used to identify those who would be helped by this program" (p. 2582).

The construct of predelinquency folded into the categories of thought embedded in Title I policy. This use of the predelinquency construct in framing Title I beneficiaries promoted viewing policy-eligible children as potentially dangerous and disruptive. This lens shaped the expectations for student misbehavior based on prejudgments of associated characteristics, such as poverty status. Certain characteristics of children, then, signaled the potential for violence, misbehavior, and illegal activity. By association, then, Title I eligibility was conceptually confounded with the potential for bad behavior.

With the newly defined problem of "predelinquent youth," schools faced tremendous obstacles in hiring and retaining teachers. Congress had to consider how Title I funds might be used to encourage, support, and reward the individuals who taught in such trying circumstances. Unlike the depiction of the dedicated and idealistic members of the Teacher Corps launched in the late 1960s, the 1970 debates painted teachers of the poor as leaving the profession in droves, based in part on the minimal monetary rewards for such difficult work. Some members of Congress focused on the need for additional pay for teachers working in schools that served low-income communities. Although teachers in resource-strapped areas often leave their schools for higher-paying neighboring districts, the focus of the teacher shortage in poor communities was on the difficulties presented by the children. To justify paying teachers to work with children who were represented as dangerous and explosive, a new metaphor was launched. Teachers in urban centers did not just need adequate pay or comparable pay: they needed "combat pay."

When Representative Edith Green (D, OR) (1969) first proposed an amendment using the military metaphor of "combat pay," she noted that "city classrooms" had been "turned into battlefields" and that in order for the country to "recruit and retain qualified teachers to engage in what amounts to actual combat duty," districts should be able to use federal policy-generated dollars to supplement their incomes (p. 9915). This metaphor, repeated several times as the amendment was discussed and debated, reinforced the notion of Title I beneficiaries as potentially dangerous and also connected employment compensation to conceptions of students as scary, difficult, and combative. By extension of the metaphor, students in poverty-stricken schools were cast as the "enemy."

In the 1970 debates, the entangled concepts of poverty and danger framed discussions of the policy beneficiaries. In contrast, representations of children as learners emerged primarily in relationship to the assessment of policy results and service delivery. Members of Congress probed whether the policy demonstrated improvement in reading, how the pullout model of instruction—in which students were removed from their classrooms to receive compensatory services—served students' academic needs, and how students were being identified for services. Occasionally representatives presented the Elementary and Secondary Education Act, and specifically Title I, in terms of its capacity to bring students to their full potential. For example, Representative Perkins (D, KY) (1969b) called this policy "opportunities for a student to achieve his maximum educational potential wherever he might live" (p. 9701), and Representative Roybal (D, CA) (1970) posited the program as one in which "all the Nation's youth will be afforded an equal opportunity to realize their full educational potential" (p. 10622). However, these representations were far less prevalent than those defining the policy beneficiaries in terms of their deficiencies, lacks, and deficits.

Out of the 1970 reauthorization came calls for a more equitable funding formula,[7] greater bureaucratic oversight, and narrower targeting of funds. Although the effectiveness of the policy was called into question through the presentation of various evaluation studies, Congress voted to continue funding Title I programs through ESEA. As noted by Representative Edward Boland (D, MA) (1969), "[m]any of the educational problems attacked under the various programs are so intertwined with problems of poverty, housing, cultural background and health that progress will indeed be slow" (p. 9909). Congress did not expect much improvement in the children served by Title I, at least not quickly. Nonetheless, elected officials authorized additional Title I funding for the next 3 years (Elementary and Secondary Education Assistance Programs, 1971).

1974: Weighing Poverty and Performance

The subsequent reauthorization debates for ESEA began on February 19, 1974, nearly 1 year after the Supreme Court upheld the constitutionality of the property-tax basis for school finance in the landmark *San Antonio Independent School District v. Rodriguez* (1973) case. Lawyers for the plaintiffs argued that the structure of school funding in Texas denied children in resource-poor areas their right to equal protection, guaranteed under the Fourteenth Amendment of the United States Constitution. The funding of education based on the property values of the areas where schools were located, they argued, produced gross inequities in per-pupil spending between school districts. The Supreme Court upheld the Texas school finance system, stating that education was not a fundamental right protected by the Constitution, and that the equal protection clause "does not require absolute equality or precisely equal advantages" (*San Antonio v. Rodriguez*). This ruling moved the potential for legal challenges to the inherently inequitable nature of school finance to the state level (for a review of judicial challenges to state school finance systems, see Reed, 2001). In the meantime, schools were left to rely on local property taxes, state categorical aid, and, in districts and schools with high concentrations of poverty, federal compensatory education funding, mainly through Title I.

During the 1974 reauthorization debates in Congress, there was no mention of the *Rodriguez* case or its potential meaning for the equity orientation of Title I policy. However, explicit considerations of Title I policy purpose did shape the debate as Congress considered a number of amendments to reorient the policy focus. In attempting to define precisely the policy goals and appropriate beneficiaries of Title I, members of Congress typically supported one of two perspectives. One camp, primarily composed of Democrats, maintained that Title I should remain a poverty policy that addressed the educational needs of poor children. The other group, largely Republicans, insisted that Title I should be an educational policy that focused on low academic performance irrespective of poverty status. Any efforts to define clearly what was meant by the previously vague definitions of "educational disadvantage" or "deprivation" resulted in polemical discussions of the needy poor or the generic struggling student. Elected officials based their perspectives, in part, on whether their constituencies stood to gain or lose Title I funding through the different conceptions of the policy purpose and beneficiary debated on the floor. Several representatives filled their presentations with numerical calculations of which states and cities stood to win and lose based on proposed funding schemes and measurement techniques.

As contentions centered around whether Title I policy should serve the "poorest of the poor" or address low academic performance regardless of poverty status, the link between poverty and performance was both reiterated and challenged throughout the debates. Some members of Congress argued that rather than measuring need through poverty indices, the policy should define its beneficiaries in terms of academic performance alone. While presenting the proposed bill put forth by the Education and Labor Committee, Representative Quie (R, MN) (1974a) (now the ranking minority member of that committee) maintained that using an income factor to determine eligibility for programs funded through a federal education policy betrayed what should be the academic focus of the legislation. Questioning the "presumption that there was a high correlation between low income and educational disadvantagement" (p. 6285), Quie proposed to base funding distribution primarily on measured student performance. Believing that "we are best served by a program which addresses itself to educational need," rather than by a "program to help redistribute income" (p. 6286), Quie suggested the use of criterion-referenced tests to diagnose "individual learners' capabilities" (p. 6285) and distribute funds accordingly. Although Quie asserted that "educationally disadvantaged students" were more concentrated among families "below the poverty level," he also claimed that "there are many more families above the poverty level . . . [therefore, causing the] total number of children who have severe learning problems to be greater in the above-poverty-level families" (p. 6285). Additionally, Representative Quie reported on districts and states throughout the country, such as Oakland, California, where "the schools containing children with the greatest educational deficits were not the schools with the financially poorest students" (p. 6286).

Another funding proposal central to the debate revolved around the measurement of need to determine eligibility for policy dollars. Thus far, the concept of need in Title I policy had been structured in relationship to the poverty level, measured by family income. Many members of Congress believed that the poverty level was an inadequate measure, and some found it inappropriate for measuring "educational disadvantage" altogether. The

1974 committee bill proposed to change the technical definition of poverty from the $4,000 ($14,929 in 2003 based on the Consumer Price Index) family income level and AFDC eligibility to a more complex formulation called the Orshansky index. Developed in 1963 by economist Mollie Orshansky, this index took into consideration family size, number of children, heads of households, rural versus urban locations, and food consumption. The Bureau of the Budget adopted it in 1969 as the official federal measure of poverty. The Orshansky index allowed greater flexibility in determining program eligibility, since it moved away from AFDC eligibility or a specific family income threshold. Ultimately, it would increase the number of students, schools, and districts eligible for Title I funds.

Discussions of the possible adoption of the Orshansky index to measure Title I eligibility highlight the constructed nature of the category commonly invoked by the word "poverty" for policy purposes. As members of Congress presented their rationales for embracing or resisting this index, their positions on how to measure poverty relied more on the consequences of possible measures for funding distribution than on any conceptual commitments or convictions. Throughout the reauthorization debates, Representative Quie (R, MN) (1974a), who wanted to distribute Title I funds more widely and base Title I funding on performance rather than poverty, argued that AFDC and census data were unreliable measures of need for compensatory education. First, he argued that certain groups and areas, especially "[B]lack children" and "non-English speaking . . . neighborhoods" (p. 6284), were undercounted by the census and were, therefore, underrepresented in Title I eligibility figures. Second, he claimed that some groups, namely "Chicanos and Orientals," did "not go on AFDC the way other minority groups do and the majority race does" (p. 6285). Therefore, he maintained, members of specific ethnic groups were deemed ineligible for Title I funds not due to their poverty or performance, but due to some notion of ethnic- or race-based distastes for public assistance. Third, Representative Quie (1974b) contended that since families go on and off public assistance frequently, the use of AFDC eligibility was inappropriate for measuring the "educational disadvantage" the policy was supposed to address. The congressman from Minnesota explained, "The average child . . . stays on AFDC for 1 month and they do not become educationally disadvantaged when they go on it and cease to become educationally disadvantaged when they drop off of it" (p. 8240).

The arguments against the Orshansky formula were also articulated on the basis of the consequences of that measure. The Orshansky index would indeed expand the numbers of eligible children and, therefore, distribute Title I dollars more widely across the nation. The use of the Orshanky index was met with sharp opposition from those representatives committed to focusing Title I funds on only "the poorest of the poor" (Perkins, 1974, p. 6277).

For example, Representative Mario Biaggi (D, NY) (1974) insisted that use of the Orshansky index was "a clear violation of the statement of purpose in the bill" (p. 6302), and that this revised funding formula would "dilut[e] our attack on the worst areas of educational disadvantage in the name of a handout for everyone who can possibly, somehow, claim a share" (p. 6301).

Within these discussions, the conceptual connection between poverty and performance was rearticulated and the poverty focus of ESEA Title I repeated as the representatives who hoped to maintain Title I funds as a remedy for poverty argued against proposals that could diffuse funds. The Orshansky formula was criticized as "a product of incredibly poor research and preparation" (Kemp, 1974, p. 6269), as well as biased against urban areas.[8] Although far less detailed than in prior floor debates, rhetorical portraits of misery and despair surfaced in efforts to sustain policy focus on the poor (see, for example, Pell, 1974, p. 14567). Even more common were reassertions of the original policy purpose, a revisiting of the Great Society programs, and a rereading of the original Elementary and Secondary Education Act, all leading to the conclusion that "the emphasis [of ESEA and Title I] is on poverty" (Young, 1974, p. 6342;[9] see also Abzug, 1974, p. 6274; Badillo, 1974, p. 6302; Koch, 1974, p. 6274; Pell, 1974, p. 14567). While use of the Orshansky index was passed, and the term "Orshansky children" (mentioned 5 times during the 1974 debate) was introduced into the policy discourse as a new conceptual category used to signify those eligible under this measure of poverty, other aspects of the committee bill that would reorient the policy toward poor academic performance and away from strict poverty measures were defeated.

An additional amendment, introduced on the floor by Representative James O'Hara (D, MI) (1974a, 1974b), proposed to remove eligibility criteria related to the concentration of poverty in a school district or school. Focusing on individual student need, rather than school- or district-based need, O'Hara aimed to "delete the emphasis on 'concentrations of low-income families' and substitute the concept of targeting the special education needs of educationally deprived children" (O'Hara, 1974a, p. 6563). This amendment, as O'Hara stated, tried to decouple poverty and performance by directing funds only toward "children demonstrating the need for educational remediation" (1974a, p. 6563) and those "who are failing to keep pace with their age group" (1974b, p. 8244) at the school level. Again, various members of Congress renounced this proposal on the grounds that it detracted from Title I's poverty focus. Representative Alfonzo Bell (R, CA) (1974) called it "the 'Reverse Robin Hood' amendment" since "it robs from the poor to give to the rich" (p. 8235). Representative Quie (R, MN) (1974b) also rejected the O'Hara proposal. Although he supported O'Hara's attempts to move away from a poverty formula to determine educational disadvantage, he thought that the proposed formula was "farther off the mark"

(p. 8246) than current approaches. "The only way to get to the mark is if we could have an assessment to find out who is actually disadvantaged," Quie continued (p. 8246). Quie lamented that this was not yet possible, as reliable assessment of educational performance was not available. The O'Hara amendments were defeated.

The 1974 debates, while calling into question the meaning of the categories of educational disadvantage and deprivation, also introduced a new, separate category of policy beneficiary that expanded the categorical conceptions of the policy beneficiaries and their needs: the "children of migratory fishermen." Inclusion of this group, introduced by Senator John Sparkman (D, AL) and supported by Senator Claiborne de Borda Pell (D, RI), was responsive to the fact that "the Office of Education definition of 'migratory agricultural workers' did not include migratory aquacultural workers" (Pell, 1974, p. 14327). The addition of yet another specific category of children to be served by the policy evolved concurrently with challenges to the wisdom of the categorical nature of the program and its efficiency at providing quality educational opportunities to students.

Reading from a *New York Times* editorial written by Congresswoman Edith Green (D, OR) (as cited in Ashbrook, 1974), Representative John Ashbrook (R, OH) (1974) argued that the federal dollars had "not brought the significant improvement we anticipated" (p. 8526). Although Representative Green had been a longtime supporter of ESEA, her article called for an "agonizing reappraisal" of the entire federal education program, and particularly its fragmented, categorical nature. The term "agonizing reappraisal" was picked up by representatives and repeated throughout the debates.

Part of the motivation for this "agonizing reappraisal" was the lack of evidence that students served by ESEA Title I were benefiting from the program. Several Republican representatives argued that students were actually worse off after participating in these programs. For example, Representative John Rousselot (R, CA) (1974) quoted a newspaper article asserting that "considerable evidence shows that . . . some youngsters in Title I programs fell further behind in basic skills" (Rabben, as cited in Rousselot, 1974, p. 8251), and Representative Earl Landgrebe (R, IN) (1974), insisted that "there is much evidence that the supposedly educationally disadvantaged really are disadvantaged after treatment by or exposure to our Government's education plans" (p. 6291). Various program supporters, largely but not exclusively Democrats, produced studies that countered these claims through evidence of improved reading scores, science achievement, and other indicators of academic performance among participants in Title I programs (see, for example, Badillo, 1974, p. 6304; Schweiker, 1974, p. 14836).

Overall, the 1974 reauthorization debates introduced the potential for reframing Title I as an educational rather than an antipoverty bill. The rival concepts of the policy beneficiaries both relied on the identification of deficit and deficiency, but with differing perspectives regarding where such deficits were located.[10] While some focused their attention on the poor academic performance of students no matter what their class status, others insisted that poverty was the organizing principle for this policy, and that Title I funds should be targeted narrowly toward the poor. After considerable debate, the poverty focus of Title I was maintained.

Given the repeated rhetoric of equal educational opportunity throughout all Title I debates, the lack of reference to the landmark *San Antonio Independent School District v. Rodriguez* (1973) school finance case as further justification for maintaining Title I's poverty focus is curious. Certainly, the Supreme Court protected the inequities and glaring inequalities inherent in a school finance system based on local property taxes. The predominant rationale for preserving the poverty orientation of ESEA, however, was rooted in assumptions about the academic performance of the poor and the daily hardships of their lives. The absence of reference to the *Rodriguez* decision is consistent with the culture of policy framework in that the articulation of need for targeted money toward resource-poor schools was located in the deficiencies of the children served rather than the systems of finance that perpetuate inequality. Justifications for maintaining Title I's poverty orientation had more to do with conceptualizations of the policy beneficiary as deficient rather than the inbuilt injustices of the overall structures of educational finance. The 1974 reauthorization maintained Title I's poverty focus based on ideas about children in poverty rather than notions of fairness and equity in educational finance.

1978: Narrowing the Definition of the "Title I Student"

The next reauthorization of ESEA occurred 4 years later. During the 1978 debates, members of Congress continued tinkering with the concept of the appropriate policy beneficiary for Title I. Proposed amendments addressed the funding formula, the focus of the program, and the administration of the program. Again, the question of whether the Title I beneficiary ought to be "poor children who are educationally disadvantaged or . . . any children who are educationally disadvantaged regardless of family income" (Perkins, 1978c, p. 38541) focused many of the speeches presented on the congressional floor. Similarly, the issues of program evaluation, administration, and implementation resurfaced as members of Congress called into question various Title I–funded educational practices, reported on research showing dismal educational performance among Title I participants and nonparticipants alike, and examined the role of the states in administering Title I.

The 1978 debates generated various proposals for defining the policy beneficiary more precisely than in prior years. For example, Representative Quie (R, MN) (1978), whose unsuccessful past proposals aimed to focus

Title I funds on educational performance rather than poverty, put forth a new proposal that prioritized the conditions of the policy beneficiaries in order to "establish some policy of the order in which we reach children" (p. H6596). Instead of focusing Title I simply on the "needs of educationally deprived children," a concept that after 10 years of policy implementation still had multiple, contradictory meanings, Quie proposed to focus on the "needs of children in the following order of priority":

> (1) educationally deprived children [evidenced through academic performance] from low-income families, (2) educationally deprived children who are not from low-income families, (3) children who are not educationally deprived but are from low-income families, and (4) children who are neither educationally deprived nor from low-income families. (p. H6596)

This proposal met resistance from Democrats who argued that Title I should continue to serve "the poorest of the poor" (Perkins, 1978b, p. H6596). They also contended that while poverty should determine how funds were distributed to states, districts, and schools, the school-based practitioners should determine the precise students eligible for the policy based on individual academic performance. Claiming that funds should be distributed "on the basis of objective poverty data," Representative Perkins (D, KY) (1978b) argued that the Quie amendment would be cumbersome to schools where at present time "any disadvantaged children" (p. H6596), regardless of the source of their disadvantage, could receive services.

The conceptual problem, again, was the policy's original assertion of a link between poverty and performance. If Title I were intended to redress inequities inherent in the property-tax–based financing of schooling, academic performance should not matter in determining Title I funding allocation. Poor districts and schools should get the money, whether or not they were doing a decent job educating children. However, the use of the correlation between poverty and performance (with only later and secondary attention to the effectiveness of school-based instructional practices) begged the question of whether the policy should serve children of all class backgrounds who struggle in school. The notion of educational deprivation as linked to academic performance rather than poverty provided a strong conceptual challenge to the policy's original constructs and assumptions. After nearly 10 years and multiple reauthorizations, Title I priorities still had not been resolved.

While the technical definition of the Title I policy beneficiary was still evolving, the discursive definitions launched by members of Congress rendered familiar theories about the children Title I had and should continue to serve. For example, Representative James Oberstar (D, MN) (1978) proposed the following definition of the category of thought—the "Title I student"—

that was by now well-established in the minds and vocabularies of politicians and educators:

> The title I students are the children who traditionally receive low grades in school. They are the pushouts, the fadeouts, the dropouts, and are probably a year or more below grade level. Testing is feared, or even hated, by these students. School attendance has been habitually poor. Title I of ESEA is intended to reach out to these students and give them the extra help needed to "make it" in the school environment. (p. H6553)

With an earlier reference to the focus on "American children in low-income areas" (p. H6552), Representative Oberstar defined the contours of the "Title I student" in terms of academic performance, with detail about students' experiences with grading, testing, and attendance. Within the struggle to define the Title I beneficiary for policy purposes, the representation of students—earlier in terms of their family culture and now in terms of their poor academic performance, habits, and emotions—developed the category of thought legislated in 1965. And the more the conception and technical definition of the policy beneficiary moved toward performance and away from poverty, the more schools would have to rely on the existence of low-performing students to secure funds for the school. If Title I eligibility were connected to performance, then schools with greater numbers of low-performing students would receive more funds. The government's policy aimed at school improvement would then contain monetary incentives for schools, districts, and states to maintain low-performing students.

As in prior reauthorizations, the definitional battle over Title I was fought mainly along partisan lines. The Republicans wanted to cut the "sacred cow [of Title I] down to size" (Proxmire, 1978, p. 27307) and to eliminate many of the categories created in prior policy iterations. The "sacred cow" metaphor provided an opportunity for Republicans to question why, after years of poor evaluation results and questionable practices, Title I policy "enjoy[ed] such immunity from criticism" (Proxmire, p. 27307). Many Republicans cited studies that questioned Title I effectiveness, instructional practices, and the various categories of children it aimed to serve. Most Democrats, however, wanted to maintain the categorical nature of the funds and increase the overall funding.

Several Republican proposals attempted to narrow the categories of children served by Title I, or, as they put it, to "reorganize, simplify, deregulate, and consolidate" (Domenici, 1978, p. 27340) Title I and move responsibility for certain categories of children to programs under other sections of ESEA. These attempts were aided by the 1975 passage of the All Handicapped Children Act, which placed the education of "handicapped children" in a separate federal act, within ESEA but outside of Title I. In response, these categories and the special needs of the children who occupied them were articulated and rearticulated by those opposing programmatic consolidation.[11]

Throughout ESEA's tenure, the issue of desegregation mandates and compliance therewith surfaced in Title I policy discussions. Typically, members of Congress questioned how the government could ensure that federal education money did not finance segregated schools. Discussions of desegregation and busing were framed mainly in terms of local compliance with court agreements and policy mandates. In the 1978 reauthorization debates, however, the issues of busing and desegregation challenged funding practices with implications for the construction of the Title I policy beneficiary. Since Title I dollars were distributed to states, districts, and schools based on measures of poverty concentration, poor students bused to wealthier schools would not be eligible for funds. As articulated by Representative Daniel Glickman (D, KS) (1978), if a poor black child were bused from a segregated school with a large concentration of poor students to a wealthier, desegregated school, she or he would not be eligible for Title I–funded services in the new school (p. H6550). Fearing the "administrative nightmare" that would result "under Title I if one undertakes to follow the child with the money" (Perkins, 1978a, p. H6550), separate policy money from the Emergency School Aid Act (under ESEA Title VI, in which approximately $300 million was allocated yearly to support desegregation efforts) was designated for poor students bused to more affluent schools.

The issues of busing and desegregation unearthed additional tension in defining the policy beneficiaries. The question was whether the target of Title I policy should be framed as poor children or as the schools that serve them. Discursively, members of Congress were more apt to characterize the policy beneficiaries as children than they were to focus on the schools that the children attended. However, the schools were the recipients of funding based on the students' poverty status, and the money stayed in the school, even if the students generating the funds left to attend elsewhere. Although the policy beneficiary was conceptualized and portrayed as poor children, the funding actually went to the schools serving such children without a necessary connection to the children themselves.

The primary focus of the debates, however, was the evaluation of Title I programs. Several congressional representatives discussed the decline in student achievement, both in and out of Title I, and some voiced concern over certain curricular programs and instructional practices, namely those focused on "social awareness and social adjustment" funded by Title I.[12] Evaluation studies, conducted by government-funded researchers and university scholars, revealed unpromising results. Media reports with titles such as "The More We Spend, the Less Children Learn" and "Is Anyone Out There Learning?" were read or summarized in the debates, demonstrating the public's concern for the lack of measurable improvement in student performance. A number of Democrats argued that the studies on which these reports were based were not reliable sources of information since the nature of local programming was hard to capture, observe, and assess. It was difficult, some insisted, to tell which students were receiving what services, making the study of all eligible students unrepresentative of the effectiveness of actual participation in a Title I–funded program. Additionally, while some programs focused on academic skill building, others addressed social, behavioral, and attitudinal issues.[13] Maintaining partisan priorities, the Democrats defended the program by presenting evidence of Title I's ability to improve schooling for the policy beneficiaries and noting a lack of standards in the evaluation studies reported by the Republicans (see, for example, Bingham, 1978, p. E3809; Chisholm, 1978, pp. H4803–4804). Addressing the issue of sound research on which to base policy decisions, the 1978 legislation included a statutory mandate for the National Advisory Council on the Education of Disadvantaged Children (NACEDC) to "review and evaluate the administration and operation" of Title I in order to inform Congress and the president of its effectives (Education Amendments of 1978, Sec. 196).

The 1978 debates moved the discussion of the Title I policy beneficiary further away from strict poverty considerations to assessment of academic performance. In fact, this reauthorization was the first to require a comprehensive assessment of students' educational needs as a means to determine which students should receive Title I–funded services at the school level. Although some states and districts had already required formal assessments of student needs, Title I policy itself had not yet made this a mandatory step in the pursuit of federal funds.

As a whole, the reauthorizations of the 1970s brought about challenges to the original conceptualization of the policy beneficiary, but little actual movement away from the poverty criteria. Title I was neither a solid educational policy nor a sound poverty policy. Simultaneously, however, each new reauthorization brought about more federal oversight, more bureaucratic mechanisms to ensure compliance with policy mandates, and more paperwork for the local practitioners. By the end of the 1970s, nearly 900 pages of the United States Code and 1,200 pages of the Code of Federal Regulations were devoted to education statutes. Additionally, the U.S. Department of Health, Education, and Welfare issued regulations to states, which circulated information to districts, which shaped the language and rituals of schooling for policy purposes. The conceptions of policy purpose and characterizations of policy beneficiaries moved from the floor of Congress through the administrative and bureaucratic mechanisms of the federal Department of Health, Education, and Welfare, the state departments of education, the districts, and ultimately the schools, thus shaping the ways in which practitioners were asked to interpret, organize, and serve eligible students. As Congress developed

Title I policy in response to the experiences of district- and school-based practitioners, the documentation of funding misuse, and the evaluative results of
local programs, the bureaucratic oversight of Title I expanded, contributing
to the culture of Title I policy in schools. The first reauthorization hearing in
the next decade attempted to address the level of bureaucratic oversight
through programmatic consolidation.

1980S: CUTTING AND CONSOLIDATING

Congress reauthorized the Elementary and Secondary Education Act only twice
during the 1980s: once in 1981 and again in 1988. With Republican presi-
dents for both reauthorizations, the congressional discourse focused in the early
part of the decade on whether to consolidate and cut federal education programs and in the latter part of the decade on how to guard against international competition and focus programs on schools with high concentrations
of poverty. The 1988 reauthorizations also demonstrate, through the significant focus on a telephone pornography service, how the priorities of small
numbers of congressional representatives can shape the contours of the debate, and move the substance of the discussion to rather tangential concerns.

1981: Combining the Categoricals

In the 1981 debates, the reauthorization of ESEA was included as part of
the Reagan administration's Omnibus Budget Reconciliation Act of 1981.
This act was an enormous piece of legislation with the overall goal of con-
solidating various policy arenas and reducing government spending in many
policy domains. The Education Consolidation and Improvement Act of 1981
(ECIA) reauthorized and renamed ESEA and merged 44 separate federal
programs under ESEA into two block grants. The first block grant, entitled
"Chapter 1," was intended to be an improved, streamlined version of Title
I with a proposed funding cut of roughly 12%. The second block grant, entitled "Chapter 2," consisted of all the remaining Titles under ESEA.
    The Omnibus Budget Reconciliation Act (1981) addressed government
spending in several policy realms, including Medicaid, student loans for higher
education, food stamps, and other domestic programs; education was only one
of the several policy arenas addressed. Within the debates on this vast act,
considerations of the Education Consolidation and Improvement Act and its
beneficiaries were notably more vague than in prior years. The theme of consolidation itself received a substantial amount of attention on the congressional
floor where elected officials argued for and against the curtailing of federal
spending through the merger of programs. The Republican authors of the ECIA
defended the proposed changes in education policy as a simplification of

administrative procedures and as a transfer of authority and responsibility to the state and local levels. Proponents of the new act insisted that federal resources could be used more efficiently and effectively toward the teaching of basic skills if the "tangle of red tape" that was "choking local enthusiasm and creativity" (Ashbrook, 1981, p. 12677) were removed.

With the proposal to cut Title I funds by nearly 12%, the floor debates focused on the benefits and drawbacks of programmatic consolidation, rather than the policy beneficiaries themselves. Instead of the typical definitional debates led by Representative Quie (R, MN) (who had now become the governor of Minnesota) and Representative Perkins (D, KY), the contours of the conceptual category of the policy beneficiary were not debated extensively. In fact, the question of "[p]overty targeting" (Chisholm, 1981, p. 14667) versus performance targeting was raised on the floor succinctly only by Representative Shirley Chisholm (D, NY), who insisted that the minority staff director change the words "educationally deprived" to "children from low-income families" in the passage that opened this chapter (Peterson, as cited in LaFalce, 1981, p. 15272). Otherwise, the debates centered on the vague "needs" of the "needy" policy beneficiaries.[14] The characterizations common to the historical conception of Title I students were leveraged only to defend the prior policy structure, as the "poor, minority, disadvantaged, and handicapped" would "be pitted against one another for a piece of an increasingly smaller pie" (Dellums, 1981, p. 14102) under the consolidated programs. Accounts of the theorized needs and neediness of the various categories of children served by Title I no longer resembled the rich portraits of prior reauthorization debates.

Although the definition of "educationally disadvantaged youth" was not clarified or debated as in past years, a definition of the term "educationally deprived children" did appear in the floor debate transcript through Representative George Miller's (D, CA) inclusion of a report entitled *Title I, Today: A Factbook* (Jung & Buhl, 1981, as cited in Miller, 1981, pp. 10610–10621) as an extension of his remarks. This report, published by the National Advisory Council on the Education of Disadvantaged Children (NACEDC),[15] had not been published in time for the floor debates, but contained a review of research on Title I effectiveness and participants nationwide. The report, which accounted for approximately one-seventh of the entire Title I-focused floor debate text in 1981,[16] sought to answer three questions: (a) Are Title I programs effective? (b) What do Title I dollars buy? and (c) Who participates in Title I projects? (p. 10611).

Consistently, the authors of this report found that "Title I students" obtain "dramatic achievement gains" in reading and mathematics skills if they participate in "[s]table Title I programs" (Jung & Buhl, 1981, as cited in Miller, 1981, p. 10610). These findings contradicted the results of earlier national evaluations. The report addressed this discrepancy in findings and provided a methodological critique of the prior studies. Basing their conclusions on work conducted by the National Institute of Education, the Stanford Research Institute, and the System Development Corporation, the authors included tables and charts that illustrate the effectiveness of Title I at providing additional funding to poor students and schools and promoting achievement gains for "Title I students." Contrary to the discouraging results of past evaluations, *Title I, Today* provided research-based evidence of Title I's success. The authors suggested that in addition to the methodological problems of past studies, the initial misuse of Title I funds; the lack of oversight, accountability, and parental input; and the limited practitioner knowledge about educating "the disadvantaged" contributed to prior evaluation outcomes that were less than promising. Now that the oversight and accountability practices were well established, the mechanisms for parental input in place, and the practitioners more able and experienced at working with "Title I students," the proposals to cut both funding and federal oversight were positioned as ill-conceived attempts to limit the federal government's commitment to education.

Jung and Buhl (as cited in Miller, 1981), the authors of this report, described the "multiple and evolving goals" (p. 10612) of Title I policy, ranging from equalizing per-pupil expenditures to breaking the cycle of poverty. In the introduction to the report, the authors reasserted the connection between poverty and performance: "Poverty and poor performance in school go hand in hand. They cause students to drop-out of school, and they foster unemployment, crime, and more poverty" (p. 10611). These familiar portrayals emerged in descriptions of the general purpose of the policy, but not when reviewing evaluation studies. While the perils of poverty were used to denote the policy beneficiaries in general terms, the evaluations of Title I measured whether "Title I students" or "low achievers" (rather than "students from low-income families" or "poor students") actually benefited from the policy. This report depicted children as economically poor when explaining their eligibility and as "low-achieving students," "Title I students," and "educationally disadvantaged students" when analyzing their academic performance gains.

The report also reviews some of the instructional practices used in Title I programs, including "smaller classes, more hours of instruction in reading and math, special teachers and aides, and more varied instructional approaches and materials" (Jung & Buhl, 1981, as cited in Miller, 1981, p. 10611). Title I legislation did not require specific instructional approaches, but rather focused on targeting services to eligible students. Although the authors reviewed a few Title I–funded instructional approaches observed in various schools, they did not provide much analysis of these approaches or how they might contribute to the performance gains or lacks thereof of participating students. And while noting the additional hours of "remedial reading and math" and the unspecified "varied instructional approaches" afforded by Title I, they provided minimal consideration of the effects of specific instructional practices. Certainly, smaller classes and more hours of instruction may only mean that students receive ineffective instruction in smaller groups for longer periods of time. The authors did address the prominent instructional strategy of the pullout model—wherein students were pulled from their classrooms to receive remedial instructional services—with the following observation:

> Most students receive their compensatory instruction outside the regular classroom. Thus, there is apparently a wide-spread but erroneous belief that the Title I law or regulations require pull-out programs—removing students from their regular classrooms for a part of the school day to obtain additional remedial instruction. (p. 10614)

Although not noted by the authors, the perception that Title I required pullout programs likely resulted from the monitoring of Title I to ensure the service of eligible students. The pullout model allowed for efficient determination of who was receiving what services, irrespective of what those students were receiving while in pullout programs. And in their treatment of instructional practices, the authors did not report what students did while in pullout programs. Similar to Title I discourse on the floors of Congress, the report focused more on the recipients of Title I than on the instructional services they received.

A section of the report entitled "Title I students" asserted that since there were not enough funds to support supplementary services for all low-performing students, the limited funds had been targeted toward "educationally deprived children attending the poorest schools" (Jung & Buhl, 1981, as cited in Miller, 1981, p. 10615). The authors of the report continued by explaining the selection process for eligible students, moving from the district selection of target schools based on poverty to the school-based selection of children with "the greatest need for remedial help" as indicated by "standardized achievement scores, teacher judgments, or some combination of methods" (p. 10615). According to the studies the report summarizes, Title I recipients tended to be poor and educationally needy. However, the report continued, not all poor students nor educationally needy students were being served by Title I.[17]

While the discursive policy focus in the report is some combination of poverty and performance, the definitions of "educationally deprived children" and "compensatory education" included in the report do not refer to poverty at all. Instead, "educationally deprived children" were defined as those "whose educational attainment is below the level that is appropriate for children of their age," and "compensatory education" was defined as "educational or support services intended to upgrade or compensate for skill deficiencies of children doing poorly in school" (Jung & Buhl, 1981, as cited in Miller, 1981, p. 10617). Although in general terms the report cast Title I as a policy that serves poor children, the definition of the policy beneficiaries and the services they are provided did not include any reference to poverty.

This framing of the policy beneficiary and the services Title I affords reveals a gradual shift in the thinking about Title I policy from its inception to the present moment. Rather than a central characteristic of the policy beneficiary, poverty now provides a backdrop for theorized special educational needs of certain children. Academic performance frames the technical definition of the policy beneficiaries. The various debates that questioned the connections between educational and economic disadvantage and deprivation clearly moved the policy from its strict poverty orientation to one of academic performance anchored in assumptions about the performance of poor children. This shift is further revealed in the differences between the Declaration of Policy in the 1965 and 1981 Acts. Whereas the 1965 Declaration focuses on poverty as the motivation, justification, and centerpiece of the policy (educational deprivation was assumed to go hand in hand with poverty), the 1981 Declaration flips the ranking of performance and poverty, asserting that "Congress recognizes the special educational needs of children of low-income families, and that concentrations of such children in local educational agencies adversely affect their ability to provide educational programs which will meet the needs of such children" (Education Consolidation and Improvement Act of 1981, Sec. 552).

In the first declaration, Congress focused on low-income children as the beneficiaries of the policy and committed to provide financial assistance to schools serving those students. In the second declaration, however, Congress committed to provide financial assistance to schools to meet the needs of "educationally deprived children," a term now devoid of any poverty status, and then recognized the "special educational needs" associated with poverty. As attention to the poor had waned since the 1960s, so did the focus of Title I on poverty.

After negotiations and revisions, the Omnibus Budget Reconciliation Act (1981) passed with only minor changes to Title I (now coined "Chapter 1"). The 1981 reauthorization debates raised fewer definitional questions than in prior years, in large part due to the structure of the Omnibus Act and the more pressing concerns about budget cuts. Although the reauthorization debates lacked serious consideration of how the policy beneficiaries were framed, the overall casting of those served by Title I had moved away from poverty and toward academic performance.

1988: Beating Around the Bush

The next reauthorized legislation was titled the Augustus F. Hawkins–Robert T. Stafford Elementary and Secondary School Improvement Amendments of 1988. This act, resulting from the House bill H.R. 5, maintained the format of the 1981 legislation with some modification in focus, and added an option to target *schools* with high concentrations of children in poverty, rather than targeting the children themselves. Chapter 1 of this act—the policy formerly known as Title I—included grant provisions for basic programs, the Even Start program (similar to the Head Start program of the 1960s), Basic Skills Improvement and Dropout Prevention and Reentry programs, and state programs for students classified as "migratory," "handicapped," and "neglected and delinquent." During the debates leading up to this reauthorization, the discourse on the policy beneficiary mirrored the educational concerns of the time: (a) international competition, (b) the education of children in areas with high concentrations of poverty, and (c) accountability for federal dollars.

Launched as a central concern in the 1983 document *A Nation At Risk* (National Commission on Excellence in Education), international competition became a primary discursive motivator for educational reform through the late 1980s. The future of the nation, members of Congress argued, relied on the schools' ability to produce skilled workers relative to the education systems of other countries (see, for example, Hawkins, 1988, p. 7454; Levine, 1988, p. 7474; Scheuer, 1988, p. 7476). Comparisons to educational practices in Asia and Europe shaped the debate and caused the alarm that other countries could dominate economically based on superior educational strategies. Fear of putting the nation at risk through nonrigorous schooling fueled proposals for better educational programs for the "gifted and talented child," the "educationally disadvantaged child," and—with the recent introduction of a new discursive category of children and thought—the "at-risk child."

Similar to the 1983 report's insistence that the nation was "at risk" of foreign domination, individual children were posited as being "at risk," but of something less specified. The term "at risk," based in the language of medicine and epidemiology, replaced the prior language of "cultural deprivation," yet seemed to garner the same vague meaning (Crosby, 1993; Placier, 1996). Typically, the term had no substantive content. Students were referred to as being "at risk" without any description or explanation of what the students were at risk of doing or not doing, becoming or not becoming. Resembling the vague meaning of educational disadvantage and deprivation, the meaning of the "at-risk" category was open to vast interpretation.

The definition of the Chapter 1 policy beneficiary was not debated extensively on the congressional floor in 1988. Rather, the only rhetorical portraiture of the policy beneficiary connected directly to poverty focused on the effects of high concentrations of poverty on schooling and the extension of Chapter 1 services to preschool students and their parents through the Even Start Program. Members of Congress made emotional pleas for focusing Chapter 1 policy on the "most needy" (Perkins, 1988, p. 7467), for addressing children with functionally illiterate parents through Even Start (see, for example, Brennan, 1988, p. 7477; Conte, 1988, p. 7476; Goodling, 1988, p. 7453; Hawkins, 1988, p. 7454), and for renewing the commitment to dropout prevention as a mechanism for "rescuing the futures of thousands of young people who otherwise would be destined to become part of society's growing underclass" (Hayes, 1988, p. 7464).

Focusing on the concentration of poverty, members of Congress, namely Democrats, reoriented Chapter 1 toward the poverty focus of the original act. This attempt narrowed the broad conceptualization of the policy beneficiary in terms of academic performance and focused on concentrations of children in poverty. Although "concentration grants" for areas with a high proportion of low-income families were established in the 1978 ESEA legislation, they were not discussed as extensively until 10 years later. This debate resulted in extension of the concentration grant formula to serve poor children in rural areas with less dense populations. Additionally, schools with 75% poverty rates were allowed to use their Chapter 1 funds to serve the entire school population, irrespective of the poverty status or academic performance of individual children. In this provision, developed in part to counter the extensive use of the pullout programs that scholars found to have detrimental effects on the education of participating students (see, for example, Eyler et al., 1983; Glass & Smith, 1977; Kimbrough & Hill, 1983), schools rather than students were framed as the unit of intervention. The schoolwide program option allowed for more flexibility in program delivery. The characterization of the policy beneficiary, again, was located in children, and now in the concentration of certain types of children (namely, poor) in schools or areas, rather than the limited resources available in communities with low property values. These ways of characterizing the policy beneficiaries were not debated as in past years.

Instead, the unrelated topic of "dial-a-porn," a telephone pornography service that members of Congress feared could be dialed by children from their homes, was debated extensively. Although disconnected substantively from matters of school improvement, poverty, or student achievement, the dial-a-porn issue consumed the bulk of the 1988 reauthorization debates. Elected officials tried to craft an intervention that could limit the availability of dial-a-porn to children, through either regulatory or technological means (e.g., devices that could make certain phone numbers impossible for children to dial without parental consent), while avoiding First Amendment violations. During dial-a-porn discussions, children were described in collective terms (e.g., "our young people," "the kids of our country") without

attention to any subgroups of children based on the classificatory schemes
that had shaped the Title I/Chapter 1 debates. An enormous amount of the
floor debates was devoted to this issue, assumed to affect "all children," and
directed attention from the core issues of the legislation.

This capture of the reauthorization debates for the purpose of discussing
solutions to a different and barely related (if related at all) policy problem was
challenged by Representative Augustus Hawkins (D, CA) and Representative
James Jeffords (R, VT). Both Hawkins and Jeffords tried to reorient the debates on the education bill at hand and "the status of those basic educational
programs which do so much for the people of this country and especially
those who live in the economically disadvantaged areas" (Jeffords, 1988,
p. 7453).

Despite this peculiar and distracting focus on the issue of dial-a-porn,
the discourse of Congress while considering the Hawkins-Stafford Amendments did demonstrate notable shifts from prior reauthorization debates.
Issues of school accountability focused less on federal or state oversight and
more on program improvements and student achievement standards. The
expectations of eligible students and their curricular opportunities were addressed directly, as was the integration of the Chapter 1 program with the
general classroom curriculum. In an attempt to build consideration for the
ways in which Chapter 1 shaped educational opportunities for eligible students, Representative Charles Hayes (D, IL) (1988) backed a policy provision to coordinate Chapter 1 services with those in the regular classroom.
Asserting that the policy beneficiaries were "those who will, someday, plan
our space missions, run our corporations, write our newspapers, and in fact,
take our places in this very Chamber," Representative Hayes supported efforts to coordinate "chapter 1 programs with regular school programs . . .
to help students master basic skills" (p. 7464). Stressing that "minority and
poor children, those often served by chapter 1, are most at-risk of being placed
in lower tracks of the regular program, misclassified, given a watered down
curriculum, and held to lower expectations than their peers" (p. 7464), Congressman Hayes called attention to the problem of lower expectations in
compensatory education services. Lower expectations for students in Chapter 1 programs impeded not only the education of the affected children, but
also the success of federal education policy. Hayes continued:

> With respect to chapter 1, enactment of H.R. 5 will mean that schools will have
> to examine the chapter 1 students' regular program and modify any features,
> including grouping practices, which may be frustrating achievement of the
> overall chapter 1 goals. (p. 7464)

Unlike past reauthorization debates, the discussions in 1988 focused
primarily on an unrelated policy issue—dial-a-porn—and paid less attention

to issues of funding formulas, budget cuts, or definitional battles over who the policy beneficiary should be. The focus on international competition, the concentration of poverty in particular areas, and accountability practices framed the issue of who should be served. The 1988 debates set the stage for the one reauthorization in the 1990s.

THE 1990S: GOING SCHOOLWIDE

The decade of the 1990s saw only one reauthorization, in 1994. The 1994 reauthorization attempted to further concentrate funds on high-poverty areas and to allow even greater flexibility in the expansion of schoolwide projects.

1994: Serving "All Children" in "High Poverty Schools"

In 1994, the Clinton administration—the first Democratic administration in the White House in 12 years—proposed a bill that would expand rather than consolidate federal education programs. In the Clinton proposal, Chapter 1 resumed its original name of Title I in the Improving America's Schools Act of 1994 and reoriented its purpose toward the improvement and reform of schools serving children in poverty, rather than the children in poverty themselves. Similar to the 1988 debates, this reorientation focused on schools with concentrations of children from low-income families. Along with the attention to "concentrations" of children in poverty was a new vocabulary for discussing educational goals, standards, and objectives. In addition to the concern for schools with large numbers of poor children, children in poverty were included under the recently launched umbrella category of "all children."

Different from the "all children" affected by the dial-a-porn issue in the 1988 debates, the new conceptual category of "all children" resulted from a recent focus on the development of goals and standards for education nationwide. Efforts toward establishing national education goals and standards for "all children" came about in part from the 1989 Education Summit of state governors, convened by the Bush administration and led by the then-governor of Arkansas, Bill Clinton. From this summit, the governors committed to a variety of reform platforms, including the creation of national education goals, the improvement of academic achievement for "all students," the development of high standards for student performance and school accountability, and increased flexibility and support in state and federal programs (Martin, 1994). The relatively new language of standards and accountability for all children shifted the discourse of the Title I floor debates away from the delineation of types of children as policy beneficiaries toward more institutional, schoolwide concerns about program goals, federal control and flexibility, and appropriate funding formulas so as to maximize the abilities of "all children" to meet high standards and achieve national goals.[18]

In attempts to counter the low expectations built into the original and ongoing policy formulation, Senator Ted Kennedy (D, MA), who in 1967 had asserted the "heritage of cultural depravity" of poor children for which educational programs needed to compensate (p. 35715), in 1994 explained that the proposed legislation for reauthorization—Senate bill S. 1513—was based on the principle that "schools should not hold disadvantaged students to a different, lower standard from the standard they apply to other students in their school" (1994, p. S9755).

One of the proposed strategies for avoiding lower expectations for eligible students was to reconfigure the funding formula to rely solely on school poverty (rather than student performance) rates and to target the funds to schools with a minimum threshold of poverty. Additionally, schools with the requisite concentrations of children in poverty could use the money to serve all students rather than only those identified as "educationally disadvantaged" due to low academic performance. While past iterations of Title I policy provided monetary incentives for maintaining low academic performance, the proposed 1994 legislation focused only on poverty, measured now through free and reduced-price lunch eligibility rather than AFDC eligibility. In order to avoid the common occurrence of schools losing their Title I monies when their test scores improved, the 1994 legislation proposed to connect eligibility exclusively to measures that would not make funding eligibility rely on low academic performance.

The poverty threshold for schoolwide eligibility was the cause of further deliberation. The administration's proposal suggested that a 30% school poverty rate or higher should denote a "high-poverty school," because, as Senator Kennedy (1994) noted, "Thirty percent is the point where research shows that the concentration of poverty affects student learning" (p. S9755). After debate, however, the threshold of 65% poverty was included in the actual bill. Also, the use of AFDC eligibility to measure poverty was changed to reliance on free and reduced-price lunch eligibility, which was measured through parents' self-reports of family income.[19]

Unlike prior Title I debates in which the focus of the policy problem was understood to be childhood poverty and the presumed cultural, social, and academic opportunities of children growing up poor, the 1994 reauthorization floor debates included commentary—albeit relatively brief—on the inherently inequitable nature of the country's school finance system. In a departure from the prior focus of Title I debates on only the compensatory role this policy was to play, Senator Orrin Hatch (R, UT) (1994) admonished the gross funding disparities built into the school finance system. Senator Hatch challenged the idea that Title I could address the gross imbalances of school funding, arguing that "the failure to deal with educational inequity" made Title I "an inefficient program" (p. S10042) that could not achieve its goals. He continued, noting that Title I was "built on the fiction of a level playing field," and that federal funds intended to supplement the education of "economically disadvantaged" (p. S10042) students could not have a great impact if the base educational programs for children in resource-poor communities were inadequate at their core. Senator Hatch then advocated for an "equalization factor" amendment to the funding formula that he argued would concentrate resources on children from low-income families more effectively than other proposed arrangements. Hatch's proposed amendment allowed states 3 years to move toward equity in their distribution of federal funds.

The technical mechanisms for targeting funding more narrowly to "high-poverty areas" were the subject of much discussion. As in prior reauthorization debates, elected officials based their support for or opposition to funding formula options on whether their constituencies stood to gain or lose from the proposed equations. Also as in prior debates, Title I was framed as a necessary intervention to enhance national security and international competitiveness. In fact, for Senator Paul Wellstone (D, MN), this form of national defense was more powerful and protective than other militaristic forms. Addressing the concern captured in *A Nation at Risk* (1983), and mimicking some of the rationale of the 1960s prioritization of education over the Vietnam War, Senator Wellstone (1994) posited the following:

> [I]f the Nation is at risk, and we are talking about national security, why do we not start investing in the health and skills and intellect and character of young people? . . . We do not need star wars. We do not need the B-2. We do not need the space station. Let us invest more in education and children. (p. S9879)

The new focus on the school as the policy target shifted the notion of poverty and its consequences from individual children to entire schools, communities, and areas. This shift, although not as pronounced as the Clinton administration had hoped for, expanded the use of the new language of "Title I school" (instead of "Title I student") and enhanced the idea that poor schools, rather than poor children, were in need of corrective intervention. Although concern about the low expectations for eligible students spurred the movement from individual student to whole-school projects, the language of policy culture at the time of policymaking moved from a casting of the individual student as lacking to a casting of a school's entire student body, and even community, as deficient.

From 1965 through 1994, the Title I policy script crafted by Congress and buffered by social scientists and practitioners promoted the conceptual connection between poverty and performance and framed "the poor" in terms of their deficiencies, deprivations, and lacks. However, within the discourse of deficit and deficiency that proliferated Title I's history, it is important to explore any alternative framings of children as talented and capable that may have emerged during the policy debates.

IN SEARCH OF A DISCOURSE OF TALENTS

Although far less common to the debates as a whole, there were some portraits of the policy beneficiaries in terms of their promise and potential. While few and far between, these framings asserted the talents and skills of children eligible for Title I due to their poverty or academic performance. In the creation of policies for "gifted and talented" education under separate title of the 1970 Elementary and Secondary Education Act, Congress asserted the category of "gifted," although these students were rarely considered to be the same children as those who occupied the category of "educationally deprived." Since the prevalence of deficit and deficiency in the characterizations of "disadvantaged" students created a sense of overlooked talent and promise among these policy beneficiaries, I went in search of any mentions in the floor debates that cast "Title I students" in promising terms.

During the first set of congressional floor debates in 1965, several speakers expressed concern for the talents of poor children that were latent, wasted, or tragically underdeveloped (see Fulbright, 1965, p. 7624; Gilligan, 1965, p. 6135; McGee, 1965, p. 7713; Montoya, 1965, p. 7328; Philbin, 1965, p. 6146; Ribicoff, 1965, p. 7532; White, 1965, p. 6149). In all, there were eight references to the policy beneficiaries in terms of their underdeveloped talents and untapped potential. These comments depart from the tenor of the entire floor debates, but provide important counterexamples to the general tendencies. All eight examples assert talent in *all* children and the responsibility of educational institutions to figure out how to develop those talents.

The subsequent reauthorization debates follow a similar tendency to focus overwhelmingly on disadvantage and deprivation, with infrequent references to the talents of students in poverty or of students in general. A few exceptions to this general tendency are noteworthy. For example, in 1978 Representative Larry Pressler (R, SD) declared, "Gifted and talented children come from all economic and language groups and from all parts of the country." He went on to assert the existence of the "gifted poor" and challenge the "tragic inequities between the opportunities of the gifted rich and those of the gifted poor" (p. H6542). Additionally, such considerations of the "gifted poor" eventually took hold in the conceptual constructs of gifted and talented education programs.

During the 1988 reauthorization debates, the Jacob K. Javits Gifted and Talented Students Education Act of 1988 (Augustus F. Hawkins–

Robert T. Stafford, 1990, Title IV, Part B) allocated funding toward the education of students identified as "gifted and talented," with the act's "highest priority" as

> the identification of gifted and talented students who may not be identified through traditional assessment methods (including economically disadvantaged individuals, individuals of limited English proficiency, and individuals with handicaps) and to education programs designed to include gifted and talented students from such groups. (Sec. 4105)

Indeed, one of the expressed purposes of this act was to identify students from "economically disadvantaged families and areas" (Augustus F. Hawkins–Robert T. Stafford, 1990, Sec. 4102). The Javits Act was maintained in the 1994 reauthorization of the Elementary and Secondary Education Act (Improving America's Schools Act of 1994). Although separate from Title I, the Javits Act did assert the existence of poor children who could be "gifted and talented." However, the general notion of poor children as harboring talents and strengths on which to build was not typical in the discourse of Title I policy.

CONCLUSION

The preceding historical treatment illustrates the struggle over Title I's purpose and how the ways of seeing the policy beneficiary evolved over time. Over three decades of Title I debates, students were defined as the policy problem that Title I was to solve. Members of Congress cast poor students as victims of their homes, as potential delinquents, and occasionally as the future of our country. The policy scripts were disseminated to local practitioners, containing imagery, language, and metaphors consistent with these views. The original focus on cultural deprivation imbedded in Title I policy talk evolved, but despite the changes in specific language, the more generalized categories of thought about deficits and deficiencies in the policy beneficiaries persisted. Through evolution of the categories of thought deployed in Title I policy (from economic to academic disadvantage), generations of policymakers cast the presumed policy beneficiaries in terms that shape their identities in school and in society.

Such categories of thought are stubborn. They fold into the commonly held biases on the part of the general public and become widely accepted ways of seeing. Although the language and behaviors generated by this policy evolved in response to new information about policy processes, emergent understandings of social problems, or contemporary agreements about appropriate discourse, the initial categories of thought rooted in

Title I policy shaped the possibilities for future political and practical thought and expression.

The cultural elements of policy practice are evident not only on the floors of Congress, but also within local educational institutions. By exposing the assumptions and premises on which policies are built, and exploring the language and behaviors that policies encourage, this review provides a context for understanding the behaviors of policy practice at the time of implementation. At the local level, we see how a policy's identity shapes the identities of the policy beneficiaries as they are constructed through daily policy practice. The following chapter brings us into the schools to show the culture of policy as reflected in the daily language and rituals of schooling.

The School

My analysis moves now from the halls of Congress to the heart of classrooms. Through investigation of classroom practices, this chapter highlights the language and routines of schooling that conform to and resist the culture of policy. In written documents, hurried hallway conversations, and general educational parlance, myriad policy-generated terms pass between practitioners, parents, and students. District and state officials perform periodic site visits to monitor compliance with policy mandates, often measuring adherence to regulations through observations of how students are categorized on paper, how familiar teachers are with the various students' policy-relevant designations, and what resulting services students receive. Educational materials, such as books and filmstrip projectors, purchased with policy-generated funds are often marked, literally, with a label or stamp of the policy source from which the item was bought. Students are also marked—literally on paper and figuratively in practice—with policy regulations that ensure conscious adherence to policy-born labels.

Over the course of its history, Title I policy has introduced language and routines that promote ways of seeing students at odds with its egalitarian goals.[1] At the local level, practitioners interpret and construct policy practices in ways that comply with and at times defy the overarching framework of the culture of policy. The words and work of practitioners reveal the range of interpretations and meanings associated with these terms. Investigations of policy-oriented budgetary practices, policy-based student labels, and policy-funded educational opportunities highlight how the policy mores launched in Congress shape the language and rituals of the classroom.

This chapter examines how the culture of policy takes form in nine elementary schools from one urban district 30 years after initial passage of Title I. Each of these schools reported over 75% free and reduced-price lunch eligibility (for demographic profiles of the schools and my methodological approach, see the Appendix). Exploring both conformity and resistance to the culture of policy among school practitioners, I consider Title I–related budgetary, labeling, and instructional practices to reveal how the culture of policy takes shape in the language and routines of schooling. My analysis focuses on four main consequences of the culture of policy: (a) the language used to mark eligible students and associated educators, (b) the overreliance on reductive measures of poverty and performance to determine eligibility, (c) the stigmatization of marked students, and (d) the rituals of policy-funded learning opportunities for eligible students. Although not all practitioners conform deferentially to this policy culture, all operate within its domain.

THE LANGUAGE AND RITUALS OF POLICY CULTURE

The culture of policy takes hold in the language and meanings of eligibility markers and the rituals of targeted service provision. However, each local entity has discernable and unique expressions of policy culture. Despite the expected variation in cultural expression between school sites, the need to contend with the culture of policy through the identification of eligible policy subjects, the demonstration of compliance with policy mandates, and the practice of policy rituals through the provision of services remained constant among the schools under study.

At the level of implementation, the same policy may take different programmatic forms, depending on the policy-relevant decisions—such as how to spend Title I dollars—and the local approach to integrating policy requirements with other practices. The same policy may also fit into the practitioners' conceptions of students differently, either confirming their prior beliefs or encouraging their previously determined oppositional stances to the ways of seeing encouraged by policy. Exploration of the daily work of schooling illustrates how students are marked, language is deployed, stigmas adhered to or challenged, and rituals observed.

Marking Eligibility and Association

At the time of this study, Title I cultural practices distinguished the individuals associated with the program as separate and different from the rest of the school population. Through budgets, time sheets, and class rosters, the adults employed by and children eligible for Title I were named and identified. Lists of affiliated adults and children were circulated throughout the schools signifying who was associated with "Title I."

The primary use of Title I funds to hire personnel contributed to the marking of adults. The nine studied schools used Title I–generated dollars primarily to fund personnel. The personnel most typically funded through Title I were resource teachers and classroom aides known as "paras" (shorthand for *paraprofessionals*). Some resource teachers had the designation of "program resource teacher" (commonly referred to as PRT) and served as

the site-based coordinators of the Title I program, having both instructional
and administrative responsibilities for its execution. In a majority of the
schools, resource teachers and program resource teachers conducted lessons
in a daily one-on-one early literacy program for a small number of first-grade
students entitled Reading Recovery.

The use of Title I to fund specific types of personnel led to an understanding of the Title I program as the work of certain, marked individuals.
Although some staff members' salaries were combinations of Title I funds,
base budgets, and/or other policy-generated program funds, all policy-funded
staff members were aware of how many hours they were hired to work for
each program and were expected to organize their daily activities accordingly. Hourly paraprofessionals filled out separate time sheets for the various programmatic revenue sources that funded their positions. Program
resource teachers noted how many hours they were supposed to be working
with "Title I" or "EDY" students. The work of these individuals, designated
on various school documents as "Title I," then, became the Title I program.

When asked to describe the school's Title I program, most practitioners
answered, "Reading Recovery and paras." This answer reveals how the culture of policy encourages the separation and marking of associated adults.
While Reading Recovery is an actual program for emergent readers, "paras"
describes a subset of school employees with no substantive programmatic
content. The work of funded practitioners, irrespective of anything they might
do programmatically, was identified as the policy's "program." The "Title I
paras," as they were often called, had a specific status, different from that of
other paraprofessionals and staff members funded through other policy-
driven and base-budget sources.

The culture of policy is also transmitted through the marking of eligible
students. For at least the first 30 years of its existence, Title I policy required
practitioners to distinguish eligible students both on paper and through service delivery. This marking became necessary in order to target services.
Eligible students were identified on paper at the beginning of the school year
through lists developed and distributed by the program resource teachers.
The format of the lists varied from school to school. In some schools, the
program resource teacher typed out a list of names for each classroom teacher
and paraprofessional under the heading, "EDY." In others, program resource
teachers tried to accommodate various policy-generated student designations
on one sheet of paper. For example, in one school, the program resource
teacher passed out class rosters on a grid with various policy-generated student designations. Across the top of this grid, the column headings read,
"student name, ethnicity, LEP, EDY, Brigance, CTBS [California Test of Basic
Skills] reading, CTBS math, GATE [Gifted and Talented Education], Birthday, 'sex,' and 'other.'" Next to each student's name, there were various check
marks and letters. For the LEP (limited English proficient) classification, "N"

signified a student who was not proficient in English, and "L" represented a student who had "limited" English proficiency. For the EDY classification, an "X" signaled a Title I–eligible student, and "no" indicated a test score that was higher than the minimal threshold for Title I eligibility. Eligibility for the gifted and talented program was marked with an "X" next to far fewer names than any other policy designation. Some teachers and paraprofessionals reported storing these lists in desk drawers and paying them little mind. Others taped the lists to the classroom walls or stored them in a binder with instructional materials to which they referred periodically. The moniker of "Title I" or "EDY" was ascribed to students as part of their school-based identity. Once students were marked with a policy-generated identity, teachers could view them through this lens.

Although the practice of marking eligible students was consistent in all the schools, the meanings of such markings differed. While a number of teachers, principals, and paras in the studied schools believed that the policy-generated labels of "EDY" or "Title I student" helped them make sense of the students and their educational needs, others saw the act of labeling students as policy-eligible to be detrimental to their academic success. Despite these schisms within the ranks of educators, all knew that they needed to use policy-generated terminology in order to secure future funding and demonstrate compliance.

Reductive Measures of Poverty and Performance

Since its inception, Title I state, district, school, and student eligibility has been calculated using a combination of poverty indicators and test performance. This process had various steps. First, Congress negotiated a funding formula—based on poverty concentrations and school-aged populations—for the distribution of Title I monies to the states. The states then allocated money, again derived from poverty measures, to the local school districts. The districts in turn distributed monies to schools, using some combination of poverty and performance measures. And the schools, based initially on test scores and later on other criteria, determined which students were to receive services.[2]

Whereas complex and multiple measures of student academic performance would best reflect what types of policy-funded learning opportunities and instructional approaches a student might need, Title I eligibility has historically been determined through simplistic and reductive measures of poverty and performance. However, point-in-time measures of poverty status do not indicate whether or not a student would benefit from any particular service, or what prior educational opportunities might have been like.[3] Measures of testing are similarly limited. One day of testing certainly does not provide diagnostic or prescriptive information on students' academic needs.

The tests provide limited information about what a student knows and can do, and one day of testing picks up effects unrelated to the skills and knowledge that the child has or has not had the opportunity and ability to learn.[4] The practice of using nondiagnostic tests to determine Title I eligibility at the individual level illustrates the reliance on measures that are reductive and misleading.

As part of the 1994 reauthorization of Title I, the measures of student poverty considered at the federal, state, and district level changed from eligibility for Aid to Families with Dependent Children (AFDC) to qualification for the federal free and reduced-price lunch program. This change moved Title I eligibility determinations from a welfare policy involving rigorous qualification processes to a federal school lunch program in which parents simply filled out forms that were never checked for accuracy. Whereas AFDC eligibility was determined by status at or below the poverty line, eligibility for the free-lunch program was based on family incomes that fell within 130% of the federal poverty guideline. Predictably, reported levels of school poverty rose. Schools had great incentives to encourage parents to fill out forms for the school lunch program so as to maximize the school's overall Title I eligibility.

The district in which the studied schools operated used a two-step process to allocate funds to schools. First, it ranked the schools according to poverty measures, prioritizing schools with higher proportions of students eligible for AFDC (until the 1994 reauthorization) or free- and reduced-price lunch (after 1994). Then it allotted funds based on the percentage of students scoring at or below the 40th percentile on the Comprehensive Test of Basic Skills in grades two through five or at or below 95% on the Brigance Test in kindergarten and first grade.[5] By this process, poverty determined school eligibility and performance determined student eligibility. At the time of this study, half or more of the student population in each school was eligible for Title I services based on both test score performance and free and reduced-price lunch eligibility. Those qualifying for Title I funds were identified as "educationally disadvantaged youth," typically with the acronym "EDY."

A new option—the schoolwide project—allowed schools to use Title I for the entire student population, rather than targeting specific children.[6] Although one might predict less use of labels and narrowly targeted services under this option, the schools eligible for this approach (those with 65% poverty or higher) still operated as "targeted assistance schools" in which funds were directed to specific students based on test scores. As mandated by Title I policy, schools interested in the schoolwide project option had to undergo a planning year. Therefore, during the 1995–96 school year, the district provided workshops to program resource teachers in order to get them ready to "go schoolwide." Prior to this year, only one school had pursued the schoolwide option. The studied schools all operated as targeted-assistance schools and were planning to "go schoolwide." District personnel instructed school-based practitioners that during the 1995–96 school year they should continue to identify their "EDY students" based on their individual test scores. Additionally, practitioners were told that students in kindergarten and first grade who scored lower than 95% on the Brigance test would now be eligible for Title I. In other words, any child who did not get 95% of the test questions correct was labeled as EDY. The combined effects of these changes resulted in a considerably higher number of students with EDY status than in prior years.

Although many practitioners in the studied schools accepted the measures used for identifying eligible students, some were openly critical of how poverty measures and test scores were used to determine policy eligibility. In one school, two teachers noted that they have had excellent students from low-income families. These teachers expressed dismay at the labeling of certain students as EDY (a term they clearly thought to be derogatory) just because they were poor. The program resource teacher at another school stated that she has "a really hard time, you know, dealing with [poverty] as the reason why [the students] are always going to have trouble in school."

A few teachers in the study were critical of the practice of standardized testing and the use of test scores to determine EDY status. One teacher, noting the traumatic response students had to testing, said she thought that making students take the CTBS was an act of "child abuse." Another teacher worried that her students' talents and skills would not be reflected in their test scores, since "the CTBS is not in compliance with what we are doing in the classroom." She explained that her students have strong emotional reactions to the testing procedure; in past years they cried and fidgeted during the testing period. This teacher's usage of the term "compliance" inverts traditional relationships of monitoring oversight. Curricular correspondence is usually the measure of appropriateness, and in some cases fairness, of a test, while the term "compliance" usually refers to local adherence to a policy mandate. Although the CTBS is intended to be an aptitude rather than achievement test (i.e., it is not necessarily designed to reflect any particular curricular content), this teacher's inversion of the compliance hierarchy reorients the concept to suggest that the criteria on which policy-generated school-based labels are assigned might not actually reflect what they claim to measure (namely student academic capabilities, rather than the learning opportunities that they were afforded).

In addition to generalized concerns about testing and its psychological effects on students, teachers voiced frustration with the use of standardized tests to determine policy eligibility. The program resource teacher and classroom teachers at one school were particularly critical of this practice, saying that the test scores did not identify which students needed the most help. The program resource teacher used the example of first-grade students to high-light some of the problems in using standardized tests to determine Title I eligibility. As she explained, first-grade students took the Brigance test in the fall and the CTBS in the spring. Both tests were used to determine Title I eligibility. Since the CTBS is a far more challenging test than the Brigance, at the beginning of first grade teachers have a short, nearly nonexistent list of "Title I students." By the end of first grade, however, they have a long list of designated students. Looking at the discrepancy in the lengths of the two lists, she exclaimed, "But these are the same kids!" The use of two different measurements rendering different academic identities exposes the potentially arbitrary nature of using static measurements to determine policy eligibility, and calls into question the labels and terms that shape students' school-based identities.

The incentives for raising test scores also contribute to student eligibility practices. For example, the teacher described above further criticized the use of tests to determine Title I eligibility, since, she suspected, the tests were manipulated to show gains. She explained that in the previous year the superintendent ordered schools to refrain from administering the CTBS to any students designated as limited- or non-English proficient (LEP or NEP) and who had been in the district for less than 36 months (3 academic years). She said that he also ordered that no first-grade students with the LEP or NEP designations should be tested, regardless of how long they had lived in the district or in this country. The only exceptions to these directives were for students whom the teachers thought "would do well" on the test. This program resource teacher suspected that the superintendent wanted to give the appearance of higher district test scores to promote his own career, although the rationale he used was that making such students take the test was unfair to them. Since eligibility relied on CTBS scores, students who were never tested on the CTBS were automatically ineligible for Title I services. The superintendent's directives, therefore, rendered any students who were identified as LEP/NEP and in the district for less than 3 academic years ineligible for Title I–supported services.

Teachers voiced additional concern when they learned that the cutoff score for kindergarten and first-grade EDY designation increased from 87% correct to 95% correct on the Brigance test. After learning about these changes, a group of kindergarten teachers complained that under this new directive the vast majority of their students suddenly "became EDY."

The program resource teachers in two other schools criticized the district's use of test information, gathered during a discrete period of time, to make broad judgments about policy eligibility. The program resource teacher in one school asserted, "It's just one day, or two days of testing and they get labeled as Title I." The program resource teacher at another school thought that her school's Title I program was out of compliance for not sticking strictly to serving students labeled EDY. Concerned about the students who needed services but performed *too well* on the CTBS to receive the EDY label, she defended her school's approach. "Just because a student happens to do well on a test one day out of the year doesn't mean that we shouldn't help them if they're having trouble with division."

School-based educators found themselves in an uncomfortable bind. Some teachers expressed concern about the stigma associated with the EDY label, and did not want to use it to describe eligible students. Simultaneously, the same teachers worried that if struggling students scored high on the CTBS, they would be denied supplementary services that they might need. Those teachers who were critical of the naming and framing rituals that cast students as deficient or deviant based on poverty indexes and/or one day of testing viewed the policy labels as constructed categories. Their focus on the changes of the requisite scores as well as the inclusion and exclusion of students from the testing program led them to see how malleable such designations were. To their minds, district-level bureaucrats and policymakers crafted these labels and determined their uses. Teachers only had professional discretion in how they used the terms and made sense of their meaning in daily interactions.

Stigmatization of Marked Students

Students who are marked for services through the reductive measures of poverty and test performance are also saddled with the stigmas of deficiency and deficit woven into the initial conceptualizations of Title I. The act of marking students for services incurs the "dilemma of difference" (Minow, 1990) reviewed in the Introduction to this book. In order to target resources to students with perceived educational needs and to provide services to those students, educators have to demarcate individuals who are eligible for policy-funded services. In so doing, however, the demarcated students are stigmatized as being different and usually deficient to the norm. Indeed, practitioners in the studied schools revealed a range of associations with the markers used to determine Title I eligibility.

When asked to describe a "typical Title I student,"[7] interviewed practitioners revealed many associations with the Title I designation, ranging from family conditions to language barriers to behavior issues. All associations were rooted in deficit thinking (see Valencia, 1997). Practitioners' interpretations of the policy and characterizations of eligible students revealed the persistence of the culture of poverty framework, not only in the establishment of Title I policy, but also in more recent educational thought.

In keeping with congressional language (see chapters 2 and 3), practitioners identified *poverty* as having a strong association with individual Title I eligibility. And in concert with the "culture of poverty" narrative, poverty was assumed to limit enrichment and support *in the home,* rather than enrichment and support in the school. The poverty narrative takes precedence over any explanatory reasoning that includes sound instructional practice on the part of teachers, adequate funding for schools, or any structural elements of resource distribution in a capitalist market economy where school finance is based largely on local community wealth. For example, in describing a typical Title I student, one resource teacher noted:

> They usually, in our school, come from a poverty background. They have not been given a lot of the enrichment and opportunities that other children might have. They don't come to school as prepared with as much background knowledge as maybe someone in a middle-class situation.

The comparison to a middle-class norm, spoken in the halls of Congress since the mid-1960s, is echoed in the halls of school in the mid-1990s. The learning opportunities provided to middle-class children at home are presented as enrichment and preparation, while the background knowledge of poor children is spoken of only in relative terms. Rather than finding the strengths or educationally useful elements of any child's background knowledge, this comparison sets up a hierarchy of experiences, valuing some background experiences as *more than,* rather than *different from,* others.

The poverty narrative dominates the minds of practitioners; even a principal who said that "there isn't really a typical Title I student" went on to say, "but I know what would come to mind . . . probably a child in the lower quartile who is living in, you know, . . . a child living in poverty, and a child in an alternative family." This principal said that she was very uncomfortable using policy labels, noting that "even as the main administrator of this school . . . I can't think that way. I mean, I can get the [EDY] lists out, but I don't want to think that way." This principal struggles within and against the culture of policy; she notes that she does not like to use policy-generated labels, yet needs to keep lists of eligible students in order to be in compliance with policy regulations. Additionally, although she does not initially acknowledge a prototypical student who is eligible for Title I services, she goes on to note characteristics about the family structure of the typical policy-eligible child and whether that structure is "normal" or, in this case, "alternative."

The culture of policy aligns Title I eligibility with assumptions about poverty and defect in the student population. The basic premise becomes that a student growing up in poverty starts school "behind." Somehow, the children—nearly all the children in some schools—fail to come prepared for the institution, rather than the institution failing to prepare for most of its students. The students and their families, instead of the schools and their faculties, are held accountable for this gap. As stated by one program resource teacher, "I think it makes sense that anyone who is academic[ally] or financially disadvantaged is disadvantaged to start within the school." The concept of "starting behind" places the onus on the students in poverty, rather than on the match between the students' actual (as opposed to imagined, assumed, or theorized) learning opportunities before they enter school and the school's instructional programs.

Connected to these notions of poverty are the associations between Title I eligibility and a troubled home life. One resource teacher typified this sentiment in her description of eligible students as "neglected nutritionally and physically," going on to say that such students "hear a lot of negative things growing up." A program resource teacher at another school noted that their "external surroundings at home are not . . . controlled." Certainly there are students who come from homes that do not meet their basic emotional and nutritional needs. Indeed, there are children of all class backgrounds who are emotionally, nutritionally, and physically neglected in various ways, and who hear a lot of "negative things" growing up. But the movement from a policy category based largely on imprecise measures of family poverty and/or academic performance to an indictment of family and community resonates with both the culture of poverty theory and the culture of policy. The connection made by the above practitioners is particularly noteworthy since Title I is not a poverty nor a family policy per se, in that it does not address poverty or family in any meaningful way. The policy provides money to schools to hire personnel to serve identified students. Associations with poverty and family conditions reveal a limited sense of perceived efficacy in addressing the theorized causes of the students' assumed deficiencies. Practitioners must then resign to providing services that do not address what they see to be the root causes of the students' "problems," problems that they define as clearly beyond their control.

This resignation is echoed by a resource teacher who noted that among the Title I–eligible students, "There're family conditions that you can't do anything about." Such interpretations expose an additional tension in the culture of policy: Many practitioners who work with students growing up poor believe that Title I policy itself could not possibly address the theorized pathologies identified in the culture of poverty thesis. Therefore, practitioners see this policy as a poor fit with the problems it presumes to solve.

Some practitioners saw certain, negative behaviors as typical of students identified for Title I services. One resource teacher in a particularly chaotic school identified a group of students as "Title I" as they ran through the school's cafeteria shrieking at a rather high pitch. Knowing that I was conducting research on this policy, she turned to me and said, "These are your Title I students. . . . Just look at them!" Many practitioners in this study expressed similar sentiments. The principal at one school claimed to know the Title I–eligible students well because they "get in trouble . . . or they get sent to the office a lot." Focusing on their negative behaviors (which he did not identify with any more precision than to say, "They do this and do that"), he suggested that his ability to know the eligible students was born out of their bad behavior.[8]

Other teachers also characterized Title I–eligible students in terms of "bad behavior." In describing the ways in which bilingual education policies shaped the school's classroom assignments, one program resource teacher noted that the non-bilingual classrooms were "loaded with mostly all those EDY kids, all the very acting out kids." In a conversation with two first-grade teachers at the same school, one explained that typical "Title I students" have a "short attention span, behavioral most of the time, mostly discipline problems. [They are] not focused." Another teacher added that she believed the Title I students "act out so they won't be embarrassed. They are slower than the other children, not able to grasp ideas." Then, implicating their home lives, this teacher noted, "There is no follow-up at their homes." She finished her thought by invoking another cultural category that was getting considerable media attention at the time: "A lot [of EDY students] are crack babies." Revealing an overall sense of futility for any educational project addressing this population, she extended her sense of professional helplessness further by asserting, "It's a known fact that crack babies will not increase in intelligence. They can only develop to a certain point, but their intelligence won't go up." These teachers' comments demonstrate the conceptual slippage between policy eligibility based on poverty measures and other possible conditions, such as misbehavior, in utero physiological addictions, and an inability to learn.

All of these characterizations reveal micro-theories of cause and effect on the part of practitioners. Students are deemed eligible for Title I–funded services. Policy mechanisms require that eligible students be marked on paper. This eligibility is associated with poverty, family hardships, and bad behavior, all damning conditions that have these students "starting behind," with limited possibility for catching up. In the case of the "crack baby" association, students are even theorized to stagnate at some low level of cognitive development. The policy label of "Title I" that starts with basic eligibility criteria now becomes part of a series of mental shortcuts used by practitioners. Such shortcuts are influenced by the categories of race and language as well. Participation in the language and rituals of policy culture contributes to lowered expectations of students in poverty, expectations that run counter to the ultimate objectives of the policy itself.

As noted in chapter 2, the historical moment in which Title I was established contributed to conceptual associations between the program and black students (Meranto, 1967). The restrictions on funding for students who were eligible for bilingual education programs furthered this association. In schools, practitioners articulated these associations as they decided which individual students should get what services. A sense of whom Title I was for and which students were, as some practitioners put it, "truly Title I" was revealed through practitioners' interpretation of and communication about policy language in practice.

For example, when asked to describe a "typical Title I student," the program resource teacher at one school noted, "Well, sadly, here, they're mostly Black." Indeed, three of the four students whom she served in the Title I–funded Reading Recovery program were black. However, in her school, 52% of the entire student body was designated as EDY or Title I–eligible, and only 27% of the same student body was identified as black. Even if every single black student were designated as EDY, there would still be nearly as many students of other ethnic and racial classifications with the same EDY designation. Blackness, performance, behavior, and Title I eligibility converged to signify deficit, defect, and limitation.

In one school, the deliberations over which students would receive what services revealed the practitioners' notions of whom this policy intended to serve. While a program resource teacher reviewed her school's lists of eligible students, she noticed that a number of students in the Chinese bilingual program were designated as EDY. Worried that the policy regulations required her to provide services to all eligible students, she complained, "These [Chinese] kids might be really smart . . . while there are so many truly Title I students." A teacher in the Chinese bilingual program in the same school said that she wondered whether the students who were designated as limited English proficient were being "lumped in with the slow students" through their eligibility for Title I. While, based on the technical criteria for Title I eligibility at that time, students from various ethnic and language groups were eligible in all of the schools, practitioners articulated clear associations with certain ethnic groups, primarily black and in some cases Latino students.

Associations between Title I and poverty, family, behavior, and race were common to many practitioners in the nine studied schools. However, there were a number of practitioners who actively resisted the cultural policy practices of labeling students for policy purposes. Of the principals in the nine studied schools, four expressed their opposition to the labeling practices generated by policy mandates, regardless of the basis for the label. For instance, when asked to describe a "typical Title I student," one principal said, "Nothing comes to mind. I don't like labels, that's why I can't think of anything." In fact, she put the onus of the "Title I" label on the school, stating that the only typical aspect of students with a Title I designation was that "we [the practitioners] haven't figured out the best way that child learns." The principal of another school expressed a similar notion. Referring to some of the typical associations with the Title I designation, she explained:

> I don't think there is a typical Title I student. You know, because the only factor at this point, until we change what Title I is about, is that this is a youngster who's not achieving. . . . They may or may not have had pre-

school. They may or may not have had kindergarten. They may or may not have home support. They may or may not go to an after-school child-care program. . . . They may or may not have two parents in the home. They may or may not, you know, I couldn't give you a typical.

Discussing the EDY designation, another principal noted, "It's an ugly name, EDY, educationally disadvantaged youth. I mean, I hate to say it. . . . I don't even like to think [it]." She went on to note that she purposefully did not know which students had the EDY designation. Rather, she believed that "whether [the students are] EDY labeled or not, if they're having difficulty in some area [they] should receive support." Her beliefs about labeling practices were firm: "[EDY is] such an ugly label. . . . I hate labels so I just sort of ignore them." However, noting the mechanisms of compliance monitoring that transmit the culture of policy between institutions, she explained, "I'm not supposed to do that [ignore the labels], but I do." The principal at a fourth school echoed her sentiments, ensuring that if asked, she could get out lists of eligible students, but "I don't want to think that way [about the students]."

Whether one accepts or resists the framing of eligible students as deficient or defective, all contend with the language of policy culture. Here a paradox emerges. Practitioners with low expectations for students use their policy-generated labels to support their perspectives on what students know and can do. Title I becomes yet another indicator of individual deficit or defect, a stigma on eligible students. On the other hand, practitioners with high expectations for students and firm commitments to their learning feel constrained by the policy mandates in their ability to meet the students' needs and acknowledge the stigmas associated with eligibility. Governed by policy regulations, some students are ineligible for Title I–supported services, but could benefit from them; others are eligible, but have to contend with a label that most practitioners associate with negative characteristics. The practice of marking children as eligible for policy-generated services hampers the work of practitioners who resist the culture of policy and bolsters the negative assumptions of those who believe that poor children cannot succeed. The greatest consequences of these practices are revealed in the rituals of service provision.

The Rituals of Service Provision

Services to students form part of daily school rituals. Marked adults have the responsibility to serve marked students. Although the mandated marking practices were relatively consistent among the studied schools, the ways in which those markings garnered meaning and translated into service provision exhibited considerable variation. In some schools, practitioners expressed the belief that only Title I–marked adults could serve Title I–marked students. In others, decisions about service provision were made based on various considerations (such as student performance, teacher capacity, and other available services) beyond Title I policy regulations. In all cases, however, practitioners struggled within the culture of policy to determine the appropriate learning opportunities and deliver them to students.

The policy-generated labels used for program delivery and compliance measures influenced the learning opportunities—through curriculum, pedagogy, and service coordination—made available to students. The services provided to students often hinged on their policy eligibility designations, especially in situations where school personnel did not question or challenge the language and routines deployed in the culture of policy. And although many policy-marked practitioners did not limit their service to policy-marked students, all Title I–funded practitioners expressed their sense of technical responsibility to serve students designated for services.

How were the rituals of practice for delivering policy-generated learning opportunities determined? Three elements of schooling contributed to these rituals: policy-driven decisionmaking strategies, staffing, and school-based approaches to policy compliance.

Policy-Driven Decisionmaking Strategies. By regulation, in order for a school to determine how to use policy-generated resources, a special school-based council consisting of teachers, administrators, and parents was to conduct a needs assessment. Site-based priorities were to drive budgetary decisions. All committee members were to participate equally. However, when asked how Title I allocation decisions were made, most school staff members reported that the principal and teachers would allocate resources and that parents basically approved the decisions made by school personnel. Many staff members complained that parents would not or could not serve on advisory boards in a meaningful capacity. Observations of committee meetings revealed rote conversations in which school staff members presented budgets quickly and with little explanation of the various terms and acronyms in the budget documents. Parents rarely raised questions.[9] Indeed, decisions seemed to be driven by dollars and employment of certain individuals, rather than by careful attention to students' learning needs as revealed through reliable indicators of performance and the appropriate programs that could meet those needs.

In such meetings, individual staff members advocated policy-program spending based on how they could make their daily work easier, how they might further their own careers, how they could protect the employment of certain individuals on staff, and, at times, how they could address students' needs and capabilities through appropriate services. Since the funds paid for the work of specific staff members, school-based personnel often felt limited in their budgetary discretion by the legacy of past budgets and the personal pressure to maintain employment for specific individuals in the school.

Staffing. The opportunities to learn provided to Title I–eligible students differed remarkably from classroom to classroom and from school to school. Although many practitioners made efforts to direct their services to students identified as eligible for Title I–funded services, it was often unclear what learning opportunities identified students received through these targeted services. These learning opportunities were shaped in large part by the staffing of schools and the various personal and professional commitments that school administrators had to employ specific individuals. Loyalty to the employment of individual adults through Title I allocations lays bare how the culture of policy provides incentives for the maintenance of a deviant population and effectively compromises learning opportunities. When money is provided to schools based on poverty measures and low scores on norm-referenced tests, and that money is used to hire adults to serve eligible students, adult employment relies on funds generated through the categorization of students as poor and underperforming. As long as Title I funds are determined primarily by low scores on standardized, norm-referenced tests, teachers and administrators work within perverse incentive structures that mitigate against providing students with meaningful educational opportunities.

A principal in one of the studied schools noted that the paraprofessionals funded by Title I were aware of the policy's goals, which he defined as helping kids raise their test scores, "but they also know that if you raise the test scores you lose the funding to a certain point." He continued to speculate on the effects of such incentives, saying, "I'm often wondering about the struggle as an employment plum, and then people safe-guarding it. But I don't know if that's true or not, or a subconscious thing."

The principal of another school noted that she overheard a paraprofessional discuss the connections between students' scores and her own employment: "Out on the schoolyard, [Ms. Jones, a paraprofessional] was saying that if our kids' scores go up we lose our jobs." This principal said that she did not find this attitude to be uncommon. Their comments suggest that the maintenance of low-performing students somehow secures the financing of their own employment. Improved student academic performance, some believe, threatens their jobs.[10]

The learning opportunities provided by paraprofessionals varied immensely and, in some schools, were hard to discern. Paraprofessionals typically worked in classrooms as aides to teachers. Originally hired to compensate for teacher shortages through clerical and "housekeeping" chores in the 1950s, the role of the paraprofessional shifted with increased federal funding to include instructional support in the mid-1960s (Pickett, 1986, 1994). Some worked in one classroom all day, while others rotated between

classrooms. Classroom teachers assigned the paras activities that varied sub-
stantially between classrooms and schools. Some paras had a designated
location in the back of a classroom, where they would meet with individual
students or small groups for reading drills. Others rotated around the classroom answering students' questions as they arose. Most had lists of students
marked as EDY in folders or taped to the wall next to their work space. One
paraprofessional explained that her work "depends on the teacher, what she
wants [me] to do with the children." She added that sometimes teachers asked
her to work with students who were not necessarily eligible for Title I services, but who were not following a specific lesson. "Otherwise," she stated,
"I work with the kids on the list." "The list" refers to the students designated as educationally disadvantaged youth (EDY), or eligible for Title I.

Research on the value of paraprofessionals reports mixed results. Some
research on paraprofessionals suggests that paras provide minimal to no improvement to the quality of instructional practice (Rubin & Long, 1994), while
other sources suggest that paras can have positive effects on student achievement (Jackson et al., 1985). A 1999 report prepared by the Department of
Education recommends "*[p]hasing out* their use in instruction and promoting
their use as parent liaisons or in administrative functions" (p. xxxi).

However, paraprofessionals have served an important noninstructional
function through their connection to the communities in which they work.
Unlike the majority of many urban teaching staffs, paraprofessionals typically live in the same communities as the students and often know students
from both inside and outside the school. Additionally, paraprofessionals tend
to reflect the ethnic/racial background of the students more closely than the
teaching staff. In the studied schools, teaching staffs were primarily of European descent, while the paraprofessional staff members were primarily of
African, Latin American, and Asian descent. More specifically, in five of the
nine schools, the paraprofessional population contributed an equal or larger
number of adults of African descent to the school's staff than did the teacher/
administrator population. The same holds for adults of Latin American and
Chinese descent in four schools.[11]

Title I–funded resource teachers and counselors, by contrast, were predominantly white. Of the 13 professional staff members funded by Title I
across the nine schools, only 1 was Asian and 1 was black. The program
resource teachers in each school supervised the paraprofessional staff, making
sure that their Title I–oriented obligations were met. They also coordinated
and maintained the Title I budgets, wrote reports on Title I, and distributed
the EDY lists to the classroom teachers and paraprofessionals.

The instructional work of the Title I–funded professional staff (resource
teachers and program resource teachers) typically focused on defined projects
with more consistent and identifiable activities than the paraprofessional staff.
In all nine schools, the program resource teachers led instructional projects

in addition to their administrative duties related to the coordination of the Title I program. These projects ranged from technology coordination and instruction for the school to early literacy instruction of students in Reading Recovery to professional development for the teaching staff. In six of the nine studied schools, resource teachers worked on a daily one-on-one literacy program entitled Reading Recovery. In two schools, Title I–funded resource teachers participated in the implementation of an instructional strategy that organized students by "ability." In one school, the instructional focus was math, in the other literacy; in both, the Title I–funded professional worked with students whom they described as "the lowest" or "the bottom." In other schools, Title I–funded resource teachers worked in literacy groups (again, with students they described as "the lowest") as counselors, and finally, as part of a classroom teaching rotation intended to reduce class size.

The connection of Title I dollars to individual employment enhances the culture of policy, providing incentives to invest in a system of meaning that defines students as defective. Professional and paraprofessional staff members, competing for dwindling federal funds, also focused on one another's perceived weaknesses. The paraprofessionals complained that the resource teachers worked with so few students and that the teaching staff did not know or understand the students. In a conversation among paras, one noted that "the teacher doesn't know [how] to discipline the kids," to which another responded, "If you're not here, [the kids] get crazy. When the para is absent, [teachers] don't know how to handle the kids because they don't know them . . . they don't even know the students." The first para continued, "Kids listen to the para instead of the teacher . . . they go with familiar faces. They trust us. We have established that relationship, that bonding with the kids."

In similar form, the resource teachers complained that the paras were undertrained for their assigned tasks. Many noted that the paras did "not really know how to help" struggling students. One resource teacher insisted, "I don't think Title I funds should be used to pay the salary of people who do not have an education . . . they don't even need a high school diploma . . . to me it's the blind leading the blind. . . . I cannot see how a person who is uneducated can work with these kids." A resource teacher at another school echoed those concerns, saying, "It's always amazed me that we have taken our children . . . who have the really biggest problems in learning how to read and learning how to understand in mathematics, and we're thinking that the paraprofessional with the least amount of training is going to be able to fix this." In only one school did a program resource teacher express confidence in the paraprofessionals' capacity to serve the students.

The staffing of schools, then, contributes to the rituals of service provision by determining which employees will serve the eligible students, and how the policy motivates their behavior. The incentives for maintaining low performance among eligible students and the economic competition between staff members of different professional statuses created bizarre educational practices only loosely connected to student learning. Certain staff members, then, had great incentive for marking students as eligible, highlighting a need for their services, and justifying the usefulness of their particular role. The professional hierarchies mirrored entrenched hierarchies of race and class. The rituals of service provision, then, folded into rituals of differentiation—of both students and educators alike.

Approaches to Policy Compliance. In each of the schools, the theme of compliance with policy mandates was articulated by various staff members funded by or administering Title I. School personnel described their approaches to Title I implementation in relationship to the concept of compliance. They highlighted practices that they developed in order to ensure compliance, and were aware when their practices did not conform to their understanding of policy regulations. Whether school personnel believed their programs to be in or out of compliance, all referred to the notion of compliance as an external, governing force that shaped school-based practices.

Despite the consistent focus on the concept of compliance, the studied schools exhibited different tendencies in their approaches to this concept. Some schools practiced "strict compliance," in which practitioners followed the letter of the law and the regulations to a tee, whether or not they believed that those practices made educational sense for students. These schools tended to provide discrete and isolated services to eligible students in a rather fragmented and disjointed school day. Other schools did not comply with policy mandates. In fact, although practitioners in these schools spoke of compliance, they did not seem to know what the policy regulations were. The policy implementation decisions made in these schools reflected a more generalized sense of chaos and disorganization. Finally, a third subset of schools practiced what I have termed "thoughtful noncompliance," in which educational decisions were based on thorough assessments of student performance and available resources. These schools knew whether their implementation strategies fell within what they believed to be the policy regulations, but focused on students' needs over policy prescriptions. Although at times out of compliance with the technical regulations, these schools provided learning opportunities to students that were integrated and meaningful.

The schools that practiced strict compliance with policy regulations ensured that Title I–marked personnel through their funding served only Title I–marked students. Although the staff members did not necessarily know the precise funding sources of various positions, all personnel hired through Title I funds were informed that they were to work with Title I–eligible students. The principal from a school that practiced strict compliance exemplified the marking of adults and their requisite work with students in the following statement:

> The Title I paras have been here for quite a while. . . . We have other kinds of paras here as well. We have some [desegregation funded paras] and some special ed paras. . . . Title I is specifically remediation, working on reinforcing with the kids that are at the lowest spectrum. That's what they're supposed to be doing.

The program resource teacher at the same school noted that the personnel funded through Title I were to work with students identified in the following manner:

> We come up with students below the 40th percentile in reading and/ or math. We develop an EDY participant list from that. Those are the people that in the past generated the funds, so they got the service from the paraprofessionals and so forth.

Indeed, in schools that practiced strict compliance, the notion of who should get what services depended in large part on who generated the policy-driven funds, rather than a more thorough assessment of student academic performance and educational need.

Teachers at the same school noted that recent policy changes allowed for more flexibility in deciding how the paraprofessionals should spend their time. These teachers noted that although the school had practiced strict compliance for many years, they now exercised more discretion in determining which adults should work with which children. One teacher explained how past Title I iterations led to a culture of policy in which even filmstrips, materials, and classroom learning spaces were allocated based on policy designations. Noting that "when visitors used to come, we were told to only use filmstrips and other materials with Title I students," the teacher explained how this policy culture translated into the organization of classroom routines. "The para was supposed to take [the students ineligible for Title I] on the rug and work with them because they weren't supposed to use any materials or receive any services funded by Title I." In accordance with the policy changes of the most recent reauthorization, the teachers knew that they could now have the paraprofessionals work with any student in their classrooms. Interestingly, however, the Title I coordinator and principal insisted that Title I–funded services were still provided only to Title I–eligible students.

Other schools practiced a second approach to compliance: the overall disregard for policy regulations. This policy practice took root in the most chaotic situations, in which crisis-driven management and leadership styles led to rather disorganized and incoherent daily school practices. The school principal and Title I coordinator knew that they were supposed to get lists of EDY students to the teachers but took a number of months doing so, as daily fights and other disruptions consumed their time. Once teachers received the lists, they did not know what to do with them. Teachers did, however, know that the term EDY meant deficit and deficiency. The cultural aspects of policy practice provide powerful messages to teaching staffs, even when the technical compliance measures are disregarded.

When the policy regulations were completely disregarded and only the meanings of policy markers were in place, the learning opportunities for students were fragmented and at times indiscernible. In fact, one first-grade teacher complained that too many resource teachers were taking students out of her classroom for supplementary services. She said that was never informed as to what the services were, why those students were selected, and when the supplementary service providers might show up to pull students for the various policy-driven compensatory and categorical programs available in the school. Responding to their perceptions of chaos in their school, some staff members thought that further adherence to policy routines might improve educational practice. For example, the Title I coordinator at a school where compliance practices were for the most part disregarded pushed for stricter policy designations for students and adults, stating, "I would like to see, like if the paras are funded two hours [by] Title I, that they really work for two hours, not all at once, with certain little groups [of eligible students] and help them get their skills."

In contrast, schools that engaged in critical, reflective discussions about the routines and language encouraged by the culture of policy developed a form of thoughtful noncompliance. Although acting in resistance to the culture of policy, the practitioners in these schools saw compliance with policy mandates as secondary to addressing the educational needs of the students whose academic performance could benefit from additional services. Issues of compliance were approached with humor or frustration. For example, in the school in which the resource teachers were part of a class-size reduction strategy, the entire school staff was under the impression that they were out of compliance with Title I regulations. At a staff meeting preceding a district committee visit, the staff was instructed that "the people who are paid by these funds should not do what the district-funded folks should do, like classroom teaching." The room erupted in laughter as all realized that their Title I use was exactly that. They were out of compliance and knew it, but they also knew why—class-size reduction was an intervention that all agreed would serve the students best. Despite their obvious resistance and thoughtful noncompliance, however, they were instructed that if anybody asked them to describe their use of Title I funds, they were to reply, "to work with the at-risk, EDY population in the lower quartile."

Even in schools that practiced thoughtful noncompliance, Title I funding influenced who practitioners thought they could serve. For example, in one school three resource teachers delivered Reading Recovery lessons to four students each. At the beginning of the school year, they worked together to determine which students should participate in the program. After collectively testing 36 different students, they determined which 4 students each resource teacher would serve. As they calculated which students scored lowest on a series of alphabet letter identification, word identification, text reading, story and word writing, and word vocabulary tests, each resource teacher discussed the students' strengths, weaknesses, and any additional perceptions that the classroom teachers had shared. When the list of participating students was finalized, the Title I coordinator paused and sighed, "Title I throws a monkey wrench in this whole thing because we don't know if these are Title I kids." Another resource teacher rolled her eyes and replied, "I thought we were going by need, not by Title I." The coordinator responded, "We are going by need, but we've all funded ourselves by Title I. . . . Let's go with this for now." The culture of policy created a situation in which practitioners weighed policy regulations against their own sense of "need" based on rigorous and meaningful diagnostic assessments that they trusted. By going with their own determination of who should receive what policy-funded services, practitioners practice resistance to the culture of policy. This resistance does not preclude providing services to eligible students, but it does demonstrate more reflective, critical approaches to issues of compliance. A paraprofessional in the same school echoed a similar approach: "As responsible paras, we try to help those children who really do need the help. . . . If they're not on [the Title I] list, they'll come up and ask for help." However, the same paraprofessional was cognizant of the expectations to serve primarily marked students. She went on to note that "as part of being Title I–funded, we are supposed to work especially with [Title I–eligible] children."

POLICY CHANGES AND THE RITUALS OF PRACTICE

Shaped by the above dynamics, Title I took form in daily rituals and routines. Paraprofessionals signed time sheets, noting how many hours of their work were funded by Title I. Title I coordinators circulated lists of eligible students to teachers. Teachers placed these lists on walls, in drawers, or in folders. Paraprofessionals met with small groups of students in the back areas of classrooms or circulated to various classrooms, meeting briefly with students who sought their help. Reading Recovery teachers removed students from their classrooms, one at a time, for daily one-on-one literacy sessions. Title I coordinators kept records of which practitioners served which students. Teachers administered tests. Schools encouraged parents to fill out and submit eligibility forms for the federal free-lunch program.

Changes in policy construction at the federal level brought new dynamics to the culture of policy as manifested through Title I. As evident in the testimony of practitioners, the time during which these schools were studied was a time of transition. Movement between 1995 and 1996 from test scores to poverty measures as the main determinant of eligibility revealed how the symbols of poverty and performance resonated with the practitioners' sense of whom they should serve and how. At the time of these observations, the transition from a focus on individual students to one on whole schools had not yet taken hold. Practitioners still thought in terms of targeting specific students and did not think of their schools as being "Title I." Those marked were individual students and practitioners, not the entire student body and teaching staff.

Importantly, Title I policy does not operate in isolation. It is just one piece of a larger culture of policy that encourages the language and routines of practice. The following vignette based on my observation at one of the studied schools highlights how this culture of policy operates for various compensatory policies:

> The principal of Jordan Elementary School called a meeting to prepare for a February site visit from a group of school district compliance monitors to provide the staff with a "refresher" on ESEA Title I and other school-based programs, "in case we get quizzed" by the district representatives. The school's Title I coordinator ran the meeting noting the various policy-generated programs in the school, including Title I, bilingual education, special education, and others. The coordinator explained how the school was allocating Title I funds to reduce class size, a use of such funds that staff members thought to be out of compliance with the district, state, and federal guidelines for this policy. "Most importantly," the coordinator noted after murmurs of concern about noncompliance, the funds paid for the salaries of staff who worked with "the at-risk, EDY population, the lower quartile."[12] The Title I coordinator then instructed the teachers to memorize which students were designated as "EDY" (educationally disadvantaged youth) and "LEP" (limited-English proficient), in case they were asked by the district monitors, and referred the staff to various lists that displayed students' names alongside their policy-generated designations. Teachers joked about the prospect of being asked to identify each student by her or his policy-based identities. One teacher suggested facetiously that staff members ask, "Could all the LEP students raise their hands?" to which another added, "We should have them all tattooed in October." (observed by author in 1994; reported in Stein, 2001, p. 142)

Indeed, practitioners operate in a policy culture where the metaphor of a permanent etching of a policy-based identity onto students' bodies surfaces in preparation for a compliance review. And while we can interpret the teacher's use of the tattoo metaphor as sardonic critique, cynical resignation, or solid support of the culture of policy, the ambiguity of its intended meaning makes an even more salient point: Policy mechanisms and compliance practices contribute to the culture of policy whether one conforms to or resists that culture. The tattoo metaphor shows how the marking of students is passed down from the various levels of government to the classroom teachers through common school practices. And, like the tattoo, the marking is easier to get than to remove.

CONCLUSION

Policy does not create bias. However, it does embody the biases of its crafters, and can reinforce the biases of its implementers. The cultural dimensions of educational policies form a critical dimension to the recursive relationship between the interpreted meanings of policy-driven language (such as the labels that mark eligible students) and the expectations that teachers hold for their students.

Within educational systems, close attention must be paid to the incentive structures inherent in any policy practice. When adults are rewarded for student underperformance, for their own low expectations, or for perpetuating a system of naming and framing students based on insufficient measures, we can expect to see those practices. What is tragic is that Title I policy, at least from 1965 to 1994, has provided incentives for language and behavior that work against student learning rather than for it.

The following chapter reviews two additional equity-oriented policies that illustrate further dimensions of the culture of policy.

"Line Up for Integration!"

This chapter considers desegregation and bilingual education policies through the culture of policy lens. Here, investigation of the simultaneous implementation of these two policies as they take shape in daily school practice provides additional illustration of the language and rituals of the culture of policy. Building on the prior analysis of ESEA Title I, this investigation of policies that promote classification schemes based on race and home language illustrates elements of the language and rituals of policy culture even more starkly contrary to egalitarian policy purposes.

The following analysis presents the daily practices of schools in which the concurrent implementation of desegregation and bilingual education policies led to classrooms that were ethnically segregated in formally integrated schools. In these schools, the culture of bilingual and desegregation policies encouraged narrow and outdated notions of race, ethnicity, and diversity as well as educationally questionable practices to achieve a symbolic and policy-driven diversity. In effect, the simultaneous implementation of these two policies led to school rituals that interrupted, quite literally, the learning opportunities made available to students. This chapter provides further evidence of how the culture of policy framework exposes how policy-driven language and routines of schooling not only conflict with stated egalitarian goals, but can actually foster rituals of stigmatization, deficit orientation, and strategies.

A brief review of the two equity-oriented policies shows how these judicial mandates came to operate in the studied schools. My investigation of school practices then demonstrates the ways in which these two policies (a) *required* the marking of students based on categories of race and language; (b) affected the organization of the school day; (c) influenced how practitioners came to understand and represent the concept of "integration"; and (d) communicated to children race-based messages that were confusing, troubling, and certainly not in keeping with the equity orientation of either desegregation or bilingual education policies. As with the prior analysis of Title I, the habitualized activities of school personnel and students were documented through interviews and observations.[1] These policies provide further examples of how, like Title I, equity-seeking policies, based on national, state, and local judicial, legislative, and administrative decisionmaking create cultural consequences for schooling.

BILINGUAL EDUCATION AND DESEGREGATION POLICIES IN THE STUDIED SCHOOLS

The historical intentions of both bilingual education and desegregation policies are linked to notions of civil rights and educational access for various racial, ethnic, and linguistic groups. Since the late 1800s, bilingual education has been a politically contested educational strategy for students whose first language is other than English (Tyack & Hansot, 1982). In the 1960s, bilingual education became part of the national discourse on civil rights for immigrants and racial/ethnic groups (Hakuta, 1986; Stein, 1986; Tyack & Hansot, 1982). The first federal policy for bilingual education was passed in 1968 as part of the reauthorization of the Elementary and Secondary Education Act (ESEA, 1968). Title VII (Bilingual Education Act) of ESEA included funding for "experimental programs" in districts that were interested in designing programs to serve students whose home language was not English (Hakuta, 1986, pp. 198–199). The goal of many of the programs initiated at the time was to maintain the home language while developing command of English.

Later, based in large part on the civil rights movement and the landmark *Lau v. Nichols* Supreme Court decision of 1974, the focus of bilingual education shifted from the maintenance of the home language while learning English to equal access to quality education for students whose limited command of the English language curtailed meaningful engagement in core curricular activities (Hakuta, 1986; Stein, 1986). The *Lau* decision mandated that limited- and non-English-speaking students receive assistance in all school districts nationwide, and spurred the development of guidelines for bilingual education under the Bilingual Education Act. This act required schools to identify children whose home language was not English, assess their proficiency in English, then use their home language as a "transitional tool" (Hakuta, 1986, p. 204) to provide access to core curricular content while they learned English. Since their inception, bilingual education programs have been implemented in many divergent forms. Beyond their direct educational significance, they have come to represent group rights for immigrants (Cardinale, Carnoy, & Stein, 1999; Hakuta, 1986) and have been criticized as "misguided policies which threaten national unity" (U.S. English, 1992, p. 146). Bilingual proponents sometimes frame antibilingual sentiments as racist attacks on specific groups, often Latinos (Cardinale et al., 1999).

Desegregation agreements have also been part of the national discourse on civil rights for specific racial/ethnic groups, namely blacks and Hispanic/ Latino Americans. Similar to bilingual education policies, desegregation advocates have represented this policy as a means to equal access to quality education for students who had previously been denied such learning opportunities. As this judicial policy, based in the landmark *Brown v. Board of Education* (1954) decision, was implemented, the policy's measure of success grew to be the integration of students from various racial and ethnic groups in school buildings, rather than the parity in learning opportunities available to all racial and ethnic groups. Scholars and activists have argued against the idea of integration as an end unto itself, one calling for abandonment of the "traditional and limited sense" of desegregation as "the mandatory mixing of certain numbers of [W]hite, [B]lack, and Hispanic pupils in all schools" (Brady, 1986, p. 28; see also Bell, 1975, 1980, 1986). Derrick Bell (1986) notes that "since the 1780s, when the first public schools opened in Boston, [B]lack parents have urged racially separate as well as integrated schools, in their quest for effective schooling for their children" (p. 71). Martha Minow (1990) further explains how

> the new generation of [B]lack leaders who started the Black Power movement favored community control of local, segregated schools. They vocally rejected assimilation as a threat to [B]lack culture and [B]lack self-consciousness. They sought to raise the status, power, and pride of their communities through self-governance. (p. 24)

Although largely resisted by some black and Latino advocates for community control of neighborhood schools as well as many white parents and schoolteachers, court-mandated desegregation arrangements garnered historical meaning as an important step toward equal educational opportunities and civil rights (see Tyack & Cuban, 1995, p. 27).

Similar to Title I, conceptualizations of deficit and deficiency among students marked as needing more for having less were implicit in both desegregation and bilingual education policies. However, unlike Title I, the notion of having "less" was not connected to material resources; it was connected to racial hierarchies. With Title I policy, the government aimed to compensate for students attending schools in resource-strapped communities. This redistributive policy aimed to alter the distribution of resources generated by a capitalist market economy. In contrast, with desegregation and bilingual education policies, the government attempted to correct state-based and state-sanctioned status hierarchies based on race and home language. Through addressing these racial and linguistic hierarchies, students with less social currency based on their race and/or command of the English language were tagged as deficient and needy through racial, ethnic, and linguistic classification schemes that were limited and reductive.

The Language of Desegregation: Marking Race and Ethnicity

The district governing the schools I studied had operated under a court-approved and monitored desegregation policy since the late 1970s. In order to comply with the policy, the schools could not exceed between 40 to 45% representation of any one ethnic group. To determine the ethnic compositions of the schools, the court established ethnicity categories that became part of every student's record. These ethnic categories came into place in the schools as a way to monitor the desegregation policy. Upon registering a child for a school in the district, the parent or guardian had to declare the student's ethnicity as one of the following: Latino/Hispanic, Other White/Caucasian, African American/Black, Chinese, Japanese, Korean, American Indian, Filipino, or Other Non-White (this category was noted to include Arabic, Samoan, and Indochinese students). District and school statistics, including test scores and "EDY" (Educationally Disadvantaged Youth) designations, were broken down by these categories as a way to keep track of how ethnic/racial groups were performing relative to one another.

These racial/ethnic classification schemes became policy markings similar to EDY status. Also similar to EDY status, these markings were reductive and slippery. As with many desegregation plans nationwide, the racial and ethnic categories at the time of the court intervention may not maintain relevance years later. Immigration patterns, community transience, and the evolutionary dimension of racial categorization schemes (Omi & Winant, 1994) all render these categories limited in their usefulness. Additionally, students of mixed racial/ethnic heritage are asked to select only one racial/ethnic marker.

Parents and teachers manipulated this policy-driven approach to racial/ethnic classification. Parents knew that there were advantages to having their students marked with certain ethnic classifications so as to manipulate the desegregation plan. Since only 13% of the elementary school population was classified as white, a child classified as such would have less competition for slots in the more desirable schools. One parent reported that she marked her daughter (of mixed white and Hispanic/Latino heritage) as white for elementary school so that she would have a greater chance of attending a "better school," and later switched her marking to Hispanic/Latino when competing for middle school placement since by that time there were fewer Latino students in the running for the middle school to which she wanted to send her daughter. This parent explained that the district allowed parents to switch their child's ethnic categorization once. A district middle school teacher reported noticing that a student who appeared to be and identified himself in daily interaction as white was marked on school records as black. This teacher called the parent to investigate what she thought might have been a mistake in reporting or recording. The parent told the teacher that although she considered herself and her child to be white, the ethnic categorization was not a mistake: she marked her child as black so as to maximize his chances of attending that school.

The behavior of the above parents reflects the incentives built into desegregation policies with superficial understandings of both desegregation and the conditions it aims to remedy. If there are a limited number of slots for high-performing schools with rigorous curricula and engaged teachers, parents who are seeking meaningful educational opportunities for their children will determine when there is a premium on identifying them as part of one or another racial/ethnic group. Some parents will game the system through the policy markings available to raise the chances that their children will receive a quality education assumed to be in limited supply. The racial and ethnic markings then become part of a strategy for accumulation of resources, rather than an indicator of individual identity, historical conditions, or community membership.

Regardless of the manipulation of the ethnic markings by a few individuals, in order for the district to comply with the desegregation plan, some students had to be bused from their neighborhoods to schools outside of their immediate communities. A movement toward neighborhood schooling had somewhat discouraged this practice at the time of this study, but compliance with the court-monitored plan still necessitated some busing. The desegregation policy also provided funds to the schools that served certain zip codes (primarily those in black residential neighborhoods) in order to improve the overall school programs. Similar to Title I policy, those marked as generating the funding—in this case, the children from predominantly black neighborhoods—were also marked as defective, deficient, and needing more than other students. Also similar to Title I, these policy-generated resources were used to buy materials and hire paraprofessionals for classroom and counseling positions. In some schools the monies generated from the integration and the Title I policies were used in very similar ways. In fact, some paraprofessionals and resource teachers were compensated in part through Title I and in part through desegregation funds.

Demographic changes in the neighborhoods and the city at large made consistent compliance with the desegregation plan challenging. The studied schools reported shifts in their student populations due to patterns of immigration, the closing of major public housing facilities, the district's location (and relocation) of specialized bilingual programs, and the move toward neighborhood-based attendance areas. A resource teacher funded entirely by her school's desegregation budget observed the shifts in her school composition due to changes in public housing as follows:

> In order to have the four major ethnic races represented, you had to
> have bused in children. . . . And the Housing Authority tenants across
> the street were predominantly African American. They tore down the
> housing project across the street and when they rebuilt it they made it
> multicultural. So we have Chinese students from across the street; we
> have Vietnamese children; we have African American; we have
> Hispanic children now who actually live in our neighborhood.

At the time of this statement, this teacher's school had two buses pull up to
the school every day: one carrying Chinese students and the other carrying
Latino students. The program resource teacher at another school described
similar changes, noting that

> [t]he area in general has changed and the main housing project has
> closed down within the last year. . . . So that changed [the school]
> considerably. We have more of an influx of Chinese people and
> Chinese students coming into our school. We're currently maxed,
> based on [the city] regs . . . we can't take any more Chinese students.

The changes described by these school personnel influenced more than
just the ethnic composition of the schools. The programming needs of the
schools were affected as well; the bilingual regulations at the time required
that a certain number of students marked as "Limited English Proficient"
(LEP) or "Non-English Proficient" (NEP) required a bilingual or English
Language Development (ELD) program, and therefore bilingual or ELD-
trained teachers and classrooms.

The Language of Bilingual Policy:
Marking Ethnicity and Home Language

The delivery strategies for bilingual education were mandated from the
superintendent's office and the office of bilingual education. The district
adopted a bilingual policy that had formerly been state law. The law ordered
that if there were 10 or more students from a language group other than
English in two consecutive grades, the school had to offer a bilingual education program. Students were tested for their English proficiency if their parents marked that their home language was other than English upon registering
them for school. Parents could also request their child's placement in or out
of a bilingual classroom. Principals, teachers, and parents noted that in some
cases students were placed in bilingual classes based primarily on their sur-
name, rather than their English-speaking capabilities.
    The predominant delivery strategy for bilingual education was to teach
core curricular materials in the students' primary language with gradual

transition to English. According to a district bilingual resource teacher, after third grade, schools were expected to redesignate students into English-only or English Language Development classrooms. However, schools had the option to continue offering self-contained bilingual classrooms beyond the third grade. The theory behind this policy is based on the transferability of skills from one language to another. Students master their first language as they develop their literacy skills and learn the curricular content in math and language arts. Once they had mastered these skills, they could transfer them to another language. A district-based resource teacher was careful to note that school-based pressures contributed to what she described as an implementation system that was "inconsistent across classes." Teachers often felt pressured to teach in English earlier than when the Office of Bilingual Education recommended. Additionally, the bilingual teaching practices differed markedly in Spanish and Chinese bilingual classes. The district policy, based in large part on research on English language acquisition for Spanish-speaking students, was in flux in its approach to Chinese bilingual education. Since the level of transferability of skills from Chinese to English was unclear, Chinese bilingual teachers delivered language arts instruction in English.

In the schools, most personnel described the bilingual education policies as inconsistent from year to year and out of sync with the staff's instructional capacity. Programs were instituted and phased out frequently. A fifth-grade Spanish bilingual teacher complained that "[t]he district just makes decisions and tells people what to do without any communication about why or encouragement of shared vision for where the district and the schools are or ought to be going." This comment demonstrates how through the culture of policy, the overriding equity concerns and central policy goals get lost. The district informs the schools about what they should be doing in order to be in compliance with policy, but does not connect the regulations or expectations for implementation practice to an overall agenda for student learning, instructional equity, or academic performance. Rather, school practitioners are instructed "what to do," without any connection to the broader principles or goals of the policies. And the notion of what the schools should be doing changes frequently according to new policy legislation constructed at the federal, state, and district levels.

The implementation of the bilingual education policy in this district had changed a number of times. Until 1994, the predominant strategy for bilingual education was to compose classrooms of students with one-third monolingual English speakers and two-thirds students who spoke another language at home (usually Spanish or Chinese). However, in response to complaints about the placement of monolingual English speakers in bilingual classrooms, in 1995 the superintendent issued a directive prohibiting the placement of students who speak English as their first language in bilingual classes. This directive was motivated by previous concerns that black students were being placed in bilingual education classes inappropriately and were not thriving academically. The assistant superintendent of elementary education explained that the district had changed policies in response to ethno-political pressures on various occasions. For example, he relayed that when the policy was to compose classes with one-third English speakers and two-thirds Spanish or Chinese speakers, a local newspaper printed an article saying that black students were being "dumped" in bilingual classrooms. In reaction to this article, the superintendent at that time "jumped up and down, saying 'How could this be?'" The assistant superintendent believed the superintendent's surprise to be odd, since the district's racial/ethnic profile along with the combined factors of the desegregation and bilingual policies made this situation practically inevitable. Indeed, since the proportionally largest English-speaking population in the district was black and one-third of the students in a given classroom were to be English-speaking, the English speakers were most likely to be black. Subsequently, the central office issued a directive to move all of the black students out of bilingual classrooms.

Following this reorganization, the court-appointed monitor of the desegregation agreement reviewed the schools and found that that there were 135 ethnically segregated classrooms in the district. According to the assistant superintendent, his former boss "jumped up and down again." The district then moved back to the two-thirds/one-third strategy. At the time of this study, a new superintendent had decided that the only students who should be in bilingual classes were those whose first language was the language of instruction. He was quoted informally by various administrators as having said, "I don't want to see any black faces in bilingual classes."

The concurrent policy mandates had a number of consequences on school organization, including the nature of teacher collaboration, the hiring of teachers, and the placement of and class size for black students. The most striking of these consequences, however, was the largely segregated nature of the classrooms within each school. Although the impetus behind the segregation was the selected approach to bilingual education, and the segregation was essentially by *language*, the fact that the language and racial/ethnic lines tended to coincide led to schools that were segregated by *race/ethnicity*. This visible segregation was so stark that one resource teacher described her school environment as "apartheid."

The ethnic markers made educationally relevant through equity-oriented policy schemes provided racialized vocabularies and routines for common school practices. Every morning, at each of these schools, students would line up with their classes to say the Pledge of Allegiance. In every school, there were ethnically identifiable lines of children assembled next to one another. Each school had classes of Chinese children lined up next to classes of Latino children. Some of the remaining classes were ethnically mixed, but most were primarily or exclusively black children. In some of these schools, adults would use racial cues to determine who was supposed to be where. For example, during a morning recess period in one school, a group of children from two different classrooms were playing on a jungle gym that had been reserved for only one of the classes (that happened to be a Chinese bilingual class). A group of girls from the assigned class approached me, saying that the jungle gym had been reserved for their classroom, but that there were "black people" on it. One of the girls asked me, "Could you please get the black people off?" Startled by the suggestion, I advised them to get their teacher. Once notified that students from outside her class were playing on the equipment, the teacher looked for the classroom aide assigned to the almost exclusively black "English-only" class. "Can you help me here?" she called out to the young black aide, waving her to come to the door where the equipment reservation sheet was posted. "My class is supposed to have the play structure today, but I think your students are on it." Looking at the mix of Asian and black children on the slide and jungle bars, the aide started pulling the students from her class off of the structure, telling them that they would have a turn another day. Of all the black children on the jungle gym, only one remained, talking with two Chinese girls. "I said get off!" the aide shouted. "The play structure is reserved for Chinese bilingual today!" The black girl jumped off the slide, startled, while two Chinese girls shouted in unison, "She's in our class!" "She's in Chinese bilingual!?" the aide questioned and before waiting for a response said to the girl, "I'm so sorry." Indeed, policies encourage confusing messages about race.

The above story would not have any racial script if the classroom compositions were not drawn along racial and ethnic lines. Indeed, if both classes were ethnically mixed, or if all students in both classes were of the same ethnicity, the play structure scenario would only represent classroom scheduling of playground equipment. However, the combined implementation of desegregation and bilingual education policies wrote a racial script onto otherwise mundane school practices.

This racial script was more pronounced in some schools than in others. In all schools with bilingual classrooms, the classes taught in either Spanish or Chinese were ethnically exclusive with only occasional exceptions. In one school, a handful of English-speaking black students were in bilingual classes. Teachers said that these placements were due to student behavior problems or parental requests.

The segregation of students led to ethnic- and race-based resentments. One principal noted how black parents at her school were furious when they saw the students lining up for classes on the first day of school. The principal explained to them that the reason for the segregation was the bilingual education policy. She apologized that she did not have any control over the situation. In another school the program resource teacher said that teachers of predominantly black students in the English-only classes resented the

Chinese teachers and students since the bilingual program left them with "all the regular ed students with problems." According to this principal, the teachers believed that "the Chinese, it's that stereotype again, that the Chinese are the easy ones to work with because they don't talk back, they don't act out, they don't do all of these things." The program resource teacher at yet another school echoed these sentiments, noting that bilingual education "ends up putting often times a lot of kids that are behavior problems into the three or four other classes and that then creates division among the staff." The associations between racial/ethnic markings and behavior are similar to those between Title I markings and behavior.

In one school, the students often fought along racial/ethnic lines. At a late November meeting between classroom aides and the principal, one aide talked about the tensions created in such a segregated structure. She told the principal that students were insulting each other with racial slurs and fighting race-based fights on the playground. Another aide complained that because lunch and recess were organized by classrooms the students did not have the opportunity to meet and get to know each other in any school capacity. Various resource teachers commented on the racial tensions they observed between students, one stating that "we have been lucky that we have not had more incidences go down by race lines." This comment indicates the expectation of race-based incidents due to the policy rituals in place. Ironically, the implementation of two policies seeking educational justice on racial, ethnic, and linguistic lines heightened both in-school segregation and racial/ethnic animosities. Teachers and administrators observed frequently that the simultaneous implementation of these policies led to practices that ran counter to the policies' goals. These efforts to remedy injustice required their own equity-seeking remedies.

REMEDY RITUALS: ORGANIZING THE SCHOOL DAY FOR "INTEGRATION"

The schoolwide rituals created to comply with these equity-oriented policies wrote a racial script onto school routines. Anything scheduled by classroom (e.g., the distribution of playground equipment, the use of school spaces, classroom performances) tended to be organized by race/ethnicity as well. When school personnel complained that the current bilingual education strategy segregated the schools by race, the superintendent created yet another policy: a set period for integrated activities that was to occupy at least 20% of each school day. According to the assistant superintendent of elementary education, this mandate came about through a meeting between the directors of the district's bilingual and integration offices. They faced the challenge of crafting a strategy that would satisfy both policies. After each program head told the other the virtues of her or his respective policies and approaches, they decided that the schools needed to implement some plan to integrate the students for a certain percentage of the day. The assistant superintendent said that they "arbitrarily" chose 20% of the school day (roughly 1 hour and 15 minutes) to be the required time period. Here, again, compliance with policy regulations seemed to take precedence over academic or instructional goals.

The rituals deployed in response to these combined policy directives varied considerably between schools and school-level practitioners. Among the eight schools I studied, there were three main integration strategies, largely determined by the school's principal and leadership teams. Some schools instituted daily schoolwide rotations scheduled at a specific time period labeled as "integration." Others relied on grade-level rotations, organized independently by teachers at each grade level. And one school had schoolwide special days of integrated activity approximately once a month (this school began a grade-level-based integration routine in March when it was noted that the special days did not fulfill the policy mandates).

In five of the eight schools, "integration" became a scheduled time of the day in which classes were divided up and regrouped into racially/ethnically integrated classes. As part of the daily routine, teachers commonly instructed students to "line up for integration" before shuffling students to the classrooms in which they would receive instruction with students from different ethnic/racial backgrounds than their own. Similar to "physical education" or "art," students had to relocate to a new learning space for "integration." The term "integration" came to signify a time to switch classrooms for a different type of learning, with different kinds of students and, often, with a different teacher.

Two schools established one fixed time of day to integrate the students. At a specified time of day—in one school, this period ran from 11:35 a.m. to 12:50 p.m. and included the lunch period and a short recess—students in each classroom would divide into predetermined groups in accordance with the number of classrooms at the same grade level. For example, if there were four first-grade classrooms, the students in each first-grade class were divided into four groups. One of the groups remained in the original classroom with the classroom teacher while each of the other groups moved to one of the other classrooms with the other first-grade teachers. The principal at one school implementing this approach explained the evolution of her school's integration program, noting that she

> decided that teachers needed to integrate their kids by grade level before lunch, so they could eat with kids from other classrooms and then play on the yard with those classrooms and then line up and then have some time of interaction and some time of learning with the kids from the other classrooms.

In accordance with her school's plan, 5 minutes before lunchtime students were told to get in four different lines for their "integration groups." Once all students were with their "integration teachers," they were escorted to the cafeteria or the play yard for lunch. At lunch, students were seated in their "integration groups." After lunch and a brief recess, they lined up with their "integration teachers" and returned to their "integration classrooms."

During daily, schoolwide "integration" class periods in both schools, teachers led a range of activities, including art projects, lessons on dental hygiene, read-alouds, reviews of the class norms from a conflict-resolution program, and various "icebreaker" activities to get students from different classrooms to interact. All integration classes were conducted in English, and core curricular materials and activities were largely absent. Teachers explained that this absence—which many of them lamented—resulted from the fact that the languages of instruction and overall curriculum for students from the various classrooms were not consistent. In other words, due to curricular and language differences between programs and materials, teachers encountered great difficulty in developing core curricular lessons from which students in all language programs could benefit.

In five schools, teachers coordinated with their grade-level colleagues to integrate students for parts of the day. In some schools, this coordination occurred on a daily basis. In others, it was scheduled irregularly or on one or two days per week. Teachers at each grade level determined how they would integrate the students, when such integration would take place, and what activities they would do with the integrated groups. For example, teachers in these schools would rotate students between classes, team-teach combined classes, and take grade-level field trips. Sometimes they would decide to meet at the same time during the school day or week. Other times they would schedule "integration" around other activities. The principal of one school using this strategy described his school's integration plan as one in which teachers "team-teach and mix the classes up, at least 20% of the day. So they do it through science or through P.E., art, music, or some of them even do it through the core subjects at times." For the most part, however, "integration" was absent core curricular materials.

At some grade levels, classroom doors had signs reading "Integration Schedule," displaying the times and locations of integrated activities. Other grade levels integrated their classrooms less frequently or regularly. For example, during my 6 weeks of observations in the first-grade classrooms of one school, the teachers integrated their classrooms on an irregular schedule for activities such as motor-perception skills classes, schoolwide assemblies, and video viewing. Whenever a first-grade teacher was going to show a video, she or he would inform the other first-grade teachers and ask whether their classes wanted to join. Since decisions were made at the grade level, the frequency of integrated activities exhibited a considerable range from grade to grade within one school.

One school began the school year with an approach to integration through schoolwide special days in which students would select an elective class (such as arts and crafts or music) and spend the afternoon in that class. Teachers selected students for programmatic options by ranking them according to their interests (as indicated on a survey), and the classes were constructed with ethnic/racial integration in mind. At various faculty meetings, the principal referred to these special days as the days "when we integrate the students." This principal described the program as an opportunity for students to have "field trips together, assemblies, where Chinese New Year would not just be Chinese children participating, it would be all of the third graders." According to this principal, the period of integrated activity lasted approximately 45 minutes to an hour and was scheduled twice monthly. At the beginning of the school year, these days were the children's only integrated activities besides weekly classes that focused on motor-perception skills.

In mid-March, this school moved to a more frequent integration schedule that approximated the grade-level integration periods observed in other schools. The observed activities during these integration periods included game-playing, singing, and arts and crafts projects. Each teacher determined individually what her or his group of students would do during the integrated activity period. After roughly a month of this practice (mid-April), the first- and second-grade teachers and paraprofessionals asked to meet with the principal to resolve some conflicts in the plan. At this meeting, the teachers explained that they could not integrate their students before lunchtime because the lunch cards would get "jumbled" and a cafeteria worker complained that the students were registered in her computer by classroom. The classroom aides added that they found it difficult to monitor the cafeteria under this arrangement since students were assigned to different tables, and not all classes arrived at the same time. The principal responded to these concerns by moving integration time to after lunch.

The multiple iterations of "integration" described above highlight additional elements of the culture of policy that build on my previous analysis of Title I. As policy language and rituals are interpreted, incorporated, routinized, and habitualized, practices absurd to the casual observer—such as "lining up for integration"—become normal, typical, and expected elements of the school day. An overall focus on technical compliance with policy regulations and reductive conceptions of difference and diversity overshadow the larger policy goals of equal educational opportunities. Indeed, students who are lining up for integration, switching classes to do so, and receive no core curricular instruction during daily integration periods lose instructional time. This practice, in very concrete and measurable ways, limits the educational opportunities of the students that policies aim to serve.

THE MEANING OF "INTEGRATION" IN
THE LANGUAGE OF PRACTITIONERS

In the culture of equity-oriented education policy, representations of the policies' equity imperatives are largely absent. Similar to the culture of Title I policy, bilingual and desegregation policy compliance often took primacy to provision of meaningful learning opportunities. "Integration" came to signify various features of classroom-scheduling practices, yet was never represented as a means to access a quality education for any students. Local practitioners were held to policy regulations that structured their students' days; they were not held as rigorously to policy-driven standards for providing meaningful and equitable instructional opportunities to children. Responding to the demands placed on them, practitioners discussed the technical issues of compliance and daily organization rather than the deeper tensions of pluralism and instructional effectiveness that challenge educators on a daily basis.

Practitioner discourse reflected the absorption and permutation of the language of policies into the schools' daily practices. Practitioners represented integration as (a) a scheduled activity, (b) a constraint, (c) an amount of lost instructional time, (d) the physical proximity and interactions of students from different classrooms, (e) a respite from a challenging teaching load, and, in a few cases, (f) a necessary inconvenience to ease racial tension.

Integration as a Scheduled Activity

Similar to lunch, art, and physical education, school practitioners and students used the term "integration" to signify a scheduled activity. In various conversations between teachers and students, the term "integration" reflected a specific time of day. Comments such as, "After recess I have integration," "I'll pick up Lorena [for Title I–funded Reading Recovery] at the beginning of integration," and "You're in my room for integration," were common to all schools with defined periods for integrated activities. A teacher trying to get students to walk quietly through the hallway ordered, "If you can't be quiet, we're going to spend our whole integration time learning how to walk." The use of the term "integration" to represent a scheduled activity became a normalized part of the schools' daily vocabularies.

Integration as a Constraint

Despite the habitualized use of the term "integration," many practitioners questioned the ritual of integration, noting that it severely constrained their daily routines and teaching strategies. Numerous teachers shared the opinion that they were asked to solve an impossible puzzle handed to them by the district. Many stated that before the most recent bilingual policies the

schools were largely integrated and that the mandated integration put additional constraints on their professional discretion. Using the terms "mandate"
and "order," principals explained to their staffs the need for scheduled integrated activities. At a meeting, one principal told her staff that the superintendent has "mandated integration," and that they will be monitored by "the
state" to see how they are integrating the students. Another principal reported
that the teachers at his school "think it's asinine." He continued to say that
parents also felt dissatisfied with and constrained by the segregated nature
of his school and the resulting integration plan, lamenting that the parents
feel "powerless in that situation . . . [but] that's the mandate, and they just
have to go along with it."

Integration as Lost Instructional Time

Not only did "integration" serve as a constraint, some teachers openly lamented
the daily loss of student learning time. To these teachers, the sole purpose of
the set-aside time was to integrate the students, a goal they saw as social rather
than academic. For example, the first-grade teachers at one school complained
that prior to the establishment of the integration period they taught reading in
the morning and math in the afternoon. Since "integration" broke up the
afternoon, they had to use a different schedule so as to have enough time to
cover the lessons that they had covered in previous years. Early in the school
year, one first-grade teacher complained to a group of her colleagues, "I'm
burnt out already. I just can't buy into giving up an hour of core-curriculum
instruction because somebody downtown thinks we need integration, and
someone else thinks we need bilingual." As the year progressed, her solution
to this situation was to use the morning recess period to do the activities that
she would have done during the integration period.

In all schools, the mere logistics of moving students from classroom to
classroom were time-consuming. From the time students were instructed to
"line up for integration" to the time that they were settled in classrooms,
several minutes passed, consuming precious instructional time. Teachers often
expressed their frustration in terms of their students' educational needs. For
example, one teacher continually bemoaned how the integration period had
"taken a lot of time away from children in my own classroom. . . . It's hard
when they move to different teachers." She also represented this attitude to
her students. During one classroom observation, she addressed her students
saying, "Boys and girls, we don't have integration today, so it's nice we have
a longer time together in the classroom." Some teachers expressed additional
frustration that the time in "integration" was rarely spent on core curricular
activities. In a meeting with her school's principal, a classroom aide in one
school commented, "I like integration, but they should do science or social
studies or P.E. during that time instead of playing."

Integration as Physical Proximity and Interactions Between Students

During integration periods, the sense of what constituted meaningful implementation was left to the individual educator. While some teachers did not call obvious attention to interracial and interethnic student contact during integrated learning or play periods, others were vocally concerned about the ways in which students from various groups related to one another. In a school with a daily, schoolwide integration period, efforts were made to ensure that during "integration" students were from a variety of ethnic backgrounds for both in-classroom activities and out-of-classroom resource services. One resource teacher who ran a Title I–funded out-of-classroom literacy skills development program included students from various backgrounds in her group, her rationale being, "I want to mix these groups because I'm doing it during integration, so I don't want all the Black kids in one group."

Some teachers expressed concern that during designated "integration" times, students tended to sit and interact with their original classmates. Teachers, therefore, tried to shape seating patterns by putting chairs between students from the same classroom or by telling students not to sit next to their classmates during integration time. During a classroom observation in one school, a teacher of an English-only class arranged for her students to watch a video in the afternoon. Over lunch, she asked the teacher of the Chinese bilingual first-grade class if she wanted to bring her students as well. As the teacher of the English-only class was seating her students in the library, the students from the Chinese bilingual classroom appeared at the door. Quickly, she moved a few empty chairs between her students, instructing them to "make room for the little Chinese people," and guiding her colleague's students to the seats interspersed among her primarily black students. In another school, a first-grade teacher told the students in her "integration group" to sit in a circle. Upon seeing that all of the students from the Chinese bilingual classroom were sitting next to one another, she told some students to move, saying, "Don't sit next to anybody from your classroom." After taking some students by the wrist and leading them to sit between children from different classrooms, she turned to me, shrugged her shoulders, and uttered, "They [the students from the Chinese bilingual class] always sit together." During another observation, one of her colleagues explained her perception of a specific need for integration: "The Oriental children only play together."

During a faculty meeting at the school that initially relied on school-wide special days to formally integrate students, teachers noted that playground activities were organized racially and ethnically. While debating methods for distributing playground equipment during lunch and recess, these teachers began addressing the lack of interaction between students from different ethnic groups. In a heated conversation about the number and distribution of Koosh balls[2] on the playground, teachers engaged in the following dialogue:

> *Teacher 1:* Only the Chinese use it [koosh balls].
> *Teacher 2:* No, my Latino kids use it, too.
> *Teacher 1:* Not in the primary grades.
> *Teacher 3:* Definitely not the African American kids.

Since in this school, as in all others, lunch and recess were intended to count toward the 20% of the school day in integrated activities, these teachers conveyed little faith that the playground constituted an integrated environment. During an interview, one school staff member commented, "They're out on the playground together, but they're not playing together." Whether in the classroom or on the playground, the physical proximity and interactions between students came to represent a broader sense of "integration."

Integration as a Respite from a Challenging Teaching Load

In some schools, "integration periods" were presented as a way to ease the teaching loads of teachers with overcrowded classrooms. In many schools, the bilingual classes tended to be smaller than the English-only and English-language-development classes, the latter of which are classes for students who are not in bilingual classes or whose native language is not offered in the bilingual education program at the school. In some cases, the difference could be up to 10 students. School administrators and resource teachers occasionally offered "integration" as a consolation for the uneven distribution of students.

Students were more equitably distributed among grade-level teachers during the "integration" classes. In addition to the uneven numbers of students between the same grade-level classrooms, some teachers expressed the feeling that certain classes were harder to teach. These teachers suggested that the English-only and English-language-development classes—which tended to be composed predominantly of black students—were more challenging and harder to teach, while the students in bilingual education—namely, the Chinese bilingual program—were well-behaved, motivated, and easier to teach. While not representative of the entire teaching staff of any one school or the studied schools more generally, the above attitude and the perception of how "integration" could make for an easier teaching load were typified in the strategy one resource teacher used to convince classroom teachers of the benefits of this program. According to him, teachers in the English-only and English-language-development classes complained simultaneously that they had to integrate their classrooms and that they did not have the opportunity to teach the Chinese students, who were almost exclusively in bilingual classrooms. He claimed to try to motivate these teachers by saying that "integration" gives them a chance to "divide up their loony tunes" and teach the Chinese students. Invoking his perception of racial preferences on the part of the teachers, he represented "integration" as a benefit to teachers who wanted the opportunity to teach students whom they otherwise would not have the opportunity to teach. Here the lenses of racism and racial essentialism (Omi & Winant, 1994, pp. 53–76) were used to explain, justify, and utilize "integration" in ways clearly contradictory to the equity-seeking policies from which this strategy emerged.[3]

Integration as a Necessary Inconvenience to Ease Racial Tension

Some school-based practitioners, and particularly those in schools without structured periods of integrated activities, discussed the value of integrated environments in faculty meetings and interviews. Noting that before the recent decisions about bilingual education, the schools were integrated "normally" or "naturally," they voiced the need for integrated activities to appease racial tension in the schools. Some educators mentioned fights "by race lines" and "derogatory racial remarks" as justification for the need for routinized and structured integrated activities. At a grade-level meeting with the principal at one school, a classroom aide shared her despair over the race-based fighting and racial slurs she had observed between first- and second-grade students. Structured integrated activities were presented as the solution.

Even with the representation of "integration" as a necessary inconvenience toward a larger social goal, not one practitioner expressed the belief that integrated periods of time, even on a daily basis, could address the powerful manifestations of segregation communicated through daily school routines, nor the possibility that these routines somehow provided more equitable educational opportunities. However, they did see bilingual education and desegregation policies as a source of the segregated nature of their schools, and recognized that these policies were based on principles of equity at their construction. During the hurried school days, the larger equity-oriented goals of bilingual education and desegregation were rarely discussed as their combined implementation created racially organized and racially oriented school practices. Instead, the culture of these policies introduced language and routines that focused on the more immediate, technical scheduling procedures, such as where students were supposed to be at given times of the day, how they were going to be transported from one place to another, what activities could be done "during integration," and the coordination of specialized services with the "integration schedule."

RACE-BASED MESSAGES IN THE CULTURE OF POLICY

The language and practice of "integration" became part of the schools' cultures. They became part of the daily routines and came to mean something quite different from the equity-minded objectives of desegregation and bilingual education policies. These representations of "integration" delivered lessons to students and became part of a hidden curriculum that they experienced on various dimensions. What were some of the hidden curricular lessons that students might have learned?

First, these schools communicated that academic activities take place in largely segregated environments. The daily enactment of proximal segregated learning naturalized racial/ethnic isolation each day as students stood in ethnically/racially homogenous lines to say the Pledge of Allegiance and walk into their classrooms. The racialization of daily school routines taught students that race/ethnicity is salient in the way we organize ourselves and are organized in schools. This is not to say that schools might be the only place where students learn the salience of race. Racial and ethnic segregation exists in neighborhoods, places of worship, and other public and private institutions in most children's lives. However, the proximal nature of within-school school segregation, where children are in classes only with others from their racial or ethnic group, and see that the class next door houses a different group, naturalizes not only segregation, but the sense that learning should be organized by race. Integrated activities were generally nonacademic. Classrooms were most predominantly integrated for lunchtime, recess, and other non-core-curricular activities. The integration periods, whether daily or not, focused largely on exercises such as conflict resolution, group games, and arts and crafts.[4] The concentration of such activities during "integration" time delivers a message to students that less structured and less academically oriented lessons are appropriate for integrated environments while serious schooling happens in largely segregated environments.

Second, the ways in which practitioners consciously tried to interrupt some students' tendencies to sit with their classmates during "integration" suggests that at times being with one's own ethnic group is a problem. Indeed, while the students learn that the natural educational condition is racially, ethnically, and linguistically segregated, they are also shown that during scheduled times of the day one should not be with one's own group or, for students in Chinese or Spanish bilingual classes, one should not speak one's home language. Whereas the bilingual classes were conducted mostly in the native language of the students, all "integration" classes were conducted in English. The times of day marked as "integration," then, had different rules for interaction and expression than the rest of the day.

Third, through the communication between practitioners and students, the more general meanings of integration as a mechanism to achieve equality of educational opportunity were reduced to classroom switching and technical school schedules and routines. Students internalized and expressed the language of "integration" similarly to their teachers, asking each other, "Who's your integration teacher?" and asking their teachers, "Can I finish this after integration?" As part of a daily routine or schedule, "integration" became one more activity parallel on a list with "school assembly," "language arts," or "math."

Fourth, the integration period as a set-aside time interrupted what practitioners represent as "normal" school practices. This representation naturalized the segregated nature of the institution and placed integrated learning time as a modified variant on typical school routines. That is not to say that all teachers believed that segregated classrooms were a natural condition: Indeed, many complained that their classes had previously been integrated, but that "the district," "bilingual education," or "policies" had segregated them. Some likened the ethnic segregation to "apartheid" and "ethnic tracking." Regardless of individual teacher resistance to the segregation, the enactments of the integration time as described above set it aside as an unusual part of the school day, outside of typical classroom learning activities.

Finally, students learned that the natural condition of public institutions is racially and ethnically segregated, a lesson that legitimates and reifies the perception of meaningful distinctions based on such variations in human characteristics. Certainly, the use of integration time to interrupt the naturalized condition suggests that such segregation is problematic, at least for a defined part of the day. Regardless of the integration schedule or approach, the institutional arrangement largely segregated students, and that segregation taught students what racial/ethnic differences mean in public institutions.

School-based educators faced the daunting task of helping students navigate the meaning of this "integration" time. However, they themselves struggled with its meaning. During my observations in the schools, the difficulty that teachers had in helping students make sense of the racially bizarre messages communicated by the culture of these policies came through at various moments. How should teachers explain that the natural condition of schooling is racial segregation, that integrated learning only happens after considerable shuffling of students, and that at times teachers will ask students to sit next to children who do not look like them? These broader navigational questions were left for the most part unexplored with children. In fact, when one first-grade teacher was asked, "What's integration?" by a student whose class had just been told, "If you're not quiet, you're not going to integration," the teacher responded, "It's when we switch classrooms."

Psychologist Beverly Tatum writes, "[w]hen we adults reflect on our own race-related memories, we may recall times when we did not get the help we needed to sift through the confusing messages we received" (1997, p. 50). Imagine the memories that these students will reflect upon as adults.

CONCLUSION

Equity-oriented education policies are rife with confusing messages about difference in race, ethnicity, language, and "ability." These messages are communicated to children through transmission of the culture of policy. When efforts to provide adequate and equitable educational opportunities in a society organized by race and class translate into judicial and legislative education policies, race-based messages are conveyed through the language and rituals of schooling. The culture of policy theory provides a framework for understanding how complicated ethnic and racial identities are reduced to rigid classification schemes and how classroom ethnic and racial compositions are organized and then reorganized based on limited, and at times educationally insignificant, information. Like Title I, the equity-oriented policies of bilingual education, desegregation, special education, and school reorganization for low-performing schools all share a tendency to categorize and mark certain students or schools, to define them as lacking and deficient, to explain difference and diversity in reductive and stigmatizing ways, and to create incentives for the segregation of the population marked as deficient in order to generate resources with which to serve them.

My observations of school-based routines and rituals reveal a culture of policy that is at times absurd, at times appalling. Readers have been dismayed at the insensitivity and bias expressed by individual teachers and the seeming comfort with which some teachers in the studied schools made inappropriate, offensive, and outright racist comments. In my view, a focus on individual behaviors without investigation of the overall policy and organizational context is misguided. It is easy to get angry at individual expressions of bias. It is far more difficult to confront systems—be they of belief, behavior, or policy—that foster, encourage, and leverage existing societal biases.

My argument is not that the words and behaviors of school-based practitioners result from the culture of policy. Rather, the culture of policy nurtures both language and ritual where individual and societal biases are exposed and reinforced through school-based practices. The policies of desegregation and bilingual education both espouse important, relevant, and necessary egalitarian and pluralistic goals. And at the school level, there are legitimate reasons to group students by instructional needs (which might require heterogeneity of relevant student characteristics at times and homogeneity of relevant student characteristics at other times). However, practitioners who operate within these policy cultures cannot ignore the cultural implications of policy-generated arrangements, such as the race-based meanings that result from the combined implementation of egalitarian polices. But what alternatives exist for practitioners who see the cultural problems in strict policy adherence and want to avoid instilling bias in the next generation?

The answer again lies in schools themselves. As with Title I, strict compliance with policy mandates leads to fragmented approaches to student instruction, with minimal attention to the central goals that framed the policy's construction. If school-based leaders and teachers were to practice thoughtful noncompliance with policy mandates, they might approximate egalitarian goals more effectively. Rather than using policy compliance as an organizing principle for the language and routines of schooling, what if practitioners were to organize for instruction and equity? What would staff meetings look like if conversations were shaped not around policy compliance, but rather around instructional approaches and equitable access to effective teaching? In order to move away from the trappings of a policy culture that provides a climate that protects and nurtures bias, school-based practitioners need different ways of seeing and orientations to their work. The following chapter addresses how practitioners might organize for instruction and equity in the context of the latest authorization of Title I: the No Child Left Behind legislation.

Possibility and Potential in the Culture of Education Policy

The preceding chapters exposed the language and rituals of policy practice. The intent of this chapter is to probe the culture of policy and craft approaches to alternative language and rituals that might better align with the stated goals of equity-seeking policies.

My review of Title I's historical trajectory illustrates the cultural mores of policy setting and how members of Congress deploy conceptions of policy beneficiaries grounded in ideological assumptions, limited understandings, and contemporary social science to support their policy proposals. Their discourse relies on multiple metaphors (poverty as illness, students as deviants, teachers as soldiers) and theories of cause and effect (if a student is poor, he or she will be "handicapped") that form the contours of policy practice in schools. These metaphors and theories are central to the policy process. While we can probe, question, and challenge the metaphors that elected officials use to justify policy proposals, we cannot wish the existence of metaphorical thinking and limited mental models away. We need to constantly challenge our understandings of a policy's supposed beneficiaries, the images we associate with those beneficiaries, and how the information we get about the beneficiaries through policy channels taints our approach to seeing and understanding their promise and potential.

Focusing on Title I policy, the language and rituals of schools—even some 30 years after the policy's inception—reveal daily reliance on policy-generated categories to label and sort students by policy-related designations. Based on eligibility criteria, funding streams, and adult employment arrangements, school-level discourse responds to the conceptions of students leveraged in Congress and enlivened in the classroom. For some practitioners, policy language and routines provide a state-sanctioned anchor—indeed, a state-authored anchor—for implicit and explicit biases against poor and minority children. For other educators, the language and routines of policy practice curtail collective abilities to provide well-integrated, meaningful, and

rigorous educational opportunities to students. Resisting the limited and lim-
iting features of organizing schools for policy compliance, these educators
practice thoughtful noncompliance with regulations and rituals that they
deem to work against student learning.

Some may argue that the tendencies I have identified in the culture of
policy framework can be remedied by better policy constructions. In fact, in
discussing and presenting the culture of policy framework, I have often been
challenged to explain how recent reauthorization schemes (and particularly
the George W. Bush administration's No Child Left Behind Act of 2001),
alternative organizational strategies, or different incentive structures might
contribute to or diminish the bizarre language and rituals shaped by policy
culture. Indeed, I am often asked whether better policy can influence better
policy culture. This last chapter, therefore, considers the possibilities of
resisting the culture of policy through new legislation and local practices.

First, I review the No Child Left Behind legislation in order to explore
whether the new schemes and incentive structures might avoid the policy-
scripted language and routines grounded in deficit thinking, perverse incentives, and superficial adherence to technical policy regulations. I focus this
analysis on the concurrent implementation of two central aspects of the recent
legislation, the identification of and proposed remedies for a new policy-
promoted category of thought—"failing schools"—and the testing of students to determine their "average yearly progress" (AYP), to evaluate the
cultural dimensions of the most recent Title I policy construction. Through
this analysis, I consider the following questions: What language and routines
does the No Child Left Behind Act of 2001 introduce in schools that differ
from past policy customs? How does this policy iteration move away from
or enhance the deficit orientation of past Title I approaches? What do we
know about the behavior of educators, administrators, and parents in response to the new legislation?

Out of this analysis, an important question arises: Are there ways out
of the culture of policy? More specifically, can institutions, organizations,
and individuals create the conditions to avoid the pernicious and anti-
egalitarian effects of the culture of policy as detailed in this book? Or are
some forms of policy culture inevitable?

THE CULTURE OF POLICY AND
THE NO CHILD LEFT BEHIND ACT

Passed in January 2002, the No Child Left Behind Act (NCLB) made notable symbolic changes to Title I policy. In the context of the movement toward educational standards, testing, and accountability practices, this policy
abandons some of the language linking poverty and student performance,

instead focusing discursively on *school* performance in the service of *all* children. Unlike its predecessors, this policy has its own Web site announcing a "new era in education," with patriotic banners, photographs of President George W. Bush and Secretary of Education Rod Paige, and links to both state and local school performance data as well as the actual legislation text (http://www.nochildleftbehind.gov). Aimed at parents and community members, the web site does not address educators, nor does it show any photographs of educators with students. Instead, the president and the secretary of education are shown in classrooms, leaning over students at computers, and making speeches. The legislation even has its own logo, in the form of two pages of an open book; on the right, the page is the blue of the United States flag with three stars above a white silhouette of what appears to be a young boy, on the left, the page dons red and white stripes. The policy is represented in this web site as the beginning of a new era of patriotism, parental involvement, and proximity to our nation's leaders,[1] rather than the distant workings of the Washington bureaucracy.

The statement of purpose for Title I, now entitled "Improving the Academic Achievement of the Disadvantaged," reads:

> The purpose of this title is to ensure that all children have a fair, equal, and significant opportunity to obtain a high-quality education and reach, at a minimum, proficiency on challenging State academic achievement standards and state academic assessments. (No Child Left Behind Act of 2001, 2002, Sec. 1001)

The text of the legislation proposes that in order for all children to have such opportunities, clear standards and accountability practices must be put into place. Noting the need to meet the specific educational needs of "low-achieving children in our Nation's highest-poverty schools, limited English proficient children, migratory children, children with disabilities, Indian children, neglected or delinquent children, and young children in need of reading assistance" (NCLB, Sec. 1001), the legislation does call attention to the categories of children listed in past policy iterations. However, the 2002 legislation focuses consistently on academic achievement and the school's responsibility for providing high-quality educational opportunities to all students.

Given the discourse of high standards and achievement for all children, and the stated desire to close the "achievement gap between high- and low-performing children, especially the achievement gaps between minority and non-minority students, and between disadvantaged children and their more advantaged peers" (NCLB, Sec. 1001), the policy continues the legacy of a stated orientation to issues of equity. And the actual policy, for the first time, contains substantive educational content, taking a position on best practices in both early literacy instruction and the measurement of academic progress, as well as insisting that instructional approaches be deemed successful based on "scientifically based research."

Irrespective of the specific approaches posited in the legislation as best practices (such as a strict, phonetic approach to early literacy instruction), the attention to explicit pedagogical, instructional, and curricular approaches and how we know that they are effective is noteworthy in the most recent legislation and notably absent in former Title I iterations. The Bush administration's bill is particularly focused on the practice of using research findings to determine the value of educational approaches. Indeed, the No Child Left Behind legislation reportedly refers to "scientifically based research" over 100 times (Traub, 2002, p. 24). The issues of what constitutes "scientifically based research" and who should conduct it (such as the curriculum developers and publishers themselves or some independent research group) are not addressed.

The legislation, which received strong bipartisan support, represents potential to move away from some of the cultural elements of past policy. First, the policy increased local flexibility in implementation practices so that schools do not need to label individual students as eligible for school-based services. Second, the legislation provides a clear orientation toward specific instructional approaches, particularly regarding early literacy instruction. And third, the problem that the policy aims to address is one of *school* performance rather than *student* performance. Indeed, if a school is deemed "failing" or if any teachers are not deemed "highly qualified" for classroom teaching (based on their teaching credential or participation in a credential program), the school principal must send letters to the parents informing them of the school's shortcomings. And according to the legislation, parents of students in "failing schools" have the opportunity to transfer their children to a higher-performing public school.

The Language and Routines of NCLB

On first blush, the discursive tendencies of No Child Left Behind (2001) are notably different than those of its predecessors. It has a clear instructional component (whether or not we agree with the approach or the level of expectations that it represents, the existence of an instructional approach in this federal education policy is novel); it does not require schools to label children for services, thus avoiding some of the naming and framing practices that stigmatized eligible students in past policy constructions; it posits the "problem" of poor performance as an institutional, rather than individual, concern; it creates accountability mechanisms for student performance through average yearly progress rather than simply focusing on service provision; and, finally, it removes past incentives for identifying a deficient or defective population of students.

In some ways, the new legislation moves away from the incentives for identifying and perpetuating deviant populations present in the initial legislation and the culture of policy framework. In fact, this policy now provides disincentives, rather than rewards, for chronic low performance among a school's student body. Instead of maximizing revenues from identifying poor performance, states and districts can only maintain federal dollars through demonstrating that their schools meet performance standards. The equity-minded observer would hope that the states, districts, and schools would abandon ineffective instructional practices, hire qualified teachers, provide them with further training in the various educational practices that best serve a full range of students, and commit to do whatever it takes to raise the performance of students so that they meet the standards determined by each state.

Unfortunately, the culture of policy has perpetuated a stubborn set of low expectations and perverse approaches to educating children in resource-strapped communities. Early observations of current Title I implementation suggest that rather than assuming the responsibility for raising student performance levels, states are instead lowering their performance standards (Robelen, 2002; Rothstein, 2002; Schemo, 2002, August 27). In fact, an article in *Education Week* after passage of NCLB asserts that "[a]t least a few states, such as Colorado, Connecticut, and Louisiana, have taken steps to set 'proficient' definitions for purposes of the federal law that are less demanding than the levels set under state law" (Robelen, 2002, p. 29). Since the category of "failing schools" is based on whether or not schools meet a set of state-drafted performance standards, grounded in test-based measures of academic proficiency, states now have incentives to lower their standards so that fewer schools are identified as failing. Now schools and states will be sanctioned rather than rewarded for identifying failure.

In fact, the sanctions in large part take resources away from "failing schools" and move them to private and for-profit providers of educational services. According to education scholar Richard Elmore (2002), the "most generous interpretation" of NCLB is that it intends to "galvanize and focus the attention of educators around the problem of failing schools"; the "less generous interpretation" is that NCLB "is designed to . . . move public education funds from public schools to privately-managed schools and supplementary service providers operated with public funds" (p. 2). However we interpret the intentions of the legislation, the moniker of "failing school" caries consequences for the ways in which resources, and students, are distributed within, and now outside of, school systems.

In addition to the consequences for material resources to schools and students, the new policy-generated label of "failing school," which is now placed not on specific individuals but on the entire institution, stigmatizes those individuals and groups of students, teachers, and community members associated with the school named as a failure. The use of the term "failing school" leverages the biases against children in poverty in more nuanced ways than the term "Title I" or "educationally deprived" student did. Critical consideration of the categories of thought embedded in this new policy again exposes how biases against children in poverty are deeply entrenched in our culture at all levels of education. For example, the lowering of state standards so that fewer schools are deemed "failing" reveals a deeply held belief that either some children just cannot meet the standards or some teachers simply cannot bring all students to high performance levels, or both. Or perhaps the assumption revealed here is that lowering standards is easier than teaching poor kids.

The proposed remedy for "failing schools" through student transfer also maintains some of the pernicious elements of the culture of policy. Part of the theory behind the student transfer option is that when parents learn that their child's school is "failing," they will demand that she or he be moved to another school, and when a number of parents demand such transfers, the bad schools will be forced to close down. This logic is similar to that of voucher proponents and advocates of other school choice schemes in which the market forces of supply and demand drive out ineffective schools. Competition for students theoretically leads to improved instructional practices and better academic outcomes. However, by providing vouchers or guaranteed transfers to children identified as being from "failing schools," we stigmatize those children as low-performing and provide a disincentive to high-performing schools to accept them (especially when school success is reliant on the same measures that deem the child's original school to be a failure). Recent newspaper reports suggest that very few districts are actually offering such transfers (due to overcrowding), very few parents are requesting such transfers (due to familiarity, convenience, and transportation), and very few high-performing schools are interested in accepting students from "failing schools" (due to fear of the students' potential for continued low performance in a high-performing school, thus compromising the performance of that school) (Rothstein, 2002; Schemo, 2002, August 28, 2002, November 27). In fact, reports from New York City suggest that middle-class parents who want their children to attend a better school than the relatively high-performing one they currently attend are temporarily placing their children in low-performing schools so they can be the first ones to transfer them to schools that are even higher-performing than their children's original school (Lucadamo, 2003, February 24). Also, in New York City high-performing schools are being forced to accept all transfers, leading to tremendous overcrowding.

Unless, however, parents signal their children as middle-class and reveal their entire strategy, they risk having their child stigmatized in the new school as low-performing. If students with transfers are marked as low-performing, and high-performing schools have some discretion over which children they admit (which in urban areas many high-performing schools do), the signal of past educational failures (even if framed as the responsibility of the institution and not the individual) provides a disincentive for schools to accept a marked, marred student. Students seeking transfers are still marked as defective or deficient based on their prior enrollment in a failing school. The labeling practices in the culture of policy continue despite deliberate schemes for eradicating what the new legislation refers to as the "soft bias of low expectations."

The new legislation, therefore, has not yet shaken the trappings or traps of the culture of policy. In an era of educational standards and accountability, the act of lowering state performance standards is firmly in keeping with the culture of policy, but discordant, yet again, with equity-oriented policy goals. Unfortunately, the way states and the federal government have approached accountability in Title I policy has prevented us from accounting for anything meaningful. We count the numbers of children served, but do not question how they are served. We analyze test-score data with minimal consideration of the opportunities to learn that policies might have provided eligible students. We rarely use any data to explore the areas of instruction that teachers have mastered or that they need to master. We do not use the data to inform instructional practices so that students can meet educational standards through mastery of content knowledge and academic skills. We may test children more, but we do not use the tests to inform instructional practice or what teachers need to learn. Despite bipartisan efforts to reframe the policy problem, the conceptualization of policy beneficiaries as deficient (now through lowered standards and the consequences of marking "failing schools" on the children associated with those schools) persists in altered form. The question for concerned educators and other equity-minded individuals, then, is how to resist the culture of policy.

RESISTING THE CULTURE OF POLICY

As demonstrated, the culture of policy permeates every level of policy authorization, interpretation, and implementation. Legislators frame social problems through provocative rhetorical portraits of policy beneficiaries based on assumptions about the lives that those affected by policy lead. Federal, state, and local bureaucrats interpret the policy regulations that are built on these assumptions, and filter them through their own theories about the lives of the populations served. Local practitioners make their own sense of policy mandates, further interpreting the policy's intent and combining or challenging the policy proscriptions with personal beliefs about the policy beneficiaries. Given the pervasive nature of the culture of policy, where should we seek to intervene? If we agree that the destructive, anti-egalitarian effects of the culture of policy are worth addressing, and hopefully minimizing, on what level of policy construction or implementation should we focus? How can we make equity-oriented policy practice more consistent with egalitarian goals?

Given the incentives that motivate elected officials, the technical trappings of bureaucracies, and the pressures placed on local school districts, it is my belief that cultural resistance at the *local school level* can best shape the practice of equity-seeking policies in ways that are in accordance with the policies' goals. In fact, I contend that in order to counter the dominant equity-oriented policy culture while benefiting from whatever resources such policies might offer, school-based practitioners must engage in forms of cultural insurgence. This approach requires both reflection and vigilance in the daily work of practitioners. While crucial, the resistance that I advocate cannot be reduced to a new silver bullet, a recipe for a change, or a checklist for improvement. Rather, it requires a concrete and relentless focus of resources on the effective instruction of students, no matter who those students are or what it takes to figure out what they already know and teachers need to teach them. It requires challenging the prior assumptions, general language, and commonly held biases that name and frame students as defective and deficient, while embracing responsibility for their learning. It means seeing students' strengths and building on those strengths through sound, adaptive instructional practice.

Our strategies for holding schools and teachers accountable for Title I delivery conceptualize the policy problem as one of student poverty and performance. At the school level, we need to reconceptualize this problem as one of effective instruction, as one centered on figuring out how students learn, and as one focused on determining how teachers should teach so that their instructional practice meets the diverse needs of individual learners. This construction of the problem requires attention to the categories of thought that govern how adults approach student learning. By making explicit the categories of thought promoted by policies and those held by practitioners, local educators can begin to challenge the ways in which policies and people explain, react to, and come to expect student underperformance. The work of articulating and challenging the often taken-for-granted language and routines of policies is difficult, yet necessary for resisting the culture of policy. Otherwise, policies simply transmit and nurture the types of bias that perpetuate the very problems they claim to remedy. So how might we initiate these difficult conversations?

The How and What of School Talk

When schools organize for policy compliance, policy language and routines are taken for granted as normal parts of school-based vocabulary and behavior. The categories of thought built into the policies circumscribe the categories of thought in practice. Compliance with policy mandates, however, leads to fragmentation of services, compartmentalization of core educational functions, and a cycle of blame in which educators, families, children, and politicians all point fingers at each other for persistent educational failure on everybody's part.

Rather than organizing for compliance, then, schools need to organize their language and rituals around instruction and equity. What, then, would the language and rituals of instruction and equity look like?

The language and routines of instruction focus on continuous, active curiosity. Focusing on teachers, principals, students, and parents as continuous, public learners, the organizing principle of instruction leads to a learning process in which where a student or teacher starts is simply a starting point. The rituals of practice then become the rituals of collaboration, of co-construction, and of coaching all school community members in the practice of thinking, of figuring out, and of analyzing. In a framework of this nature, practitioners resist generalizations and assumptions, and openly and honestly explore their own biases.

The preceding chapters raise a number of fundamental questions for the schools under study. For example, how should education be provided in different languages within one school, if not in segregated classrooms? How should students divide their day to enable communication across language boundaries and barriers? How should schools organize for effective education of children with less material resources than most schools account for in their curricular design and delivery?

There are no easy answers to any of these questions. However, schools that organize for instruction and equity can approach these quandaries through reflective dialogue about how to assess students' learning needs, assess teachers' learning needs, and devise a strategic plan for thoughtfully and effectively addressing the needs of the adult learners in the service of the student learners. The real challenge is cultivating the reflective dialogue, and demonstrating how thoughtful noncompliance better serves the needs than strict compliance with policy mandates might. The work I am advocating here requires a strong school-based leader who is comfortable enough with her or his instructional leadership to acknowledge, observe, and struggle publicly with the language and rituals deployed by the culture of policy.

In my work with aspiring principals for New York City schools, I have found that typical, compliance-based attention to policy-driven language and rituals has often caused some form of cultural conflict within and between well meaning future school leaders. The following exchange between an aspiring principal (currently a teacher) and myself highlights the cultural gear-grinding necessary to confront and challenge policy-driven language and routines, and how challenging a simple term such as "at risk" unravels an entire belief system based on labeling and sorting for instructional purposes.

The exchange begins with my comments on a collaborative assignment submitted by a group of aspiring leaders that detailed their plans for professional development in a school. Included in their plan were special services for "at-risk students." Seeking to challenge the future principals' use of the term "at risk" as a way to probe the assumptions built around policy-generated language, I wrote to my students the following comments:[2]

> When you refer to students as "at risk," you leave vague what exactly the issue is for instruction. Additionally, this term and other similar labels tend to lower teachers' expectations for what students can do. If you frame the issue in concrete terms of the students' academic performance (a temporary, action-oriented designation, rather than descriptive), you provide the teachers with more room to work and set a tone for communication about children at your school. We tend to take these terms for granted, use them as codes for all kinds of shared and unshared conceptions of students, and often forget what we are really trying to describe.

My intention in writing the above to my students was to call into question the language of risk that is institutionalized by district and state policy constructions. Although school-level practitioners are frequently required, by externally crafted regulations and policies, to identify and count students who are considered "at risk," I wanted these future principals to struggle with this policy-speak as they constructed plans for serving students more effectively. Indeed, I wanted them to see that in order to serve students in meaningful and effective ways, it would be necessary to confront, probe, and challenge this policy-speak, as its use has been linked to lowered teacher expectations. After receiving my comments, one of the group members responded:

> Dear Sandra,
> Since you questioned the term "At Risk" as vague, (and because this was my contribution), I'd like to clarify. As a member of the Pupil Personnel Team [a committee typically composed of guidance counselors, psychologists, teachers, and social workers] of [my school] for the past several years, we regularly identify "At-Risk" students, who are struggling academically and/or who [are] exhibiting behavioral, emotional or attention difficulties; thus, I feel it is my responsibility to clarify.
> In [the district where I work], the term "At Risk" is commonly used at Pupil Personal Team (PPT) meetings and at all schools in [my district] (and by now, probably all other schools in [the city]). Each school in [the state] is required by law, under The New Continuum [a new set

of policies for special education] to form PPTs to identify and service "At-Risk students," who clearly need help (academic or counseling) . . . According to The New Continuum [special education policy], which went into effect last September, "At-Risk" students must be identified, and a plan of action is formed that is custom-tailored to service the child's needs . . . Sometimes parents-in-denial are very resistant to signing permission to evaluate for Special Education services and their children flounder in the large classes without help; thus, servicing the children as "At-Risk" is a way to circumvent the parent's objection [to the] Special Education referral and give the student the much needed help . . . Parents who do not like the term "Special Education" seem quite comfortable if their child gets help from the "Support Teacher," which has become the new nickname for "Special Education Teacher Support Service."

I've been intimately involved in this process for the last several years, and as a PPT member at my school since its inception, I feel qualified to state that "At Risk" is a term used, not as a put-down, but to identify students who need help, pinpoint the specific service needed, and assign staff to help the struggling student . . . Perhaps because I've been doing this for so long, and by now most general educators are also familiar with the term "At Risk," I do not think it is vague. As a Special Educator for 21 years, I do not "take those terms for granted;" nor do I "use them as codes for kinds of shared and unshared conceptions of students."

The aspiring principal's response to my inquiry reveals the language and rituals built into the culture of policy at the school level. She begins by attempting a concrete definition of the term "at risk," which includes academic, behavioral, emotional, and attention problems. Unfortunately, this definition spans such a wide range that it further demonstrates the vague nature of the construct, even in the context of an attempt to concretize the definition. It is a language of certainty rather than a language of inquiry. Rather than posit the challenge as one of figuring out what adults need to know in order to best meet the learning needs of the students, "at risk" is presented with certainty—and several years of experience to back that certainty—as a meaningful category of thought, no matter how imprecise its definition. With such an amorphous conception of school-based struggle, the definition must rely on an implicit norm. The sense of that norm at this particular educator's school might be quite different than the norm at a different school, further rendering the construct of "at risk" meaningless. From this attempt at a definition, the educator moves on to describe what is "required by law" and how at-risk students "must be identified." She clearly invokes the external policy forces that require her use of this language. Then, after defending her use of the term on definitional and legalistic grounds, she asserts her professional competence and ties her sense of her own competence to the mastery of these terms.

Now, it is unfair to take my analysis here as a vilification of this individual practitioner. She is simply responding to the cultural tendencies and incentive structures of the institution in which she works. Noting the above, I responded with the following:

> Dear [Aspiring Leader],
> I appreciate the time and thought you took to respond to my comment. Let me clarify my point in calling attention to the terms and categories that we use to identify students in schools. The issue of [the at-risk] term (as well as any other term that is generated from a federal, state, or district policy) is one of shared meaning . . . If you ask a group of practitioners working in the same school with the same students what the children are "at risk" of, you can hear anything from (depending on the grade, age, and programs available in the school) "not meeting standards" to "dropping out of school" to "getting AIDS" to "getting pregnant" to "I don't know, they're just at-risk." It is often presented as a condition itself, rather than an indicator of performance . . . I do not dispute that these are common terms in your professional practice. In fact, it is because they are so common, and often imposed on school personnel by policy-makers, that I highlight them in your work. Please be clear that this suggestion on my part did not contribute to my assessment of your project . . .
>
> I highlight these issues to generate some thinking about the language and tone you want to set as leaders. As we [prepare] the next generation of educational leaders, we want people to take a critical look at the language known to some as "education-ese" and to think about how through the use of these terms, a school leader sets a tone about how students are discussed in public forums and documents . . . As you know, many documents will ask you to identify your "at-risk students" (and as you certainly know from your 21 years of practice, the terms that we use have and will continue to change). To my mind, sticking to the core issues of student performance when describing the students rather than the categories in which we place them (such as "at-risk" which in and of itself has no substantive meaning—we are all at risk of a lot of things) helps focus the faculty on the core issues of instruction without contributing to dynamics that . . . lower teachers' expectations of what children can do.

My intention in the above message was to further probe the use of the term "at risk" by highlighting the inconsistencies and incongruities in the definition. I then wanted to tie the term's use to issues of leadership, and how leaders shape the ways in which teaching staffs, students, and parents use these terms. Finally, I wanted to highlight how terms like "at risk" interfere with teachers' expectations of students, which contribute negatively to the educational process. Her response was as follows:

> Dear Sandra,
> Your points are well taken and I concur that overuse and misuse of "education-ese" may lower teachers' expectations of student achievement. I also concur that the principal sets the tone of how students are discussed in meetings and documents. From my observations, there are more often misconceptions among general educators, who bandy around terms (often inaccurate) to describe struggling academic[ally] and/or behaviorally challenged students.
>   Although some educators are quick to categorize, often inaccurately, I've always stuck to descriptive terms of student's performance and functioning. Describing a student in observable terms academically and socially/emotionally is what I've done for every student annually while writing IEPs [individualized education plans] and meeting with general education teachers. The academic and behavioral goals must be written in ways that progress can be assessed.
>   My point is if the audience was general education teachers, then I wholeheartedly agree with you, that the term "At Risk" must be defined. However, a Superintendent would only need clarification if the "risk" is academic (being specific) or an emotional/social/interpersonal-skill issue. However, since you assured me that the grades for the Action Plan will not be affected by my choice of words, I won't belabor the point anymore.

Her statements here are particularly revealing of the incentive structure and routines in which she works. First, she draws a distinction between herself and some "general educators" who, in her estimation, label and categorize students erroneously. She then rightfully defends the practice of describing students in observable terms and setting measurable performance goals. She then takes on the question of audience (the general educators need a clear definition of the "at risk" term, while the superintendent would only need substantive clarification). And, finally, since this entire conversation was inspired by my reaction to a graded assignment, she stated that since her use of the term "at risk" did not affect her grade, she would drop the dialogue.

Now, whether or not this particular exchange made any difference in how she thinks about, talks about, or writes about students cannot be measured easily. In fact, I include this rather lengthy and somewhat parochial exchange because it demonstrates how difficult it is to engage in the type of dialogue that is necessary for resisting the culture of policy.

But what if school faculties were to engage consistently and collectively in dialogues that pried loose the biases built into the language and routines of policy compliance and questioned the underlying assumptions of practice? What if educators' "grades," so to speak, were connected to their instructional practice and the implications that their naming and framing of children have for that practice? I do not pretend to know how to create widespread incentive structures that discourage the use of labels and confront the deeply held and policy-nourished categories of thought that compromise teachers' abilities to provide meaningful learning opportunities to all students, and especially students whom policies typically name and frame as deficient or defective. However, I think it is important that equity-minded educators engage in the challenging conversations that expose our assumptions and assist us in focusing our efforts continually on educating children.

The question arises, then, of where opportunities for challenging the language and rituals of schools exist on a day-to-day basis. In what capacity can schools engage in a type of cultural insurgency against the language and routines of policies that work against children's growth? How can we all become more cognizant of the categories of thought that govern our interactions with students and each other?

I have observed how local practitioners who resist the culture of education policy can leverage any and all resources to the benefit of student learning. Practitioners who challenge the core assumptions about poverty and potential that are built into equity-oriented policy constructions can align resources for sound instruction without condemning students through lowered expectations. Communities of practitioners, who do the daily work of facing their biases, probing them, and dismantling them for the sake of building on students' strengths, work against policy culture no matter the particular definition of the policy beneficiary or monetary streams. Strong school-based leadership is crucial to this endeavor. Principals have to be prepared to facilitate the difficult conversations, and create a culture in which challenging someone's bias is seen as a gift to that person, and the language and routines are organized around instruction and equity.

Although my analysis of Title I's historical trajectory and school-based practices leads me to the conclusion that any policy scheme that signals, separates, and stigmatizes children as needing more for having less will fall into the traps of the culture of policy, I also believe that there are local practices of cultural resistance that can mitigate their negative effects on students' learning. Simply asking what all the labels mean and questioning how they shape daily practice is an important start.

APPENDIX

Methodology

Since this book explores the language and routines of both Congress and the classroom, I relied on two types of methodology: (a) content analysis of congressional discourse, and (b) multisite qualitative policy analysis of school-based practices. This appendix provides the details of how I collected and analyzed the data from both sources.

CONTENT ANALYSIS OF CONGRESSIONAL DISCOURSE

Chapters 2 and 3 highlight the language and routines of Congress. The data used in these chapters are transcripts of congressional floor debates from the authorization (1965) and reauthorizations (1966, 1967, 1970, 1974, 1978, 1981, 1988, 1994) of Title I of the Elementary and Secondary Education Act. The entire federal education acts, in their various iterations, contain numerous Titles; Title I (or Chapter 1 in 1981 and 1988) received the most attention within the floor debates in every authorization and reauthorization year. Since the focus of this book is on the language and routines of Title I, I analyzed only the sections of the floor debates that referred substantively to the reauthorized act(s) as a whole or specifically to the Title I portion of the act. Also, since various members of Congress read portions of the proposed bill text as part of the floor debates, early iterations of the bill texts formed part of the congressional discourse. I, therefore, included these readings of the draft and final bill texts in my analysis. Similarly, I only included discussions of the multiple amendments introduced during the reauthorizations when they were directly related to Title I.

Each floor debate was read to discern and analyze the themes of that particular reauthorization year, focusing on how the policy beneficiaries were described and their policy-relevant needs depicted. Next, using the QSR NUD*IST® software program for qualitative data analysis, the data were scanned for each mention of the policy beneficiaries (including *child, children, student, students, youth, youngsters, young people, kid, kids, pupil,* and *pupils*), and then coded into categories based on how the policy beneficiaries were characterized. From my review, various analytic categories emerged that typify the content of the social constructions of the policy beneficiaries on the congressional floor. These categories are not mutually exclusive (i.e., some mentions of the policy beneficiary were double- and triple-coded), but provide my best attempt at an exhaustive list of how members of Congress depicted the policy beneficiaries throughout the years of debates. Table A.1 shows the various characterizations of the policy beneficiaries, a description of each category, and illustrative examples from the actual floor debate text.

Once coded, we counted the number of mentions in each category to determine whether the qualitative analysis of congressional discourse was consistent with this more quantitative analysis. The coding exercise revealed various trends echoed in the qualitative analysis. First, the primary characterizations of the policy beneficiaries were commonly in terms of "disadvantage." And second, the portraits of the policy beneficiaries tended to focus on deficits rather than assets. This analysis also allowed us to identify each time that members of Congress discussed students in a particular way (such as when they described the students eligible for Title I as "gifted and talented," which contributed to the analysis in chapter 3).

MULTISITE QUALITATIVE POLICY ANALYSIS OF SCHOOL-BASED PRACTICES

Chapters 4 and 5 of this study evolved out of my dissertation project on the local meanings of Title I in nine urban elementary schools. The methodology for these chapters relied on the techniques of multisite qualitative policy analysis. In this type of analysis, researchers use similar data collection and analysis procedures to address one research question in various settings. Firestone and Herriott (1983, 1984) and Herriott and Firestone (1983) highlight the differences between this type of methodology and traditional qualitative research: (a) this approach emphasizes the codification of questions and variables before fieldwork, as opposed to during fieldwork; (b) it uses standard data collection procedures through semistructured interviews and observations, as opposed to unstructured interviews and observations; and (c) it emphasizes the reduction of verbal narrative to codes and categories, rather than the emphasis on uncoded or loosely organized verbal narrative (Firestone & Herriott, 1983). Although initially this study was based largely on the methods highlighted by Firestone and Herriott, it evolved during my 9 months of data collection. The following sections highlight some of the modifications I made in this methodology while still retaining its essence.

TABLE A.1. Characterizations of Policy Beneficiaries with Descriptions and Examples

Characterization	Description	Example
Abused	Students are described as suffering abuse at home	"abused children" "neglected children"
Academics	Students are characterized in terms of their academic performance	"children who have special problems with reading and math" "low-achieving children"
AFDC (Welfare)	Students are identified as being from families receiving welfare benefits	"AFDC children" "children being supported by the state" "children on welfare"
Age	Students are identified by age or youth	"young students" "school-age children"
Behavior	Students are characterized in terms of their (in most cases negative) behavior	"criminal, unruly and violent students" "hard-core problem children" "delinquent children"
Bilingual	Students are characterized in terms of their command of the English language	"limited English proficiency" "non-English speaking children"
Collective	Children are cast as being part of a collective, part of the country, and/or understood as a collective responsibility	"all American students" "our children"
Desegregation	Students are described based on their participation in desegregation efforts	"children in schools undergoing desegregation"
Disadvantaged	Children are depicted in terms of their poverty and disadvantage (this category was the most prominent of all the characterizations)	"poor children" "disadvantaged students"
Dropout	Students were framed based on their status of having dropped out of school	"dropouts" "out-of-school youth"

(continued)

TABLE A.1. (continued)

Characterization	Description	Example
Eligibility and participation	Students are described based on their eligibility for and participation in Title I programs	"eligible children" "students served by Title I"
Entitlement	Students are described as entitled to or deserving of federally funded education programs	"deserving students" "children who require programs"
Gifted	Children are characterized as being gifted and/or talented	"gifted children" "gifted and talented children"
Handicapped	Students are described based on having physical, mental, or emotional handicaps	"crippled children" "deaf-blind children"
Home-schooled	Foremost in 1994; typically stated as "parents who choose to educate their children at home"	"home-schooled students"
Immigration	Children are described based on their immigration status, typically their lack of documentation	"illegal immigrant children"
In school	Students are described in terms of their enrollment in school	"youth in elementary and secondary school" "schoolchildren" "school system children"
Migratory	Children are described as having parents who are migrant workers	"children of migratory agricultural workers"
Military	Children are described as having parents in the U.S. armed forces	"children of military personnel"
No characterization	Mention of the policy beneficiary without any modification, description, or characterization	"children" "students"
Numbers/rates	Children are referred to in rates, counts, percentages, and numbers	"percentage of students" "child poverty rate"
Orphan/foster	Children are described as living away from their biological parents, as wards of the state	"children in foster homes" "children living in facilities for orphans"

Characterization	Description	Example
Potential	Children are described as holding potential or representing potential for the country	"youth whose futures are bright" "schoolchildren who are our national future and most important investment"
Previously served	Students are characterized as having participated in Title I services that are no longer available to them	"children who lost Title I services"
Rural	Children are portrayed in terms of their residency in a rural area	"children from rural outposts"
Race/ethnicity	Children are identified as being from a particular racial/ethnic group	"minority children" "children of color" "Indian children" "Black children"
School type	Students are referred to in terms of the type of school they attend	"home-schooled students" "private school students" "religious school students"
Specific children	Children are described as those of a particular parent, or a particular set of parents	"her children" (of a particular woman, named by the congressional representative "children of postal workers"
Specific locale	Children are portrayed in terms of a particular location	"the students of Des Moines" "young people in California"
Suburban children	Children are portrayed in terms of their residency in a suburb	"children in every sizable suburb"
Their children	Students are mentioned using the possessive pronoun of "their," most commonly with reference to parents	"parents who choose to educate their children at home"
Transient children	Children are represented in terms of their geographic mobility	"students coming into . . . as a result of border settlement"
Urban children	Children are portrayed in terms of their residency in a city	"children in city public schools"

Operationalization

In line with Firestone and Herriott's (1983, 1984) approach, I developed operational definitions of various concepts and constructs prior to entering the schools for data collection. These definitions were grounded in past research on Title I delivery methods (Millsap, Moss, & Gamse, 1993; Rowan, Guthrie, Lee, & Pung Guthrie, 1986), teacher expectations (Cooper, Baron, & Lowe, 1975; Finn, Gaier, Peng, & Banks, 1975; Marwit, Marwit, & Walker, 1978), and opportunity to learn (Porter, 1993; Traiman, 1993), yet they were tailored to the specific nature of my project. In a focus on what I then termed "objective" and "subjective" constructions of Title I, I divided my study into "objective" aspects of this policy—student composition, racial/ethnic composition of Title I students, delivery methods, and written policy documents—and "subjective" aspects of this policy—the explanations, expectations, rationales, intentions, justifications, and attitudes of school-based personnel about Title I. My project was originally to look at how the "objective" and "subjective" aspects ultimately influenced the opportunities to learn afforded by Title I.

Commonly during qualitative research, initial conceptual definitions shift during data collection. Indeed, when I put my concepts and constructs to use in the schools, I noted that I could enrich my operational definitions of them with information gathered in the field. In fact, some of the concepts I used initially seemed to be an incomplete piece of a larger notion I attempted to describe. I modified these constructs accordingly. I realized that instead of discussing Title I in terms of "objective" and "subjective" aspects, which were hard to discern and disentangle, it was more analytically fruitful to think in terms of the mechanics (technical requirements) and meanings of Title I. This focus grew out of my observations of Title I in terms of the language and rituals engendered by this program. My observations and interviews led me to focus my analysis on the site-based budgets, with particular attention to the funded personnel, the use of policy labels or student designations based on eligibility for targeted services, and the multiple, interacting programs and policies that meet at the school site, such as desegregation and bilingual education policies.

Techniques and Tools

The tools and strategies I used for data collection were developed before entering the schools, yet were adapted and improved as I progressed through the school year. I started my project with the goal of studying three schools in which I would spend a total of 6 weeks (in 3 nonconsecutive sets of 2-week periods) and six other schools in which I would spend 1 week each. This sample allowed me to understand the emic perspectives of the three focus schools while drawing cross-site comparisons with a larger sample. With an approach based on Fetterman's *Ethnography: Step by Step* (1989), I entered the schools with a notebook and pen in hand, ready to jot down any information about the schools and their Title I programs. As my carefully designed project met the complex and ever-changing empirical world, I had to make adjustments to most of my strategies.

Time in Schools

Since my research project called for substantial amounts of time in schools, I had to focus on a small number of cases. However, I did not want to limit my study's power or generalizability by presenting a few case studies. Rather, I wanted to study as large a sample as was feasible for one researcher to handle while allowing for in-depth observations of a few sites. I, therefore, decided to approach my project through a nested sample design.[1] This design allowed me to immerse myself in the cultures and contexts of three sites, and to draw basic cross-site comparisons with a larger sample. My immersion in the focus schools provided greater depth of understanding when I approached the six other schools, and my weeks in the nonfocus schools provided analytical perspective and context for the focus schools.[2]

Sampling and Entry

In order to choose the schools, I first had to select a district.[3] I identified three large, urban districts from which I was to choose one. I wanted a district with a considerable range in racial/ethnic representation and with many schools that qualified for Title I funds. My first-choice district, located in a California city, had a formal application procedure for conducting research projects.[4] A woman in the district's Office of Research and Evaluation who was new to her position of reviewing research proposals reviewed and approved my project, contingent on approval from the director of State and Federal Funded Projects. The director read and approved my proposal (I recall her saying, "Let's do it") and wished me luck in finding school principals to agree to the project.

In the school selection, I controlled for socioeconomic status by eliminating all schools that qualified for the schoolwide project option. At the time of sampling, Title I eligibility was determined first by eligibility for Aid to Families with Dependent Children (AFDC) and then by standardized test scores (on the Comprehensive Test of Basic Skills—CTBS—or the Brigance test[5]). The district ranked the schools by proportional AFDC eligibility to determine their prioritization for funding distribution, and distributed funds based on the percentage of students scoring at or below the 40th percentile on the CTBS or scoring less than 95% on the Brigance.[6] After reviewing the district statistics on AFDC for the 1993–94 academic year—the most recent available documents at that time—I found a population of 12 schools that reported a poverty level (as measured by AFDC) somewhere between 35% and 65%.

I first approached the principals of these 12 schools by letter and then by follow-up phone calls at the end of the school year preceding the year I was to do data collection. Four agreed to meet with me to discuss the project. Upon meeting with them and reviewing the project, all four agreed to let me do my research in their schools. During our meetings, I explained my project focus on the ways in which teachers and administrators "make sense" of Title I. I told the principals that I wanted to look at the meanings of Title I, the purpose school personnel think this policy has, and the people they think it is supposed to serve. These initial conversations often revealed a degree of confusion over the policy and its historical propensity for monitoring and compliance. I explained many times that I was not evaluating the program to see "whether it works" or whether the schools were compliant with the regulations (two frequent questions and occasional misrepresentations of my project as school staff members introduced me to their colleagues). I insisted that my interest was in "what this policy means here; how you all make sense of Title I." "Do we?" was a common reply.

During a discussion of my project, one principal showed me new district statistics that had just been disseminated. The 1994–95 school profiles reported very different poverty measures and Title I eligibility for all of the schools I had visited. In fact, according to these numbers, all four were eligible for the schoolwide project option under the new federal regulations. Further, the district had switched from using AFDC eligibility to using free and reduced-price lunch eligibility to rank the schools for Title I priority. Test scores were no longer going to be used in the following year. The principal also told me that the district was trying to encourage more neighborhood-oriented schools and less busing where possible; he was not sure who would be showing up the following year. I realized that the statistics for the following year would also be different. I decided to wait and see what the statistics were for the 1995–96 school year while planning to continue in the schools where the principals had already granted me permission.

As the school year approached, I called the principals to set up a more formal data collection schedule. Upon calling, one of the principals told me that she was extremely busy and confronting a huge crisis with her teaching staff. She asked me to call her later in the school year. Her request left me with three schools at the beginning of the year, and all three agreed to my proposed data collection schedule. These schools would be the nested sample. I began my research on the first day of school of the 1995–96 academic year.

As I had noticed, the three nested sample schools had rates of Title I eligibility (based on free and reduced-price lunch measurements) that qualified them for the schoolwide project option. However, the district's director of State and Federal Projects told me that none of these schools had "gone school-wide." One of the schools had 75% eligibility, one had 85% eligibility, and one had 95% eligibility for free and reduced-price lunch and therefore Title I. Early in the year, the district disseminated its ranking of schools according to free and reduced-price lunch eligibility. To determine the six other schools in which I would conduct my research, I chose the two schools with eligibility rates closest to each of the schools in my sample and contacted their principals. I scheduled my weeks in the schools and presented them to each principal for approval. Table A.2 shows the actual schedule.

The weeks I spent in schools were not necessarily 5 consecutive days from Monday to Friday. They were interrupted by school vacations, holidays, scheduled time for analysis and district-level interviews, conferences, and, in one case, the need to find a new school.[7] All told, I spent 119 days in schools during 1 academic year with a total of 30 days (in two-week intervals) in each of the focus schools and 4 or 5 days in each of the nonfocus schools. I also observed two school board meetings, five District Advisory Committee meetings (for parents concerned about Title I and other school programs), and six districtwide workshops about the new Title I legislation for program resource teachers. Tables A.3 and A.4 present demographic information on the nine studied schools. Although there are some notable differences between the schools in terms of the ethnic/racial/linguistic compositions, programs offered, and eligibility rates, the schools are relatively similar in the context of the district and the larger population of all elementary schools.

Within the schools, I selected classrooms for observation based on the ways in which Title I funds were used. Since many schools used Title I funding to pay for Reading Recovery services in the first grade, I conducted most of my classroom observations in classrooms from which Reading Recovery students were pulled. In most schools, this selection process led me to first-grade classrooms that were designated "English-only" or "English-language Development." In fact, my classroom sampling based on Title I–funded services only led me to a Chinese bilingual classroom in one school (the only school where Title I funded the counselor). For the sake of consistency and comparability, even when Title I funds were not used for Reading Recovery services, I did at least 1 day of observations in first-grade classrooms. All told, I conducted observations in 17 first-grade classrooms.

When Title I funds were used for administrative purposes, I shadowed the administrator (program resource teacher) during his or her duties. I also observed paraprofessionals in various classroom settings and the counseling services in one school. Finally, when Title I funds were used for ability grouping or class-size reduction, I followed the Title I–funded personnel (usually the program resource teacher or a resource teacher) during their provision

TABLE A.2. Observation Schedule

School	Dates	Days	Reading Recovery	Classroom Observation	Literacy Group	Faculty Meeting	School Site Council	Other Parent Meeting	School Improvement Program	Semistructured Interviews/ Focus Group
1	9/6–9/19/95	10	8	5		2	1	1		
2	9/20–10/6/95	10	7	5		1				1
3	10/10–10/23/95	10	9	14		1				
1	10/30–11/10/95	10	6	5	2	1				4/2
2	11/13–11/28/95	10	5	5		1			1	4/1
3	11/29–12/12/95	10	4	5		1		1		3/2
4	1/22–1/26/96	5	4	4		1				3
5	1/29–2/2/96	5	4	3			1			1/1
6	2/5–2/9/96	5		3		1	1			2
7	2/20–2/23/96	4	2	4	1			1		2
8	2/26–3/1/96	5		3		1				2
9	3/11–3/15/96	5		4		1				2
1	3/18–3/29/96	10	4	5	3	2	1			1
2	4/15–4/26/96	10	3	5		2			1	1
3	4/29–5/10/96	10	4	5		1		1		1

Note: In Reading Recovery lessons, faculty meetings, School Site Council meetings, other parent meetings, and teacher in-service days, my observation periods lasted the duration of the lessons or meetings. For classroom observations, my observation periods ranged from 1 to 3 hours in a classroom.

TABLE A.3. Sample Schools by Title I Student Eligibility as per Test Scores and Economic Measures and Total Title I Dollars, 1995–96*

School (Number of students)	Students scoring in 40th percentile or lower on CTBS/ Brigance (%)	Students eligible for AFDC (%)	Students eligible for free and reduced-price lunch (%)	Total TI (in U.S. dollars)
1 (689)	50.99	14.61	75.43	172,149
2 (467)	64.81	35.34	94.12	156,499
3 (548)	52.26	8.15	82.39	152,586
4 (280)	71.33	56.01	93.50	84,444
5 (372)	52.05	18.07	81.69	108,194
6 (447)	68.91	41.87	77.38	108,918
7 (303)	57.14	13.58	82.61	89,378
8 (416)	57.07	36.82	93.40	143,294
9 (324)	54.74	6.37	77.69	88,292

Note: Adapted from District Department of State and Federally Funded Programs and District and School Profiles [psuedonyms], 1995–96.

* Note that the reported figures appear differently in different district documents. Additionally, principals at two schools told me that the numbers presented by the district were not accurate. Since the focus here is on Title I eligibility, the figures from the Department of State and Federal Funded Programs were used. However, these numbers are not agreed upon within the district documents or the site-based staffs.

of these services. The sampling of specific classrooms and individuals, then, was driven by the school-based Title I budget allocations.

Interviews

I conducted semistructured and informal interviews with key actors. Again, the key actors were determined by Title I allocations at the school level, the school organizational structures, and my observations of roles and responsibilities among the school staff. In each school, I interviewed the program resource teacher (PRT), who served as the site-based administrator of Title I. In the focus schools, I interviewed the PRT twice, once in the middle of the year and once at the end of the year. I also interviewed the principals at each school but one (due to personal circumstances of that principal) and all of the Title I–funded resource teachers. In the focus schools and in two of the other schools, I conducted group or individual interviews with first-grade teachers who had students in the Title I–funded Reading Recovery program.[8]

TABLE A.4. Ethnic Breakdown (in percentages)* and Bilingual Program Offering by School

School	Latino/ Hispanic	Other White	African American/ Black	Chinese	Japanese	Korean	American Indian	Filipino	Other Nonwhite	Bilingual Program **
1	27.6	4.6	18.6	26.7	0	0	0.3	12.2	10.0	Spanish and Chinese
2	20.3	1.3	30.6	39.6	0	0	0.2	0.6	7.3	Spanish and Chinese
3	27.7	5.7	26.8	17.2	0	0	0.7	14.1	7.8	Spanish and Chinese
4	46.8	6.1	35.4	2.9	0	0.7	0	0.7	7.5	Spanish
5	21.0	2.7	48.1	7.3	0	0.5	1.3	13.4	5.6	None
6	44.1	3.6	34.7	6.7	0	0	0.7	3.8	6.5	Chinese
7	8.3	9.2	38.0	32.7	0	0	1.0	4.0	6.9	Spanish
8	8.7	2.4	18.5	45.0	0	0	0	13.2	12.3	Chinese
9	41.0	6.8	27.2	9.0	0.3	0	0.3	10.5	4.9	Spanish

Note: Adapted from District and School Profiles [pseudonym] document for 1995–96.

* Totals may not equal 100% because of rounding.

** Schools with bilingual programs did not necessarily have a bilingual classroom in every grade.

I also interviewed the Title I–funded paras in focus groups at the three focus schools. All of these interviews were taped and transcribed unless the interviewee requested otherwise. One principal and two first-grade teachers requested that their interviews not be taped; they did, however, allow me to take notes. All interviewees signed consent forms granting me permission to interview them. Table A.5 presents the formal, semistructured interviews I conducted in the nine schools.

At the school sites, I also conducted many informal, untaped interviews with various teachers, paraprofessionals, and resource teachers. Outside of the schools, I interviewed the director of State and Federally-Funded Projects, district resource teachers from the State and Federal Office, the assistant superintendent of Elementary Education, and the director of the Reading Recovery program.

Observations

A typical day of data collection involved arriving at school approximately 15 minutes before the bell rang. I walked around the yard with the students and teachers assigned to yard duty or went inside to talk with a teacher or resource teacher. I watched the students say the Pledge of Allegiance, heard the morning announcements, and usually walked with a first-grade class into their classroom. Sometimes I stayed in the classroom all morning, other times I shadowed a resource teacher or PRT through Reading Recovery lessons or literacy groups. During morning recess, I met with teachers, helped to monitor the yard, or wrote up notes about my morning observations. After morning recess, I observed a classroom, a Reading Recovery lesson, or some other Title I–funded service. At lunch, I worked in the cafeterias and ate lunch in the teachers' lunchroom. Some of my most interesting insights were sparked while observing or participating in lunchroom conversations. After lunch, my schedule proceeded in similar fashion; I observed classrooms or Title I–funded services. After the school day was over, I stayed for faculty meetings (which were usually held on Mondays), talked with school personnel, or left to go home. Once home, I normally typed up and elaborated on my notes from that day.

The Human Instrument in Participant Observations

My initial goal was to conduct participant observations, but I was unclear how to be a participant in these schools. Once in the schools, however, it became clear to me that potential roles for participation abounded. With so many competing urgencies, there were many jobs that I could fulfill, and I offered to perform tasks as needs seemed to arise. After a few observations in which I helped out by working with students or photocopying papers, some

TABLE A.5. Interviews in Sample Schools

School	Interviews	Notes
1	Principal (n = 1) Program resource teacher (n = 1) Other resource teachers (n = 2) Teachers with students in Reading Recovery (n = 4) Paraprofessional focus group (n = 6)	Teachers with students in Reading Recovery were interviewed in a focus group. The PRT, other resource teachers, and all paras were funded in full or in part by Title I.
2	Principal (n = 1) Program resource teacher (n = 1) Other resource teacher (n = 1) Intervention specialist (n = 1) Teacher with students in Reading Recovery (n = 1) Paraprofessional focus group (n = 8)	All Reading Recovery students were pulled from the same classroom at time of interviews. At the paraprofessional focus group, two of the eight paras did not speak. The PRT, other resource teacher, and all paras interviewed were funded in full or in part by Title I.
3	Principal (n = 1) Program resource teacher (n = 1) Teachers with students in Reading Recovery (n = 2) Bilingual teacher (n = 1) Paraprofessional focus group (n = 6)	Teachers with students in Reading Recovery were interviewed in a focus group. All paras were funded in full or in part by Title I.
4	Principal (n = 1) Program resource teacher (n = 1) Teachers with students in Reading Recovery (n = 1)	All Reading Recovery students were pulled from the same classroom. The PRT was funded in full or in part by Title I.
5	Program resource teacher (n = 1) * Teachers with students in Reading Recovery (n = 2)	One of the interviewed teachers was also the Reading Recovery teacher in the afternoons. This teacher's Reading Recovery salary was funded by Title I.
6	Principal (n = 1) Program resource teacher (n = 1)	The program resource teacher was funded in full or in part by Title I.
7	Principal (n = 1) Program resource teacher (n = 1)	The program resource teacher was funded in full or in part by Title I.
8	Principal (n = 1) Program resource teacher (n = 1)	The program resource teacher was funded in full or in part by Title I.
9	Principal (n = 1) Program resource teacher (n = 1)	The program resource teacher was funded in full or in part by Title I.
Totals:	Total principals (n = 8) Total program resource teachers (n = 9) Total other resource teachers (n = 3) Total intervention specialists (n = 1) Total first-grade teachers (n = 11) Total paraprofessionals (n = 20)	

Note: PRT = program resource teacher.

* Due to personal circumstances, the principal was unavailable for an interview.

teachers requested my presence in their classrooms. "Can you please observe me today?" one asked. "My para's out sick."

There are also many limitations to this approach. Absorbed in the immediacies of the school worlds, I sometimes became more of a participant than an observer and wished that I could be in more than one place at a time. Obviously, as I observed Reading Recovery lessons, I missed classroom observations; as I participated in district workshops, I did not see school meetings. My inability to see everything at once made me wonder about the data I was not collecting as well as the data I was. Additionally, since all observations and interviews were conducted after seeking approval from those to be observed, and the Title I programs were different in the nine schools, it was difficult to be systematic in my observations. For example, in one of the focus schools, I did many more classroom observations during my first 2 weeks of data collection than in the other 2, since I had already learned a great deal about the district and its approach to Title I during my time in the other two schools. Additionally, the Reading Recovery program at this school only served four students, and the teachers continually asked me to help out in their classrooms. Furthermore, some districtwide events, such as Back-to-School Night and CTBS testing, happened only once or twice during the year. I witnessed these events only in the schools in which I was observing during that day or week.

In addition to inevitable variation in school observations, I was also concerned about my own lenses for taking in and recording information. In qualitative research, the researcher becomes the instrument of data collection, introducing myriad biases, prior assumptions, and messages. My personal and institutional identities influenced how I perceived and was perceived, what information I took in, and what information I was provided. The school communities regarded me through the cultural categories available to them. As a 30-year-old woman, dressed in casual yet professional-enough "teacher clothes," I projected a physical message about who I was. As a Stanford doctoral student who had never been a classroom teacher but had experience working with children, I had clear institutional affiliations and associations. As a Spanish speaker, I overheard conversations that I was assumed not to understand or was included in conversations that would not have otherwise been available to me. As a white researcher in schools serving mostly Latino, black, and Asian students and with teaching staffs that were predominantly white, I was privy to information and attitudes that may not have been expressed to a person of color. Similarly, I am certain that there were attitudes and information that were not expressed to me and that may have been shared with a person of color, a former teacher, a parent, or a government official. I can identify many times when I was provided with information because I occupied one of the above cultural categories. I can only begin to imagine what information was not available to me for the same reasons.

Besides the limitations based on my identities as understood by others, my own personal information and lack thereof also shaped my observations. There were some elements of schooling that I did not understand or with which I was not familiar, and others of which I did have previous experiences and opinions. I tried to compensate for my lack of knowledge and temper my prior assumptions by representing the voices and actions of teachers with direct quotations and low-inference observations.[9] Additionally, I had some teachers read parts of my write-ups or asked them specific questions about my notes to determine whether my perceptions and understandings were consistent with theirs.

After conducting a study of this nature, I realized how present I was in all of my observations and some of my most compelling data. For example, some of the quotations I found to be most poignant were said directly to me, rather than to another school staff member. My presence certainly influenced the topic and nature of conversations. After all, I was asking many questions about Title I. By including myself in my presentation of the data, I let the reader see that I indeed interacted within this world; I shaped it as it shaped me. Just as I have taken care to represent all of the layers and inconsistencies in the school practices, here I articulate the complexities and idiosyncrasies in my research project. My focus on ranges of practice and behavior encourages consideration of the particular and exceptional along with the regular and ordinary.

There were moments when I could see how my previous biases and prejudices influenced my work. On occasion, teachers would make what I thought to be offensive comments about certain ethnic groups (including my own). I had trouble maintaining a distant researcher role on those occasions. In fact, I have always had the personal conviction that my silence is my consent—in Spanish there is a phrase "*él que calla otorga*," meaning "he/she who is quiet, accepts"—and in the role of researcher, I kept quiet against my gut instinct. Indeed, there were moments when I felt that my personal integrity was being tested as I observed blatantly racist behavior or what I considered to be unethical practices. I was surprised by the ease with which a few school staff members acted or spoke in ways that I found to be so controversial or offensive in front of a researcher. Although there were many more teachers who did not act as such, those who did challenged my ability to uphold my carefully delineated role. When observing one particularly troubling teacher, I felt like an accomplice to her racist attitudes by virtue of being another white adult in a room full of students of color. Colleagues told me that I was getting great data. I must admit, this role was not always an easy one for me.

Validity, Reliability, and Generalizability

In empirical research, validity, reliability, and generalizability are of central concern. Researchers aim to show that their research is valid (that it actually measures and represents what it says to measure and represent), reliable (that the study can be replicated by someone else using the same methods and obtaining the same results), and generalizable (that the study results pertain to a population larger than the sample studied).[10] In this study, these issues take on a particular nature, reflective of the unique role of the participant observer.

In very basic terms, to convince the reader that this study is valid, I would have to show that the data about budgets and labels, race/ethnicity, and opportunities to learn really reflect the empirical world and that the words of school-based personnel provide insight into the content of meaning about Title I. Similarly, in order to show my study's reliability, I would have to argue that if I or somebody else were to do it all over again, the same results would emerge. Finally, in order to address concerns about generalizability, I would have to persuade the reader that the patterns observed in the studied schools could be found in other, comparable contexts. Some of these arguments are easier to make than others.

Extensive observations and interviews provided insight into the policy-generated language and routines. These data collection techniques furnished information about the ways Title I programs take form in schools and the meanings associated with Title I policies. This information was communicated through both words and actions.

There is a great deal of face validity in this type of research. By highlighting multiple meanings through the actual spoken words of school personnel (taken from transcribed interview audio recordings) and observed actions (recorded with low-inference descriptions), I conveyed the ways in which the worlds of schools are represented. To further ensure face validity, I triangulated data that were presented to me as "facts" (as opposed to opinions) and asked teachers and/or principals to review any assertions I made of which I was unsure.

Analysis of this study's reliability surfaces more complicated and challenging issues. Were I or another researcher to conduct this study again, would we arrive at the same conclusions? There is no simple answer to this question. Questions of reliability imply that there is a concrete, timeless reality that can be observed and measured in replicable ways.[11] Aspects of the methodological approach taken here could certainly be replicated. However, since so many elements of the schools and the policy itself were in flux even during the time of data collection, it is unlikely that another researcher's results would be identical to mine. And, of course, the frames for analysis that guided my observations may not be shared by others.

The question of reliability in qualitative research, then, becomes one of compensating for the difficulties associated with replicating studies so potentially influenced by characteristics of the researcher. LeCompte and Goetz (1982) identify a handful of strategies, some of which were employed in this study. These strategies are (a) the use of low-inference descriptors, (b) the combined efforts of multiple researchers, (c) the practice of reflecting with local "informants" on the observed practices and beliefs, (d) peer review with other researchers in similar settings, and (e) mechanically recorded data (pp. 41–43). In this study, I was careful to use low-inference descriptors in all field notes, and put any thoughts that I considered to be beyond descriptions (i.e., judgments, suspicions, perceptions, and viewpoints) in brackets. Unable to use multiple researchers on this project, I did rely on the reflections of key practitioners—especially resource teachers, teachers, and principals—in confirming or challenging my perceptions of the schools and how Title I took shape there, in the meanings communicated through language and routines.[12] I also discussed my findings with other researchers and teachers in various urban settings. Finally, I audiotaped (when granted permission) and transcribed all interviews and typed field notes into a computer text program.

Generalizability poses yet another challenge for research of this nature. The specific cultural and organizational elements of each school make generalizations difficult, even across the relatively homogeneous study sample. However, what is generalizable in this study is the range of patterns in thought and behavior and the ways in which the culture of policy takes shape in different contexts. My basic premises, I argue, are generalizable. The language and routines of schooling do matter, and the culture of policy limits and distorts the opportunities that those very policies afford.

Notes

Chapter 1

1. This quotation is taken from an interview transcript of a teacher who participated in the research reported in chapters 4 and 5.

2. Experimental research from the 1970s and 1980s highlights how school-based labels can be damaging to children (for a review, see Gillung & Rucker, 1977; Palmer, 1983; Salvia, Clark, & Ysseldyke, 1973) and how they produce stereotypes and biases on the part of teachers (Gallagher, 1972; Mercer, 1973; Reynolds & Balow, 1972). This research raises concerns about how the labels become self-fulfilling prophecies for student achievement. For the work that inspired much of this research, see Rosenthal and Jacobson (1968). See also Cuban (1989), Frost (1994), Gans (1995), Rose (1989/1990), and Wang, Reynolds, and Walberg (1994). Others, however, are not convinced that the use of such labels is problematic and argue that labels are necessary for efficient program delivery (e.g., see Fogel & Nelson, 1983; Graham & Leone, 1987). In order to target programs to specific groups and individuals effectively, they argue, defining and naming that group is somewhat inevitable. For an excellent analysis of the dilemmas of labeling, see Minow (1990). For an application of Minow's argument to the "at-risk" label, see Frost (1994).

3. Compensatory education lends itself nicely to analysis of the notion of "compensatory legitimation" (Weiler, 1983). In order to maintain its own legitimacy in the eyes of its public, the capitalist state has an interest in providing compensation to those disfavored by a capitalist structure. Rather than interrogate the structures of capitalism or the financing of public education based on community wealth, the government provides limited funds to signal its commitment to the poor. The state's legitimacy needs are fulfilled through this gesture while the inequitable structures remain intact.

4. The incentives I note here have also been identified by conservative analysts and reporters such as Butler and Dennis (1986), Charles Murray (1994), Tierney (2000), and others. However, I strongly part company with such analysts on two fronts. First, I do not believe that the social policies these analysts critique should be abolished without serious consideration of the inequitable structures of resource distribution in a capitalist economy. Second, in proposing such incentive structures as part of the *culture* of policy, I acknowledge the possibility for resistance to that culture. In chapters 4 and 6, I discuss both uncritical acceptance of and vigilant resistance to the culture of policy among school-based practitioners.

5. Fullan and Rolheiser (2001) use the term "union of insufficiencies" to describe considerations for reforming student assessment. Shulman (1988) also made the term "union of insufficiencies" popular in his theory and practice of teacher assessment.

6. I discuss these conditions at length in chapter 4.

7. The literature on labels and labeling—or, for my purposes, "policy markings"—is connected to studies of the influence of teacher expectations on student performance (see, for example, Finn, Gaier, Peng, & Banks, 1975; Rosenthal & Jacobson, 1968).

Chapter 2

1. Carl Kaestle and Marshall Smith (1982) argue that the passage of ESEA Title I was actually a continuation of a centralization movement in education that dates back to the 1700s. These authors contest the notion that ESEA passage was a meaningful break from past policy approaches (pp. 386–390).

2. In his revised version, Banfield (1974) argued that such cultural patterns presented "constraints which the policymaker must take into account and which limit what he may accomplish" (p. 53).

3. In his later work, Moynihan claims that Kenneth Clark originally used the language of the "tangle of pathology" in Harlem Youth Opportunities Unlimited (HARYOU) reports and then *Dark Ghetto*, published in 1965 (O'Connor, 2001, p. 333, note 27).

4. The issue of "necessary poverty" has been analyzed in my use of this quotation in chapter 1.

5. The actual votes were as follows: In the Senate, 73 in favor, 18 opposed; in the House, 263 in favor, 153 opposed (Meranto, 1967, p. 93).

Chapter 3

1. The precise definition of "handicapped children" used in the debates was: "mentally retarded, hard of hearing, deaf, speech impaired, visually handicapped, seriously emotionally disturbed, crippled, or other health impaired children who by reason thereof require special education and related services" (Elementary and Secondary Education Amendments of 1966, Sec. 602).

2. For a detailed political analysis of the 1967 ESEA reauthorization, see Thomas (1975).

3. For a review of additional early Title I evaluation studies, see Jeffrey (1978, pp. 143–178).

4. The phrase "supplement, not supplant" was first mentioned in the 1965 authorization debates by Senator John McClellan (D, AR) (1965, p. 7613).

5. The term "social dynamite" comes from the work of chemist and former president of Harvard University James Bryant Conant (1961). Conant used this term to describe children who were receiving substandard education as having the potential for considerable destruction. Conant was cited directly by Senator Jacob Javits (R, NY) (1970, p. 8906), Senator George Murphy (R, CA) (1970, p. 3599), and Representative Carl Perkins (D, KY) (1969a, p. 4182).

6. Senator Dominick (R, CO) was likely referring to controversial research that claimed that men with double Y (XYY) chromosomes were predisposed to violent behavior. For an example of this type of research, see Cook (1973).

7. Various members of Congress complained that the funding formula based on counts of children in poverty and on AFDC was inherently inequitable. Since the "count of children [eligible for Title I] involve[d] the welfare program which varie[d] from State to State" (Steiger, 1969, p. 9909), wealthier states could afford to have more children on AFDC, and, therefore, more children deemed eligible for Title I.

8. According to historian Alice O'Connor (2001), Mollie Orshansky "had never meant her measures as official government standards. . . . [And] Orshansky took pains to recognize that her work was at best an 'interim standard,' 'arbitrary, but not unreasonable,' and minimalistic at best" (p. 184). Even members of Congress noted Orshansky's caution in using this measure. For example, according to Representative Jack Kemp (R, NY) (1974), "Ms. Orshansky herself, testifying before the Special Education Subcommittee, recommended that 'further analysis' of her poverty index be conducted before it is used for the purposes of this formula" (pp. 6269–6270). Other members of Congress made similar arguments (see, for example, Biaggi, 1974, p. 6302; Peyser, 1974, p. 4448; Young, 1974, p. 6340).

9. Here, Representative Andrew Young (D, GA) was reading the dissenting views of Representatives Badillo, Biaggi, Chisholm, Daniels, and Peyser.

10. An interesting anomaly in the discursive representation of the policy beneficiaries during the 1974 debates surfaced in the representation of children funded under Title VII of ESEA (the Bilingual Education Act). Unlike characterizations of "the poor" or "disadvantaged children" launched in Title I, members of Congress made efforts to cast the children served by Title VII in terms of their strengths and to frame their culture as an asset on which to be built. For example, the statement of policy in the proposed amendments to Title VII read:

> The term "children of limited English speaking ability" is used merely as a term of statutory reference, and in no way the term intended to imply any sense that children who share a linguistic and cultural background different from the majority of students are somehow inferior. Thus, the congressional findings in the bill include: First, that there are large numbers of children of limited English-speaking ability, second, the many of such children have a cultural heritage which differs from that of English-speaking persons, third, that a primary means by which a child learns is through the use of such child's language and cultural heritage, fourth, that, therefore, large numbers of children of limited English-speaking ability have educational needs which can be met by the use of bilingual educational methods and techniques, and fifth that, in addition, children of limited English-speaking ability benefit through the fullest utilization of multiple language and cultural resources. (Cranston, 1974, p. 24916)

11. Other categorical distinctions that raised questions in the debates included whether students identified as "children with limited or non-English speaking ability" (a term changed to "children with limited English language skills" and then "children of limited English proficiency") should be considered to be "educationally deprived." Representative George Miller (D, CA) (1978) asked:

> Specifically, Mr. Chairman, does the phrase, "educationally deprived" include children of limited or non-English speaking ability?
>
> I believe that the inclusion of limited or non-English speaking children is wholly consistent with the intent of the special incentive grant provision.
>
> Clearly, Mr. Chairman, these students are not performing at grade level, and are therefore educationally deprived. (p. H6602)

Categorizing these children as such would increase the funds that they generate for schools, so it was seen to be in the school's interest to consider the "children of limited English proficiency" to be "educationally deprived."

12. According to Senator Orrin Hatch (R, UT) (1978b), the problems of public education arose when "schools started becoming more concerned with children's attitudes, beliefs and emotions rather than providing them with basic education" (p. 26682).

13. For Republican arguments against Title I–funded nonacademic programs, see Ashbrook (1978, pp. 3586–3587), Hatch (1978a, p. 8369; 1978b, p. 26682), and Holt (1978, p. 3627).

14. Students were frequently described as "needy" without any substantive definition of need several times throughout the debate. Representative Mario Biaggi (D, NY) (1981) asserted the clearest definition of need as the need for "compensatory educational services" (p. 10576), a definition also lacking substance or specificity.

15. The NACEDC was established in 1965. The council consisted of presidential appointees and had the purpose of "reviewing the administration and operation of this title, including its effectiveness in improving the educational attainment of educationally deprived children, and making recommendations for the improvement of this title and its administration and operation. These recommendations shall take into consideration experience gained under this and other Federal educational programs for disadvantaged children and, to the extent appropriate, experience gained under other public and private educational programs for disadvantaged children" (Elementary and Secondary Education Act of 1965, Sec. 212). The council was to produce annual reports on Title I programs and make recommendations for further programmatic and policy improvement.

16. This proportion was calculated by dividing the number of words in the *Title I, Today* report (10,592) into the number of words in the entire floor debate text regarding Title I (71,206).

17. Table II in the report shows that 40% of children identified as both poor and low-achieving receive Title I–funded services. Although not emphasized in this largely positive report, this figure could be used to argue that less than half of the primary target population was receiving services at the time of the study.

18. Other issues debated on the congressional floor included sex education, school prayer, the English proficiency of bilingual teachers, disciplinary procedures for gun-carrying students (including those who are "disabled"), "opportunity to learn" standards, and the impact of teacher certification provisions on home schooling.

19. Qualifying for Title I through eligibility for the free-lunch program was far more common than qualifying for Title I through eligibility for AFDC. As chapter 4 will demonstrate, the rates of school poverty jumped considerably once the measurement of poverty was changed.

Chapter 4

1. Although the research for this section took place in nine schools in the same school district, various practitioners in districts across the country have reviewed the findings. While some of the specific terms and bureaucratic arrangements may be different between districts and states, the overall approach to Title I implementation and the meanings associated with the policy and eligible students seem rather consistent.

2. Testing has also been used to determine Title I's effectiveness. Indeed, various scholars trace the emergence of state and national testing programs to the passage of ESEA. See, for example, Gifford (1993); Peters, Wixson, Valencia, and Pearson (1993).

3. Many studies have documented the relationship between poverty and student achievement (Brooks-Gunn & Duncan, 1997; Hanushek, 1986; Kennedy, Jung, & Orland, 1986; Lee & Burkam, 2002; Orland, 1990). However, the measures of poverty used in research and educational practice oversimplify complex phenomena (O'Connor, 2001). For example, point-in-time measures of poverty overlook the potentially disparate influences of long-term and short-term childhood poverty (Orland, 1990).

4. In a *New York Times* article, Richard Rothstein (2000) explains the misleading nature of standardized testing through the analogy of batting averages. Mike Piazza, a celebrated baseball player, wins numerous accolades because of his career batting average. But, Rothstein posits, "[W]hat if the team decided to pay him based not on overall performance but on how he hit during one arbitrarily chosen week? How well do one week's at-bats describe the ability of a true .330 hitter?" (p. B11). Predictably, Piazza's record is not consistent from week to week. We rely on the averages over a period of time, rather than the scores of an isolated moment, to determine batting capability. Extending Rothstein's analogy to Title I policy, let's say we test Piazza during a week in which he is not performing well. Unfortunately, our tests cannot determine why he is not performing to our expectations. Nonetheless, by not doing so, he generates funding for services that might help him bat more effectively. We tell his coaches that he is deficient or lacking in batting, take him out of regular practice, and have him practice his sport in a different space from the rest of his teammates. Based on one week of batting, we determine that Mike Piazza needs remedial help, and provide monetary incentives to his coach to perpetuate that need by giving him separate services. If he continues batting poorly, his coach gets more funds.

5. Schools used the CTBS scores of the prior year to determine eligibility. For example, a student deemed eligible for Title I in the second grade scored at or below the 40th percentile on the CTBS in the first grade test administered the April before. Additionally, in the studied district, Title I eligibility based on the Brigance test changed from 87% or higher to 95% or higher in 1995. With this change, only students with near-perfect scores were not designated as Title I–eligible in kindergarten and first-grade classrooms.

6. The option was made available first in the 1988 reauthorization of ESEA and then expanded in the 1994 reauthorization.

7. At times this question was posed to practitioners as, "What comes to mind if I ask you to describe a 'typical EDY student'?" At other times, I asked, "What

comes to mind if I ask you to describe a 'typical Title I student'?" I based my use of the term "EDY," "Title I," or "Chapter I" on the term that the practitioner used during earlier parts of the interview.

8. In this school, 57% of the 416 students had the EDY designation based on their test scores and 93% qualified for free and reduced-price lunch. Based on the principal's claim, then, somewhere between 237 and 386 students were sent to the office on a regular basis. Either his associations between Title I eligibility and bad behavior were grossly overextended, or this school had a serious and disconcerting level of student behavior problems.

9. These observations are consistent with Betty Malen's (1994) research on school community power relations.

10. While I was presenting these observations at a conference, a veteran teacher in the audience reported that her principal ordered her to "slow down with these kids" so that the school could retain the Title I revenues that funded her position.

11. This tendency underscores the need for certified teachers of African, Latin American, and Asian descent, since in some of the schools, teachers outnumbered the paraprofessionals by as many as 4:1, yet there were still more paras from these communities than certified teachers.

12. These labels refer to the following: *At-risk* is a general catchall label used commonly to describe anything from grades to behavior to family poverty to drug use (see Frost, 1994); *EDY* is an acronym for "educationally disadvantaged youth," a term used in the studied schools to designate students eligible for Title I services; the *lower quartile* refers to students who scored in the 25th percentile or lower on standardized, norm-referenced tests such as the Comprehensive Test of Basic Skills or the Brigance.

Chapter 5

1. The information here is based on eight of the nine schools reviewed in chapter 4, also during the 1994–95 school year. The one school that is not represented in this analysis did not have a bilingual program and therefore did not exhibit similar tendencies.

2. "Koosh balls" are small, handheld balls made up of many strands of a thin, rubber-band–like substance.

3. According to Omi and Winant (1994), racial essentialism refers to "a belief in real, true human essences, existing outside or impervious to social and historical context" (p. 187, n. 57).

4. I do not mean to suggest in any way that these activities are not valuable or worthwhile. Indeed, I believe they are both.

Chapter 6

1. Given findings about what many have come to call the "digital divide" in Internet access between the "information rich (such as Whites, Asians/Pacific Islanders, those with higher incomes, those more educated, and dual-parent households)" and the "information poor (such as those who are younger, those with lower in-

comes and education levels, certain minorities, and those in rural areas or central cities)" (National Telecommunications and Information Administration, 2000), the use of this web site to communicate with parents of children in low-performing, high-poverty schools seems disconnected from the studied realities of the technological resources available to such families.

2. I have edited my communication with this aspiring leader in an effort to preserve the flow of our communication and to maintain the focus on the language and routines of policy-speak.

Appendix

1. By "nested sample," I mean a sample within a sample. In other words, within my entire sample of schools, I would use more extensive data collection techniques on a few.

2. This design, involving nonconsecutive weeks in various sites, is based on past work adapting ethnographic techniques to evaluation (see, for example, Fetterman, 1984, 1986).

3. I did not want to introduce district variation into my analysis, so I controlled for such variation by studying schools in the same district.

4. Stanford University's Human Subjects Review Board also approved this project prior to district contact.

5. These tests are described in chapter 4.

6. This Brigance test cutoff score was changed from 87% during the 1995–96 academic year.

7. While reviewing the budgets at the school that was intended to be the ninth school in my sample, I noted that this school did not have any federal Title I dollars. Instead, they had state compensatory monies. This school received state funds rather than Title I funds because their proportional eligibility for Title I (based on free and reduced-price lunch eligibility) was lower than their proportional eligibility for state compensatory funds (based on CTBS test scores). In an effort to spread the money across schools, the district allocates funding from either the state or the federal government, usually corresponding to the funds for which there is a higher eligibility rate. When I explained why I did not want to introduce any variation of that nature into my sample schools, the principal told me that when I had described my project to her over the phone she didn't think that the funding source would matter, since the funds were used to purchase similar services.

8. I decided to conduct focus groups based on the teachers' scheduling preferences and my own interest in their individual and collective meanings of Title I.

9. By "low-inference observations" I mean observation notes that describe a setting or behavior without inferring beyond descriptive details. For example, instead of describing a classroom as "chaotic," I would write, "two students are crawling on the floor. Three students are chasing each other around desks. Five students are throwing crumpled-up pieces of paper at each other," and so on.

10. The particular nature of these issues in qualitative research has been discussed by various scholars of ethnography and qualitative methodologies (see Grumet, 1990; Jackson, 1990; LeCompte & Goetz, 1982; Wolcott, 1990).

11. In qualitative research, even when the observations and descriptions of two different researchers at distinct time periods seem similar, questions arise. For example, Mary Louise Pratt (1986) describes the controversy about similar accounts of the Yonomamo Indians put forth by two different anthropologists. The anthropologist presenting the second account was eventually questioned for plagiarism in part because her descriptions of the Yonomamo were so similar to those of the first anthropologist.

12. Issues of confidentiality made this reflection delicate at times. In order to avoid any breaches of confidentiality, I either asked for feedback and reflection on my thoughts in very broad terms or with specific focus on an observation I had made or an interview question response of the person at hand.

References

Abzug, B. S. (1974). *120 Congressional Record* (5), 6274.

Albert, C. B. (1965). *111 Congressional Record* (5), 6130.

Anderson, J. B. (1965). *111 Congressional Record* (5), 5732.

Anderson, V. (1997, May). Fallout from Title I switch. *Catalyst: Voices of Chicago school reform, 8*(8) [Online]. Available: http://www.catalyst-chicago.org/05-97/057main.html

Arnold, R. D. (1990). *The logic of congressional action.* New Haven, CT: Yale University Press.

Ashbrook, J. M. (1974). *120 Congressional Record* (7), 8526.

Ashbrook, J. M. (1978). *124 Congressional Record* (3), 3586–3587.

Ashbrook, J. M. (1981). *127 Congressional Record* (10), 12677.

Augustus F. Hawkins–Robert T. Stafford Elementary and Secondary School Improvement Amendments of 1988. (1990). Pub. L. No. 100–297, 102 Stat. pp. 130–431

Badillo, H. (1974). *120 Congressional Record* (5), 6302, 6304.

Bailey, S. K., & Mosher, E. K. (1968). *ESEA: The Office of Education administers a law.* Syracuse, NY: Syracuse University Press.

Bandstra, B. A. (1966). *112 Congressional Record* (10), 12984–12985.

Banfield, E. C. (1968). *The unheavenly city: The nature and future of our urban crisis.* Boston: Little, Brown.

Banfield, E. C. (1974). *The unheavenly city revisited.* Boston: Little, Brown.

Bartlett, E. L. (1965). *111 Congressional Record* (6), 7326.

Bell, A. (1965). *111 Congressional Record* (5), 5961.

Bell, A. (1974). *120 Congressional Record* (6), 8235.

Bell, (1975). Waiting on the promise of Brown. *Law & Contemporary Problems, 39,* 341.

Bell, D. A. (1980). Brown v. Board of Education and the interest-convergence dilemma. *Harvard Law Review, 93,* 518.

Bell, D. (1986). Heretical thoughts on a serious occasion. In L. P. Miller (Ed.), *Brown plus thirty: Perspectives on desegregation* (pp. 70–72). New York: Metropolitan Center for Educational Research, Development, and Training.

Berlo, D. K. (1960). *The process of communication: An introduction to theory and practice.* New York: Holt, Rinehart and Winston.

Biaggi, M. (1974). *120 Congressional Record* (5), 6301–6302.

Biaggi, M. (1981). *127 Congressional Record* (8), 10576.

Bingham, J. B. (1978). *124 Congressional Record* (106) (daily edition), E3809.

Boland, E. P. (1969). *115 Congressional Record* (8), 9909.

Bourdieu, P. (1991). *Language and symbolic power.* Cambridge, MA: Harvard University Press.

Bow, F. T. (1965). *111 Congressional Record* (5), 5993.

Brady, N. M. (1986). Brown thirty years later: The Chicago story. In L. P. Miller (Ed.), *Brown plus thirty: Perspectives on desegregation* (pp. 25–29). New York: Metropolitan Center for Educational Research, Development, and Training.

Brennan, J. E. (1988). *134 Congressional Record,* 7477.

Brooks-Gunn, J., & Duncan, G. J. (1997). The effects of poverty on children. *The Future of Children, 7*(2), 55–71.

Brophy, J. (1988). Research linking teacher behavior to student achievement: Potential implications for instruction of Chapter 1 students. *Educational Psychologist, 23,* 235–286.

Brown v. Board of Education of Topeka, 347 U.S. 483 (1954). [Online]. Available: http://laws.findlaw.com/us/347/483.html

Burke, K. (1965). *Permanence and change: An anatomy of purpose* (2nd rev. ed.). Indianapolis, IN: Bobbs-Merrill.

Butler, S. M., & Dennis, W. J. Jr. (Eds.). (1986). *Entrepreneurship: The key to economic growth.* Washington, DC: Heritage Foundation and The National Federation of Independent Business.

Byrd, R. C. (1965). *111 Congressional Record* (6), 7708.

Cardinale, K., Carnoy, M., & Stein, S. (1999). Bilingual education for limited English proficiency students: Local interests and resource availability as determinants of pedagogical practice. *Qualitative Studies in Education, 12*(1), 37–57.

Carnoy, M., & Levin, H. M. (1985). *Schooling and work in the democratic state.* Stanford, CA: Stanford University Press.

Chisholm, S. A. (1978). *124 Congressional Record* (82) (daily edition), H4803–4804.

Chisholm, S. A. (1981). *127 Congressional Record* (10), 14667.

Clark, J. S. (1965). *111 Congressional Record* (6), 7339.

Comfort, L. K. (1982). *Education policy and evaluation: A context for change.* New York: Pergamon Press.

Conant, J. B. (1961). *Slums and suburbs.* New York: McGraw-Hill.

Connecticut State Department of Education, Office of Program Development. (1967). Abstract. In *State annual evaluation report, Title I, ESEA, fiscal year 1967* (BBB02612). (ERIC Document Reproduction Service No. ED034826)

Conte, S. O. (1966). *112 Congressional Record* (19), 25344.

Conte, S. O. (1988). *134 Congressional Record,* 7476.

Cook, E. B. (1973, January 12). Behavioral implications of the XYY genotype. *Science, 179,* 139–150.

Cooper, H., Baron, R. M., & Lowe, C. A. (1975). The importance of race and social class information in the formation of expectancies about academic performance. *Journal of Educational Psychology, 67,* 312–319.

Cranston, A. (1974). *120 Congressional Record* (19), 24916.

Crosby, E. A. (1993). The at-risk decade. *Phi Delta Kappan, 74,* 598–604.

Cuban, L. (1989). The 'at-risk' label and the problem of urban school reform. *Phi Delta Kappan, 70,* 780–784, 799–801.

Dellums, R. V. (1981). *127 Congressional Record* (8), 14102.

Domenici, P. V. (1978). *124 Congressional Record* (20), 27340.

Dominick, P. H. (1965). *111 Congressional Record* (6), 7331.

Dominick, P. H. (1970). *116 Congressional Record* (2), 2581–2582.

Edelman, M. (1988). *Constructing the political spectacle.* Chicago: University of Chicago Press.

Education Amendments of 1978. (1980). Pub. L. No. 95-561, 92 Stat., pp. 2143–2380.

Education Consolidation and Improvement Act of 1981. (1982). Pub. L. No. 97-35, 95 Stat., pp. 463–482.

Elementary and Secondary Education Act of 1965. (1966). Pub. L. No. 89-10, 79 Stat., pp. 27–58.

Elementary and Secondary Education Amendments of 1966. (1967). Pub. L. No. 89-750, 80 Stat., pp. 1191–1222.

Elementary and Secondary Education Amendments of 1967. (1968). Pub. L. No. 90-247, 81 Stat., pp. 783–820.

Elementary and Secondary Education Assistance Programs. (1971). Pub. L. No. 91-230, 84 Stat., pp. 121–195.

Elmore, R. F. (2002). *Doing the right thing, knowing the right thing to do: The problem of failing schools and performance-based accountability.* Unpublished draft.

Elmore, R. F., & McLaughlin, M. W. (1988). *Steady work: Policy, practice, and the reform of American education.* Santa Monica, CA: Rand Corporation.

Eyler, J., Cook, V., & Ward, L. (1983). Resegregation: Segregation within desegregated schools. In C. H. Rossell & W. D. Hawley (Eds.), *The consequences of school desegregation* (pp. 126–162). Philadephia: Temple University Press.

Farbstein, L. (1965). *111 Congressional Record* (5), 5962.

Fascell, D. B. (1967). *113 Congressional Record* (10), 13597.

Feighan, M. A. (1967). *113 Congressional Record* (10), 12659.

Fetterman, D. M. (1984). Doing ethnographic educational evaluation. In D. M. Fetterman (Ed.), *Ethnography in educational evaluation* (pp. 13–20). Beverly Hills, CA: Sage.

Fetterman, D. M. (1986). The ethnographic evaluator. In D. M. Fetterman & M. A. Pitman (Eds.), *Educational evaluation: Ethnography in theory, practice, and politics* (pp. 21–47). Beverly Hills, CA: Sage.

Fetterman, D. M. (1989). *Ethnography: Step by step.* Newbury Park, CA: Sage.

Finn, J. D., Gaier, E. L., Peng, S. S., & Banks, R. E. (1975). Teacher expectations and pupil achievement: A naturalistic study. *Urban Education, 10,* 175–197.

Fiorina, M. P. (1974). *Representatives, roll calls, and constituencies.* Lexington, MA: Lexington Books.

Firestone, W. A., & Herriott, R. E. (1983). The formalization of qualitative research: An adaptation of "soft" science to policy world. *Evaluation Review, 7*(4), 437–466.

Firestone, W. A., & Herriott, R. E. (1984). Multisite qualitative policy research: Some design and implementation issues. In D. M. Fetterman (Ed.), *Ethnography in educational evaluation* (pp. 63–88). Beverly Hills, CA: Sage.

Fogarty, J. E. (1966). *112 Congressional Record* (2), 2091–2092.

Fogel, L. S., & Nelson, R. O. (1983). The effects of special education labels on teachers' behavioral observation, checklist stores, and grading of academic work. *Journal of School Psychology, 21,* 241–251.

Foley, D. E. (1997). Deficit thinking models based on culture: The anthropological protest. In R. R. Valencia (Ed.), *The evolution of deficit thinking: Educational thought and practice* (pp. 113–131). London: Falmer Press.

Fong, H. L. (1965). *111 Congressional Record* (6), 7568.

Ford, W. D. (1965). *111 Congressional Record* (5), 5964.

Fraser, Nancy. (1989). Talking about needs: Interpretive contests as political conflicts in welfare-state societies. *Ethics, 99,* 291–313.

Frost, L. E. (1994). "At-risk" statuses: Defining deviance and suppressing difference in the public schools. *Journal of Law and Education, 23,* 123–165.

Fulbright, J. W. (1965). *111 Congressional Record* (6), 7624–7625.

Fullan, M., & Rolheiser, C. (2001, May 11–12). *Breaking through change barriers* (Conference proceedings). Toronto, Canada: Ontario Institute for Studies in Education of the University of Toronto.

Gallagher, J. J. (1972). The special education contract for mildly handicapped children. *Exceptional Children, 38,* 527–535.

Gans, H. J. (1995). *The war against the poor: The underclass and antipoverty policy.* New York: Basic Books.

Geertz, C. (1973). *The interpretation of cultures.* New York: Basic Books.

Gifford, B. (1993). Introduction. In B. Gifford (Ed.), *Policy perspectives on educational testing* (pp. 3–17). Boston: Kluwer Academic Publishers.

Gilbert, J. H. (1965). *111 Congressional Record* (5), 5970.

Gilligan, J. J. (1965). *111 Congressional Record* (5), 6135.

Gillung, T. B., & Rucker, C. N. (1977). Labels and teacher expectations. *Exceptional Children, 43,* 464–465.

Glass, G. V. (1970). *Data analysis of the 1968–1969 survey of compensatory education (Title I).* Washington, DC: United States Office of Education, Bureau of Elementary and Secondary Education.

Glass, G. V., & Smith, M. L. (1977). *"Pull-out" in compensatory education* (Paper prepared for the Office of the Commissioner, United States Office of Education). Boulder, CO: University of Colorado, Laboratory of Educational Research. (ERIC Document Reproduction Service No. ED160723)

Glickman, D. R. (1978). *124 Congressional Record* (104) (daily edition), H6550.

Good, T. L. (1987). Two decades of research on teacher expectations: Findings and future directions. *Journal of Teacher Education, 38*(4), 32–47.

Goodell, C. E. (1970). *116 Congressional Record* (2), 2580–2582.

Goodling, W. F. (1988). *134 Congressional Record,* 7453.

Gordon, E. W., & Jablonsky, A. (1968). Compensatory education in the equalization of educational opportunity, I. *Journal of Negro Education, 37,* 268–279.

Grabowski, B. F. (1965). *111 Congressional Record* (5), 5994.

Graham, S., & Leone, P. (1987). Effects of behavioral disability labels, writing performance, and examiner's expertise on the evaluation of written products. *Journal of Experimental Education, 55,* 89–94.

Green, E. S. (1965). *111 Congressional Record* (5), 5989.

Green, E. S. (1969). *115 Congressional Record* (8), 9915.

Griffin, R. P. (1965). *111 Congressional Record* (5), 6004.

Grubb, W. N., & Lazerson, M. (1988). *Broken promises: How Americans fail their children.* Chicago: University of Chicago Press.

Grumet, M. (1990). On daffodils that come before the swallow dares. In E. W. Eisner & A. Peshkin (Eds.), *Qualitative inquiry in education: The continuing debate* (pp. 101–120). New York: Teachers College Press.

Hakuta, K. (1986). *Mirror of language: The debate on bilingualism.* New York: Basic Books.

Haley, J. A. (1967). *113 Congressional Record* (10), 13817.

Hanushek, E. A. (1986). The economics of schooling: Production and efficiency in public schools. *Journal of Economic Literature, 24,* 1141–1177.

Harrington, M. (1962). *The other America: Poverty in the United States.* New York: Macmillan.

Hatch, O. G. (1978a). *124 Congressional Record* (7), 8369.

Hatch, O. G. (1978b). *124 Congressional Record* (20), 26682.

Hatch, O. G. (1981). *127 Congressional Record* (8), 8285.

Hatch, O. G. (1994). *140 Congressional Record* (101) (daily edition), S10042.

Hawkins, A. F. (1988). *134 Congressional Record,* 7454.

Hawkridge, D. G. (1968). *A study of selected exemplary programs for the education of disadvantaged children.* Palo Alto, CA: American Institutes for Research in Behavioral Sciences.

Hayes, C. A. (1988). *134 Congressional Record,* 7464.

Herriott, R. E., & Firestone, W. A. (1983). Multisite qualitative policy research: Optimizing description and generalizability. *Educational Researcher, 12,* 14–19.

Holland, E. J. (1967). *113 Congressional Record* (8), 10534.

Holt, M. S. (1978). *124 Congressional Record* (3), 3627.

Improving America's Schools Act of 1994. (1995). Pub. L. No. 103-382, 108 Stat., pp. 3518–4062.

Indianapolis Public Schools. (1970). Abstract. In *Programs to improve the quality of education in the Indianapolis public schools from 1962–1970.* (ERIC Document Reproduction Service No. ED060162)

Jackson, C., et al. (1985). *The effectiveness of assistant teachers as an agent of change in the reading, language, mathematics, and spelling achievement of Black first and second grade students.* (ERIC Document Reproduction Service No. ED 265128)

Jackson, P. (1990). Looking for trouble: On the place of the ordinary in educational studies. In E. W. Eisner & A. Peshkin (Eds.), *Qualitative inquiry in education: The continuing debate* (pp. 101–120). New York: Teachers College Press.

Jacobs, A. Jr. (1965). *111 Congressional Record* (5), 5742.

Jacobs, A. Jr. (1967). *113 Congressional Record* (10), 13844–13845.

Javits, J. K. (1966). *112 Congressional Record* (6), 7956.

Javits, J. K. (1970). *116 Congressional Record* (7), 8906.

Jeffords, J. M. (1988). *134 Congressional Record,* 7453.

Jeffrey, J. R. (1978). *Education for children of the poor.* Columbus, OH: Ohio State University Press.

Jencks, C. (1965, October 14). The Moynihan report. *The New York Review of Books, 5*(5), 39–40.

Joelson, C. S. (1965). *111 Congressional Record* (5), 5987.

Joiner, L. M. (1970). Abstract. In *Final report of the evaluation of the 1969–1970 homework-helper program: Programs and patterns for disadvantaged high school students; ESEA Title I.* Brooklyn, NY: New York City Board of Education. (ERIC Document Reproduction Service No. ED063449)

Jussim, L., & Eccles, J. S. (1992). Teacher expectations: Construction and reflection on student achievement. *Journal of Personality and Social Psychology, 63,* 947–961.

Kaestle, C. F., & Smith, M. S. (1982). The federal role in elementary and secondary education, 1940–1980. *Harvard Educational Review, 52,* 384–408.

Katz, M. B. (1989). *The undeserving poor: From the war on poverty to the war on welfare.* New York: Pantheon Books.

Kauffman, C. (1989). Names and weapons. *Communication Monographs, 56,* 273–285.

Kelley, R. D. G. (1997). *Yo' mama's disfunktional!: Fighting the culture wars in urban America.* Boston: Beacon Press.

Kelman, S. (1987). *Making public policy: A hopeful view of American government.* New York: Basic Books.

Kemp, J. F. (1974). *120 Congressional Record* (5), 6269–6270.

Kennedy, E. M. (1967). *113 Congressional Record* (26), 35715.

Kennedy, E. M. (1994). *140 Congressional Record* (100) (daily edition), S9755.

Kennedy, M. M., Jung, R. K., & Orland, M. E. (1986). *Poverty, achievement and the distribution of compensatory education services: An interim report from the national assessment of Chapter 1.* Washington, DC: Office of Educational Research and Improvement, U.S. Department of Education.

Kennedy, R. F. (1965). *111 Congressional Record* (6), 7330.

Kimbrough, J., & Hill, P. T. (1983). *Problems of implementing multiple categorical education programs.* Santa Monica, CA: Rand Corporation.

Koch, E. I. (1974). *120 Congressional Record* (5), 6274.

LaFalce, J. J. (1981). *127 Congressional Record* (12), 15272.

Landgrebe, E. F. (1974). *120 Congressional Record* (5), 6291.

Lau v. Nichols, 414 U.S. 563 (1974).

Leacock, E. B. (1971). Introduction. In E. B. Leacock (Ed.), *The culture of poverty: A critique* (pp. 9–37). New York: Simon & Schuster.

LeCompte, M., & Goetz, J. P. (1982). Problems of reliability and validity in ethnographic research. *Review of Educational Research, 52*(1), 31–60.

Lee, V. E., & Burkam, D. T. (2002). *Inequality at the starting gate: Social background differences I achievement as children begin school.* Washington, DC: Economic Policy Institute.

LeTendre, M. J. (1991). Improving Chapter 1 programs: We can do better. *Phi Delta Kappan, 72,* 576–580.

Levine, M. E. (1988). *134 Congressional Record,* 7474.

Lewis, O. (1959). *Five families: Mexican case studies in the culture of poverty.* New York: Basic Books.

Lewis, O. (1961). *The children of Sanchez: Autobiography of a Mexican family.* New York: Random House.

Lewis, O. (1964). The culture of poverty. In J. J. TePaske & S. N. Fisher (Eds.), *Explosive forces in Latin America* (pp. 149–173). Columbus, OH: Ohio State University Press.

Lewis, O. (1965). *La Vida: A Puerto Rican family in the culture of poverty—San Juan and New York.* New York: Vintage Books.

Lipsky, M. (1976). Toward a theory of street-level bureaucracy. In W. Hawley & M. Lipsky (Eds.), *Theoretical perspectives on urban politics* (pp. 196–213). Englewood Cliffs, NJ: Prentice-Hall.

Lipsky, M. (1980). *Street-level bureaucracy: Dilemmas of the individual in public services.* New York: Russell Sage Foundation.

Lucadamo, K. (2003, February 24). Pupils seek to get into failing schools. *The New York Sun.* [Online]. Available: http://www.nyfera.org/news/FERA2-24-03NYSUN pupilsseektogetintofailingschools.pdf.

Madden, R. J. (1965). *111 Congressional Record* (5), 5732–5733.

Malen, B. (1994). The micropolitics of education: Mapping the multiple dimensions of power relations in school politics. *Journal of Education Policy, 9*(5), 147–167.

Martin, R., & McClure, P. (1969). *Title I of ESEA: Is it helping poor children?* Washington, DC: Washington Research Project & The NAACP Legal Defense and Educational Fund.

Martin, S. R. (1994). The 1989 Education Summit as a defining moment in the politics of education. In K. M. Borman & N. P. Greenman (Eds.), *Changing American education: Recapturing the past or inventing the future?* (pp. 133–159). Albany, NY: State University of New York Press.

Marwit, K., Marwit, S., & Walker, E. (1978). Effects of student race and physical attractiveness on teachers' judgments of transgressions. *Journal of Educational Psychology, 70*(6), 911–915.

Matsunaga, S. M. (1965). *111 Congressional Record* (5), 5765.

Mayhew, D. R. (1974). *Congress: The electoral connection.* New Haven, CT: Yale University Press.

McClellan, J. L. (1965). *111 Congressional Record* (6), 7613.

McDermott, R. P. (1996). The acquisition of a child by a learning disability. In S. Chaiklin & J. Lave (Eds.), *Understanding practice: Perspectives on activity and context* (pp. 269–305). Cambridge, MA: Cambridge University Press.

McGee, G. W. (1965). *111 Congressional Record* (6), 7713.

McLaughlin, M. W. (1975). *Evaluation and reform: The Elementary and Secondary Education Act of 1965, Title I.* Cambridge, MA: Ballinger.

Meranto, P. (1967). *The politics of federal aid to education in 1965: A study in political innovation.* Syracuse, NY: Syracuse University Press.

Mercer, J. R. (1973). *Labeling the mentally retarded: Clinical and social system perspectives on mental retardation.* Berkeley, CA: University of California Press.

Miller, G. (1978). *124 Congressional Record* (105) (daily edition), H6602.

Miller, G. (1981). *127 Congressional Record* (8), 10610–10621.

Miller, S. M., & Roby, P. (1968). Poverty: Changing social stratification. In D. P. Moynihan (Ed.), *On understanding of poverty* (pp. 64–84). New York: Basic Books.

Millsap, M. A., Moss, M., & Gamse, B. (1993). *The Chapter 1 implementation study: Final report: Chapter 1 in public schools.* Washington, DC: U.S. Department of Education, Office of Policy and Planning.

Mink, P. T. (1965). *111 Congressional Record* (5), 5765.

Minow, M. (1990). *Making all the difference: Inclusion, exclusion, and American law.* Ithaca, NY: Cornell University Press.

Mondale, W. F. (1965). *111 Congressional Record* (6), 7571.

Montoya, J. M. (1965). *111 Congressional Record* (6), 7328.

Moorhead, W. S. (1967). *113 Congressional Record* (10), 13822.

Morse, W. L. (1966a). *112 Congressional Record* (4), 5092.

Morse, W. L. (1966b). *112 Congressional Record* (19), 25261–25262, 25471.

Morse, W. L. (1967a). *113 Congressional Record* (10), 13799.

Morse, W. L. (1967b). *113 Congressional Record* (25), 34910.

Morse, W. L. (1967c). *113 Congressional Record* (26), 35074.

Morse, W. L. (1967d). *113 Congressional Record* (27), 37034.

Mosbaek, E. J., et al. (1968). *Analysis of compensatory education in five school districts: Summary.* Washington, DC: General Electric, TEMPO Division.

Moynihan, D. P. (1967). The Negro family: The case for national action. In L. Rainwater & W. L. Yancey (Eds.), *The Moynihan report and the politics of controversy* (pp. 39–124). Cambridge, MA: MIT Press.

Moynihan, D. P. (1968). The professors and the poor. In D. P. Moynihan (Ed.), *On understanding of poverty* (pp. 3–35). New York: Basic Books.

Murphy, G. L. (1970). *116 Congressional Record* (3), 3599.

Murray, C. (1994). *Losing ground: American social policy, 1950–1980* (2nd ed.). New York: Basic Books.

National Advisory Council on the Education of Disadvantaged Children. (1966). *Report of the National Advisory Council on the Education of Disadvantaged Children* (GPO 911–478). Washington, DC: U.S. Government Printing Office.

National Advisory Council on the Education of Disadvantaged Children. (1969). *Title I – ESEA: A review and a forward look—1969* (OE–37043). Washington, DC: U.S. Government Printing Office.

National Commission on Excellence in Education. (1983, April). *A nation at risk: The imperative for educational reform* [Online]. Available: http://www.ed.gov/pubs/NatAtRisk/risk.html

National Telecommunications and Information Administration. (2000, October). Falling through the net: Defining the digital divide [Online]. Available: http://www.ntia.doc.gov/ntiahome/fttn99/execsummary.html

No Child Left Behind Act of 2001. (2002). Pub. L. No. 107-110, 115 Stat [Online]. Available: http://www.ed.gov/legislation/ESEA02/index.html

Oakes, J. (1985). *Keeping track: How schools structure inequality.* New Haven, CT: Yale University Press.

Oberstar, J. L. (1978). *124 Congressional Record* (104) (daily edition), H6552–H6553.

O'Connor, A. (2001). *Poverty knowledge: Social science, social policy, and the poor in twentieth-century U.S. history.* Princeton, NJ: Princeton University Press.

O'Hara, J. G. (1974a). *120 Congressional Record* (5), 6563.

O'Hara, J. G. (1974b). *120 Congressional Record* (6), 8244.

Ohio State Department of Education. (1970). Abstract. In *Title I in Ohio: Fourth annual evaluation of Title I (ESEA), fiscal year 1969* (BBB09108). (ERIC Document Reproduction Service No. ED081795)

Omi, M., & Winant, H. (1994). *Racial formation in the United States from the 1960s to the 1990s* (2nd ed.). New York: Routledge.

Omnibus Budget Reconciliation Act of 1981. (1982). Pub. L. No. 97-35.

Orland, M. E. (1990). Demographics of disadvantage: Intensity of childhood poverty and its relationship to educational achievement. In J. I. Goodland & P. Keating (Eds.), *Access to knowledge: An agenda for our nation's schools* (pp. 43–58). New York: College Entrance Examination Board.

Palmer, D. J. (1983). An attributional perspective on labeling. *Exceptional Children, 49*, 423–429.

Passow, A. H. (Ed.). (1963). *Education in depressed areas.* New York: Teachers College, Columbia University.

Pell, C. de B. (1974). *120 Congressional Record* (11), 14327, 14567.

Penner, B. (1996, February 9). The school lunch plunder. *Statewide* [Online]. Available: http://net.unl.edu/swi/pers/lunch.html

Perkins, C. D. (1965). *111 Congressional Record* (5), 5736, 6004.

Perkins, C. D. (1966a). *112 Congressional Record* (4), 4426.

Perkins, C. D. (1966b). *112 Congressional Record* (19), 25328–25329.

Perkins, C. D. (1969a). *115 Congressional Record* (4), 4179–4180, 4182.

Perkins, C. D. (1969b). *115 Congressional Record* (7), 9701.

Perkins, C. D. (1974). *120 Congressional Record* (5), 6277.

Perkins, C. D. (1978a). *124 Congressional Record* (104) (daily edition), H6550.

Perkins, C. D. (1978b). *124 Congressional Record* (105) (daily edition), H6596.

Perkins, C. D. (1978c). *124 Congressional Record* (28), 38541.

Perkins, C. D. (1988). *134 Congressional Record,* 7467.

Peters, C., Wixson, K. K., Valencia, S. W., & Pearson, P. D. (1993). Changing statewide reading assessment: A case study of Michigan and Illinois. In B. Gifford (Ed.), *Policy perspectives on educational testing* (pp. 295–391). Boston: Kluwer Academic Publishers.

Peyser, P. A. (1974). *120 Congressional Record* (4), 4448.

Philbin, P. J. (1965). *111 Congressional Record* (5), 6146.

Pickett, A. L. (1986). Certified partners: Four good reasons for certification of paraprofessionals. *American Educator, 10*(3), 31–34, 47.

Pickett, A. L. (1994). *Paraprofessionals in the education workforce* (Report prepared for National Education Association) [Online]. Available: http://www.nea.org/esp/resource/parawork.html

Placier, M. (1996). The cycle of student labels in education: The cases of culturally deprived/disadvantaged and at risk. *Educational Administration Quarterly, 32*(2), 236–270.

Porter, A. C. (1993). School delivery standards. *Educational Researcher, 22*(5), 24–30.

Powell, A. C. Jr. (1965). *111 Congressional Record* (5), 5734–5735.

Pratt, M. L. (1986). Fieldwork in common places. In J. Clifford & G. E. Marcus (Eds.), *Writing culture: The poetics and politics of ethnography: A school of*

American research advanced seminar (pp. 27–50). Berkeley, CA: University of California Press.

Pressler, L. L. (1978). *124 Congressional Record* (104) (daily edition), H6542.

Pressman, J. L., & Wildavsky, A. B. (1984). *Implementation* (3rd ed.). Berkeley, CA: University of California Press.

Prouty, W. L. (1965). *111 Congressional Record* (6), 7321, 7625.

Proxmire, W. (1978). *124 Congressional Record* (20), 27307.

Pucinski, R. C. (1967). *113 Congressional Record* (10), 13870.

Quie, A. H. (1965). *111 Congressional Record* (5), 6019.

Quie, A. H. (1966). *112 Congressional Record* (19), 25337.

Quie, A. H. (1970). *116 Congressional Record* (1), 668.

Quie, A. H. (1974a). *120 Congressional Record* (5), 6284–6286.

Quie, A. H. (1974b). *120 Congressional Record* (6), 8240, 8246.

Quie, A. H. (1978). *124 Congressional Record* (105) (daily edition), H6596.

Reed, D. S. (2001). *On equal terms: The constitutional politics of educational opportunity*. Princeton, NJ: Princeton University Press.

Reid, C. T. (1965). *111 Congressional Record* (5), 6135.

Rein, M. (1970). *Social policy: Issues of choice and change*. New York: Random House.

Reynolds, M. C., & Balow, B. (1972). Categories and variables in special education. *Exceptional Children, 38*, 357–366.

Ribicoff, A. A. (1965). *111 Congressional Record* (6), 7532.

Riessman, F. (1962). *The culturally deprived child*. New York: Harper & Row.

Robelen, E. W. (2002). Paige scolds states for skirting ESEA goals. *Education Week, 22*(9), 29.

Roe, E. (1994). *Narrative policy analysis: Theory and practice*. Durham, NC: Duke University Press.

Rose, M. (1989/1990). *Lives on the boundary: A moving account of the struggles and achievements of America's educationally underprepared*. New York: Penguin Books.

Rosenthal, R., & Jacobson, L. (1968). *Pygmalion in the classroom: Teacher expectation and pupils' intellectual development*. New York: Hold, Rinehart and Winston.

Rossi, P. H., & Blum, Z. D. (1968). Class, status, and poverty. In D. P. Moynihan (Ed.), *On understanding of poverty* (pp. 36–63). New York: Basic Books.

Rothstein, R. (2000, September 13). How tests can drop the ball. *The New York Times*, p. B11.

Rothstein, R. (2002, September 18). How U.S. punishes states that set higher standards. *The New York Times*, p. B8.

Rousselot, J. H. (1974). *120 Congressional Record* (6), 8251.

Rowan, B., Guthrie, L., Lee, G., & Pung Guthrie, G. (1986). *The design and implementation of Chapter 1 instructional services: A study of 24 schools*. San Francisco, CA: Far West Lab for Educational Research and Development. (ERIC Document Reproduction Service No. ED293965)

Roybal, E. R. (1970). *116 Congressional Record* (8), 10622.

Rubin, P., & Long, R. M. (1994, Spring). Who is teaching our children? Implications of the use of aides in Chapter 1. *ERS Spectrum*, 28–34.

Ryan, W. (1967). Savage discovery: The Moynihan report. In L. Rainwater & W. L. Yancey (Eds.), *The Moynihan report and the politics of controversy* (pp. 457–466). Cambridge, MA: MIT Press.

Ryan, W. F. (1967). *113 Congressional Record* (10), 13874.

Salvia, J., Clark, G., & Ysseldyke, J. (1973). Teacher retention of stereotypes of exceptionality. *Exceptional Children, 39,* 651–652.

San Antonio Independent School District v. Rodriguez, 411 U.S. 1 (1973). [Online]. Available: http://laws.lp.findlaw.com/getcase/US/411/1.html

Schemo, D. J. (2002, August 28). Few exercise new right to leave failing schools. *The New York Times,* pp. Λ1, Λ17.

Schemo, D. J. (2002, November 27). New federal rule tightens demands on failing schools. *The New York Times,* pp. A1, A18.

Scheuer, J. H. (1988). *134 Congressional Record,* 7476.

Schneider, A., & Ingram, H. (1993). Social construction of target populations: Implications for politics and policy. *American Political Science Review, 87*(2), 334–347.

Schneider, A., & Ingram, H. (1997). *Policy design for democracy.* Lawrence, KS: University Press of Kansas.

Schweiker, R. S. (1974). *120 Congressional Record* (11), 14836.

Shore, C., & Wright, S. (Eds.). (1997). *Anthropology of policy: Critical perspectives on governance and power.* New York: Routledge.

Shulman, L. S. (1988). A union of insufficiencies: Strategies for teacher assessment in a period of educational reform. *Educational Leadership, 46*(3), 36–41.

Sisk, B. F. (1965). *111 Congressional Record* (5), 5727–5728.

Slavin, R. (1991). Chapter 1: A vision for the next quarter century. *Phi Delta Kappan, 72,* 586–589, 591–592.

Smith, H. W. (1965). *111 Congressional Record* (5), 5729.

Spraggins, T. L. (1968). New educational goals and direction: A perspective of Title I, ESEA. *Journal of Negro Education, 37,* 45–54.

Steiger, W. A. (1969). *115 Congressional Record* (8), 9909.

Stein, C. B. (1986). *Sink or swim: The politics of bilingual education.* New York: Praeger.

Stein, S. J. (2001). "These are your Title I students": Policy language in educational practice. *Policy Science, 34,* 135–156.

Talcott, B. L. (1967). *113 Congressional Record* (10), 13853.

Tatum, B. V. (1997). *"Why are all the Black kids sitting together in the cafeteria?": And other conversations about race.* New York: Basic Books.

Thomas, N. C. (1975). *Education in national politics.* New York: David McKay.

Tierney, J. (2000, December 19). The big city: When crutch for education is an anchor. *The New York Times,* B1.

Timpane, M. (Ed.). (1978). *The federal interest in financing schooling.* Cambridge, MA: Ballinger Publishing.

Traiman, S. L. (1993). *The debate on opportunity-to-learn standards.* Washington, DC: National Governors' Association, Education Policy Studies, Center for Research.

Traub, J. (2002, November 10). Does it work? *The New York Times* (Education Life Supplement), p. 24.

Tyack, D., & Cuban, L. (1995). *Tinkering toward utopia: A century of public school reform*. Cambridge, MA: Harvard University Press.

Tyack, D., & Hansot, E. (1982). *Managers of virtue: Public school leadership in America, 1820–1980*. New York: Basic Books.

U.S. Department of Health, Education, and Welfare, Office of Education. (1970). *Improving education through ESEA: 12 stories* (OE 20122). Washington, DC: U.S. Government Printing Office.

U.S. Department of Labor, Office of Policy Planning and Research. (1965). *The Negro family: The case for national action*. Washington, DC: U.S. Government Printing Office.

U.S. English. (1992). In defense of our common language: A source book on the official English controversy. In J. Crawford (Ed.), *Language loyalties* (pp. 143–149). Chicago: University of Chicago Press.

U.S. Office of Education & Office of Economic Opportunity. (n.d.). *Education: An answer to poverty*. Washington, DC: Author.

Valencia, R. R. (Ed.). (1997). *The evolution of deficit thinking: Educational thought and practice*. London: Falmer Press.

Valentine, C. A. (1968). *Culture and poverty: Critique and counter-proposals*. Chicago: University of Chicago Press.

Wang, M. C., Reynolds, M. C., & Walberg, H. J. (1994). Serving students at the margins. *Educational Leadership, 52*(4), 12–17.

Waxman, C. I. (1977). *The stigma of poverty: A critique of poverty theories and policies*. New York: Pergamon Press.

Weiler, H. S. (1983). Legalization, expertise, and participation: Strategies of compensatory legitimation of educational policy. *Comparative Education Review, 27*, 259–277.

Wellstone, P. D. (1994). *140 Congressional Record* (100) (daily edition), S9879.

White, R. C. (1965). *111 Congressional Record* (5), 6148–6149.

Wolcott, H. (1990). On seeking—and rejecting—validity in qualitative research. In E. W. Eisner & A. Peshkin (Eds.), *Qualitative inquiry in education: The continuing debate* (pp. 121–152). New York: Teachers College Press.

Yanow, D. (1996). *How does a policy mean?: Interpreting policy and organizational actions*. Washington, DC: Georgetown University Press.

Yarborough, R. W. (1965). *111 Congressional Record* (6), 7616–7618.

Yarborough, R. W. (1966a). *112 Congressional Record* (10), 12716.

Yarborough, R. W. (1966b). *112 Congressional Record* (19), 25479.

Young, A. J. Jr. (1974). *120 Congressional Record* (5), 6340, 6342.

Index

About the Author

Dr. Sandra J. Stein currently serves as Academic Dean of the New York City Leadership Academy, where her attention is focused on the creation, development, and delivery of instructional and transformational leadership programs for aspiring, new, and incumbent principals in New York City schools. Prior to the Academy's inception, she was the founding director of the Aspiring Leaders Program at Baruch College, a preparatory program for aspiring school administrators in the New York City public school system. Her approach to teaching using problem-based simulations has contributed to the preparation of hundreds of current and aspiring principals in New York City and beyond. Dr. Stein is known nationally for her rigorous, meaningful, and relevant training that focuses on strong instructional leadership. She has been recognized through grants and awards and has published in the field of educational policy and practice through various articles, book reviews, productions, and presentations. Dr. Stein is the co-director and producer of *Creating Counterparts*, a video-documentary about the power of ordinary youth to transcend distance and embrace difference through an artistic collaboration. This documentary was featured on national news and in a 5th-grade social studies text, *Our Nation*, published recently by Macmillan/McGraw-Hill. Her recent book, entitled *Principal Training on the Ground: Ensuring Highly Qualified Leadership* (co-authored with Liz Gewirtzman), describes how districts and universities can work together to develop effective principals. Dr. Stein holds a Ph.D. in Education Administration and Policy Analysis from Stanford University.